The
Great Revolt
of 1381

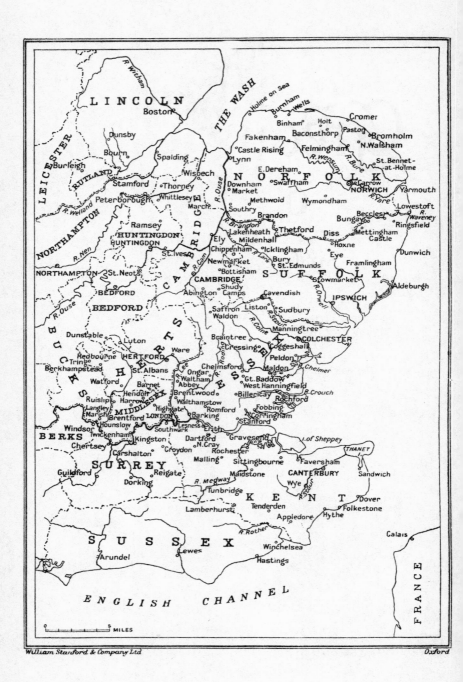

The Great Revolt of 1381

Sir Charles Oman

K.B.E. HON. D.C.L. OXFORD.
HON. LL.D. CAMBRIDGE AND EDINBURGH. F.B.A.
FOR SIXTEEN YEARS BURGESS FOR THE UNIVERSITY OF OXFORD.
CHICHELE PROFESSOR OF MODERN HISTORY.
FELLOW OF ALL SOULS COLLEGE AND
HONORARY FELLOW OF NEW COLLEGE. F.S.A., ETC.

RICHARD II. (SURNAMED OF BORDEAUX.)

RICHARD II. From a Painting in the Old Jerusalem Chamber in the Palace at Westminster.

GREENHILL BOOKS, LONDON
PRESIDIO PRESS, CALIFORNIA

This edition of *The Great Revolt of 1381*
first published 1989 by Greenhill Books, Lionel Leventhal Limited,
Park House, 1 Russell Gardens, London NW11 9NN
and
Presidio Press,
31 Pamaron Way, Novato, Ca. 94947, U.S.A.

British Library Cataloguing in Publication Data
Oman, Sir Charles, 1860-1946
The Great Revolt of 1381
1. England. Peasants' Revolt
I. Title 942.03'8

ISBN 1-85367-045-6

Publishing History
The Great Revolt of 1381 was first published in 1906 (Oxford University Press)
and is reproduced now exactly as the original edition, complete and unabridged,
with the addition of illustrations.

Printed by Antony Rowe Limited,
Chippenham, Wiltshire.

PREFACE

IF André Réville had survived to complete his projected history of the Great Revolt of 1381, this book of mine would not have been written. But when he had transcribed at the Record Office all the documents that he could find bearing on the rebellion, and had written three chapters dealing with the troubles in Norfolk, Suffolk, and Hertfordshire, he was cut off by disease at the early age of twenty-seven. All his transcripts of documents, together with the fragment relating to the three shires above named, were published by the Société de l'École des Chartes in 1898, with an excellent preface by M. Petit-Dutaillis.[1] The book is now out of print and almost unattainable. It is with the aid of Réville's transcripts—a vast collection of records of trials, inquests, petitions, and Escheators' rolls—that I have endeavoured to rewrite the whole history of the Rebellion. The existing narratives of it, with few exceptions, have been written with the Chroniclers alone, not the official documents as their basis: I must except of course Mr. George Trevelyan's brilliant sketch of the troubles in his *England in the Age of Wycliffe*[2] and Mr. Powell's *Rising of 1381 in East Anglia*,[3] the fruit of much hard work at the Record Office. By an unfortunate coincidence André Réville had completed his East Anglian section, and that section only, at the moment of his lamented and premature death, so that the detailed story of the revolt in Norfolk and Suffolk has been told twice from the official sources, and that of the rest of England not at all.

Réville's collection, together with the smaller volumes of documents published by Messrs. Powell and Trevelyan in 1896

---

[1] *Le Soulèvement des travailleurs d'Angleterre en* 1381, par André Réville: études et documents, publiés avec une introduction historique par Ch. Petit-Dutaillis. Paris, 1898.

[2] *England in the Age of Wycliffe*, by G. M. Trevelyan. London, 1899.

[3] *The Rising of* 1381 *in East Anglia*, by Edgar Powell. Cambridge, 1896.

and 1899,[1] and certain other isolated transcripts of local records[2] lie at the base of my narrative. I may add that there is also some new and unpublished material in this book, the results of my own inquiries into the Poll-tax documents at the Record Office. I think that I have discovered why that impost met with such universal reprobation, how the poorer classes in England conspired to defeat its operation, and how the counter-stroke made by the Government provoked the rebellion. The records of the Hundred of Hinckford, printed on pages 167–82, as my third Appendix, are intended to illustrate the falsification of the tax-returns by the townships and their constables. The fourth Appendix, the 'Writ of Inquiry as to the Fraudulent Levying of the Poll-tax' of March 16, 1381 (never before printed, as I believe), is all-important, as showing the manner in which the Government prepared to attack the innumerable fabricators of false returns. This writ, with its threats of imprisonment and exactions levelled against a large proportion, probably a majority, of the townships of fifteen shires, may be called, with little exaggeration, the provocative cause of the whole revolt. Urban and rural England were alike seething with discontent in 1381, but it required a definite grievance, affecting thousands of individuals at the same moment, to provoke a general explosion, such as that which I have here endeavoured to narrate. Without that writ of March 16 town and county would have gone on indulging in isolated riots, strikes, and disturbances, as they had been doing for the last twenty years, but there would probably have been no single movement worthy of being called a rebellion.

I have ventured to insert as my fifth and sixth Appendices two long documents which have already been published, but which are not very accessible to the student, because the volumes in which they are to be found are out of print. They are of such paramount importance for the detailed

---

[1] *The Peasants' Rising, and the Lollards.* Unpublished Documents. Edited by Edgar Powell and G. M. Trevelyan. London, 1899.

[2] Such as the Documents in *Archaeologia Cantiana*, vols. iii and iv, and Essex Archaeological Society's Proceedings, new series, i. p. 214, &c.

history of the rebellion that no student can afford to neglect
them. The first is the so-called 'Anonimal Chronicle of
St. Mary's, York', of which Mr. George Trevelyan published
the French text in the *English Historical Review,* part 51.
I have made an English translation of it, and by his kind
permission, and the courtesy of Dr. Poole, the editor,
and Messrs. Longmans, the proprietors, of the Review,
am allowed to reproduce this most valuable document.
This chronicle appeared after Réville's death, so that his
narrative chapters were written without its aid. The second
is the long inquest of November 20, 1382, on the doings of
the chief London traitors, Aldermen Sibley (or Sybyle),
Horne and Tonge, and Thomas Farringdon. This document formed part of André Réville's transcripts : the Société
de l'École des Chartes, who possess the copyright of his
Collections, granted me leave to republish it. All previous
narratives of the London rebellion have to be rewritten, in
view of this most interesting revelation of the treachery
from within that opened the city to the rebels.

I have to acknowledge kind assistance given me by the
following friends, to whom I made application on points of
difficulty—Mr. C. R. L. Fletcher of Magdalen College, Oxford,
Professor W. P. Ker of All Souls College and London University, Mr. Hubert Hall of the Record Office, Dr. F. G.
Kenyon of the British Museum, and Dr. Murray of the
Oxford English Dictionary. Last, but not least, must come
my testimony to the untiring assistance of the compiler of
the Index—the seventh made for me by the same devoted
hands.

C. OMAN.

Oxford,
May 3, 1906.

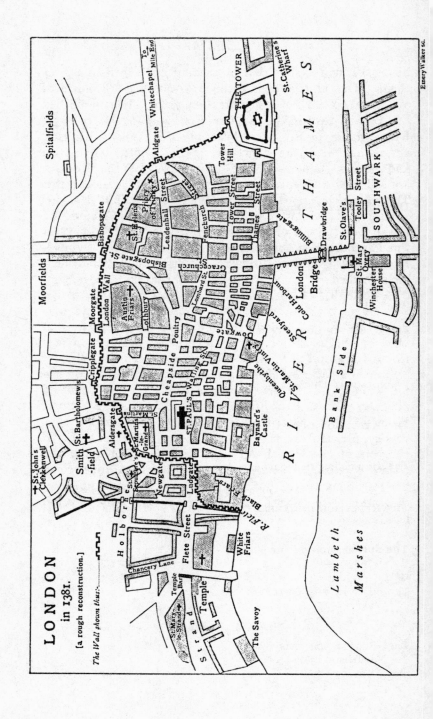

LONDON
in 1381.
[a rough reconstruction.]

The Wall shown thus: ....

TABLE OF CONTENTS

APPENDICES

The
Great Revolt
of 1381

THE GREAT REVOLT OF 1381

CHAPTER I

INTRODUCTORY

ENGLAND IN 1381

FEW of the really important episodes of English history are so short, sudden, and dramatic as the great insurrection of June 1381, which still bears in most histories its old and not very accurate title of 'Wat Tyler's Rebellion'. Only a short month separates the first small riot in Essex, with which the rising started, from the final petty skirmish in East Anglia at which the last surviving band of insurgents was ridden down and scattered to the winds. But within the space that intervened between May 30 and June 28, 1381, half England had been aflame, and for some days it had seemed that the old order of things was about to crash down in red ruin, and that complete anarchy would supervene. To most contemporary writers the whole rising seemed an inexplicable phenomenon—a storm that arose out of a mere nothing, an ignorant riot against a harsh and unpopular tax, such as had often been seen before. But this storm assumed vast dimensions, spread over the whole horizon, swept down on the countryside with the violence of a typhoon, threatened universal destruction, and then suddenly passed away almost as inexplicably as it had arisen. The monastic chroniclers, to whom we owe most of our descriptions of the rebellion— Walsingham and his fellows—were not the men to understand the meaning of such a phenomenon ; they were annalists, not political philosophers or students of social statics. They only half comprehended the meaning of what they had seen, and were content to explain the rebellion as the work of Satan, or the result of an outbreak of sheer insanity on the part of the labouring classes.   When grudges and discontents have been working for many years above or below the surface, and then suddenly flare up into a wholesale conflagration, the ordinary observer is puzzled as well as terrified.   All the causes of the great insurrection, save the Poll-tax which precipitated it, had been operating for a long time.   Why was the particular month of June 1381 the moment at which they passed from causes into effects, and effects of such a violent and unexpected kind ?   What the Poll-tax was, and why it was so unpopular, we shall soon see.   But its relation to the rebellion is merely the same as that of the greased cartridges to the Indian Mutiny of 1857.   It brought about the explosion, but was only one of its smaller causes.   Things had been working up for trouble during many years—only a good cry, a common grievance which united all malcontents, was needed to bring matters to a head.   This was what the Poll-tax provided.

The England which in 1381 was ruled by the boy-king Richard II, with Archbishop Sudbury as his chancellor and prime minister, and Sir Robert Hales as his treasurer, was a thoroughly discontented country.   In foreign politics alone there was material for grudging enough.   The realm was at the fag-end of an inglorious and disastrous war, the evil heritage of the ambitions of Edward III.   It would have puzzled a much more capable set of men than those who now served as the ministers and councillors of his grandson to draw England out of the slough into which she had sunk. Her present misfortunes were due to her own fault : as long as her one ruling idea was to brood over the memories of Crecy and Poitiers, Sluys and Espagnols-sur-Mer, and dream of winning back the boundaries of the Treaty of Bretigny, no way out of her troubles was available.   The nation was obstinately besotted on the war, and failed to see that all the circumstances which had made the triumphs of Edward III possible had disappeared—that England was now too weak and France too strong to make victory possible.   Ten years of constantly unsuccessful expeditions, and ever-shrinking boundaries, had not yet convinced the Commons of England that to make peace with France was the only wise course. They preferred to impute the disasters of the time to the incapacity of their governors. But it was useless to try general after general, to change the personnel of the King's Council every few months—it had been done thrice since King Richard's accession—to accuse every minister of imbecility or corruption. The fault lay not in the leaders, but in the led—in the insensate desire of the nation to persevere in the struggle when all the conditions under which it was waged had ceased to be favourable.

The various ministers of Richard II had, ever since his reign began, been appearing before Parliament at short intervals to report again and again the loss of some new patch of England's dwindling dominion beyond the seas, to confess that they could not even keep the South Coast safe from piratical descents of French corsairs, or guarantee the Northumbrian border from the raiding Scot, or even maintain law and order in the inward heart of the realm. Yet they were always forced to be asking for heavier and yet heavier taxation to support the losing game. Naturally each one of their financial expedients was criticized with acrimony. The classes who took an intelligent interest in politics demanded efficiency in return for the great sacrifices of money which the nation was making, and failed to get it. The far larger section of Englishmen who were not able to follow the course of war or politics with any real comprehension, were vaguely indignant at demands on their purse, which grew more and more inquisitorial, and penetrated deeper down as the years went on.

All nations labouring under a long series of military disasters are prone to raise the cry of 'Treason', and to accuse their governments either of deliberate corruption or of criminal self-seeking and negligence. The English in 1381 were no exception to this rule : they were blindly suspicious of those who were in power at the moment. John of Gaunt, the King's eldest uncle, the most prominent figure in the politics of the day, had not a clean record. He had, in the last years of his father's reign, been in close alliance with the peculating clique which had surrounded the old king and battened on his follies.   It was natural to suspect the ministers of 1381 of the same sins that had actually been detected in the ministers of 1377 : while John of Gaunt continued to take a busy part in affairs this was inevitable.   As a matter of fact, however, the suspicion seems to have been groundless.   The ministers of 1381 were, so far as we can judge, honest men, though they were destitute of the foresight and the initiative necessary for dealing with the deplorable condition of the realm.   Archbishop Sudbury, who had been made chancellor at the Parliament which met in January 1380—' whether he sought the post of his own freewill or had it thrust upon him by others only God can tell ' [1]— was a pious, well-intentioned man—almost a saint.   He would probably have been enrolled among the martyrs of the English calendar if only he had been more willing to make martyrs himself.   For it is his lenience to heretics which forms the main charge brought against him by the monastic chroniclers.   They acknowledge that he possessed every personal virtue, but complain that he was a half-hearted persecutor of Wycliffe and his disciples, and hint that his terrible death in 1381 was a judgement from heaven for his lukewarmness in this respect.   Sudbury was sometimes proved destitute of tact, and often of firmness, but he was one of the most innocent persons to whom the name of Traitor was ever applied.   Of his colleague, Treasurer Hales, who went with him to the block during the insurrection, we know less—he was, we are told, ' a magnanimous knight, though the Commons loved him not ' [2]; no proof was ever brought that he was corrupt or a self-seeker [3].   None of the minor ministers of state of 1380–1 had any such bad reputation as had clung about their predecessors of 1377.   But the nation chafed against their unlucky administration, 'and vaguely ascribed to them all the ills of the time.

---

[1] *Chron. Angl.* 255.   [2] Walsingham, i. 449.
[3] Hales did not take over the Treasury till just after the Parliament of Northampton.

Yet if the political and military problems had been the only ones pressing for solution in 1381 there would have been no outbreak of revolution in that fatal June. All that would have happened would have been the displacing of one incompetent ministry by another—no more capable than its predecessor of dealing with the insoluble puzzle of how to turn the French war into a successful enterprise.

The fact that the political grievances of England had come to a head at a moment when social grievances were also ripe was the real determining cause of the rebellion. Of these social grievances, the famous and oft-described dispute in the countryside between the landowner and the peasant, which had started with the Black Death and the ' Statute of Labourers ' of 1351 was no doubt the most important, since it affected the largest section of Englishmen. But it must not be forgotten that the rural community was not a whit more discontented at this moment than was the urban. There were rife in almost every town old grudges between the rulers and the ruled, the employers and the employed, which were responsible for no small share of the turbulence of the realm, when once the rebellion had broken out. They require no less notice than the feuds of the countryside.

It was customary a few years ago to represent the rural discontent of the third quarter of the fourteenth century as arising mainly from one definite cause—the attempt of the lords of manors to rescind the agreements by which their villeins had, during the years before the Black Death, commuted their customary days of labour on the manorial demesne for a money payment [1]. Later research, however, would seem to show that this, although a real cause of friction, was only one among many. Such commutations had been local and partial : in the majority of English manors

---

[1] This, of course, was Professor Thorold Rogers's great theory, and for twenty years it was accepted by economic writers without criticism. It will be found repeated in *Social England*, ii. 328–9, and by Professor Cunningham. But it would seem to be grounded on data of insufficient number : if such troubles can be traced in certain manors, recent research has discovered a much larger list of cases where they do not appear, and where other causes of discontent must be sought. See Ashley, ii. 265, and Réville, xxxiii–v.

they had not been introduced, or had only been introduced on a small scale, before the fatal year 1348-9. It seems far from being a fact that the lords in general made a desperate attempt, after the Black Death, to rescind old bargains and restore the régime of corvées in its entirety. In many cases the number of holdings on the manor which lay vacant after the pestilence was so great, that the landowner could not get them filled up by any device.[1] There was bound, therefore, to be a permanent deficit in the total of days of service that could be screwed out of the villeins. In sheer despair of finding hands of any sort to till their demesne-land, many lords actually introduced the custom of commuting service for rent soon *after* the year of the Plague—so that its result in their manors was precisely the reverse of what has been stated by Professor Thorold Rogers and his school. It is dangerous to formulate hard and fast general statements as to the way in which the landowning class faced the economic problem before them. Conditions varied from manor to manor, and from county to county, and the action of the lords was dependent on the particular case before them. It is certain that many abandoned the attempt to till the demesne either with villein-labour or with hired free labour, and let out holdings for rent, often on the ' stock and land lease ' system—by which the tenant-farmer took over not only the soil but the animals, implements, and plant required to till it.[2] Others threw their demesne, and even the vacant crofts of extinct families of villeins, into sheep farms, on which rural public opinion looked askance. But it would appear that in the majority of cases, where the old customary services had never been abolished or commuted before the Black Death, the landowner went on enforcing them as stringently as he could, supplementing the corvée-work of the villeins by hiring free labour, though he wished to use as little of it as he could contrive. The main design of the Statute of Labourers is to enable the employer to obtain that labour as cheaply as possible. The hirer is prohibited by it from

---

[1] For cases in Norfolk see details in Jessop's *Coming of the Friars*, 193-200.
[2] Merton College had leased out all its land on such terms by 1360.

offering, or the labourer from demanding, more than the old
average rates of payment that had prevailed before 1348.
Moreover, in an excess of unwise economy, the Statute
estimates the old rate at its lowest instead of its highest
average—at 2d.–3d. a day instead of at 3d.–4d. There
would have been much more prospect of carrying out the
scheme with success if something had been conceded to the
labourer—but he was offered only the worst possible bargain.

One generalization however is permissible. The Black
Death permanently raised the price of labour—despite of all
statutes to the contrary—though its effects would have been
much greater if they had not been checked by the legislation
of Parliament. On the other hand, the price of agricultural
produce had remained comparatively stationary—at times
it had even shown some signs of falling. The profits of the
landowner, therefore, were no larger, while his expenses were
decidedly heavier, than they had been in the earlier days of
Edward III. Even in manors where the old services of the
villeins had never been commuted, and still remained exigible, the lord had to seek a certain amount of supplementary
labour, and could not buy it so cheaply as in the years before
1348. If legislation had not intervened, the period would
have been a sort of Golden Age for the labourer, more especially the free labourer. He was quite aware of the fact,
chafed bitterly at the artificial restrictions which prevented
him from taking full advantage of the state of the market,
and set his wits to work to evade them by every possible shift
and trick.

To understand the standing quarrel between employer and
employed, which made bitter the whole thirty years between
the passing of the Statute of Labourers and the outbreak of
' Tyler's Rebellion ', we must distinguish with care between
the two classes of working-men with whom the landowner
had to deal—the villein who held his strips of soil on condition
of discharging all the old customary dues, and the landless
man, who had no stake in the manor, and lived not on the
produce of his holding, but by the sale of the work of his
hands. The latter might be a mere agricultural labourer,

or a handicraftsman of some sort, smith, thatcher, tiler, carpenter, mason, sawyer, and so forth. From the villein the lord wished to exact as stringently as possible his customary corvées, and the petty dues and fines incident on his tenure. From the landless labourer he wished to buy his services at the lowest possible rate—that stipulated in the Statute of 1351. Conversely we have the villein desiring to be quit of customary work and customary dues, in order that he may become a tenant at a fixed rent, and the landless labourer determined that at all costs he will get from his employer something more than the miserable pay allowed him by law.

In these simple facts lie the causes of thirty years of conflict.. Both parties were extremely obstinate : each had a vague moral conviction that it was in the right. Neither was very scrupulous as to the means that it employed to obtain what it considered its due. The landowners grew desperately cruel, as they saw wages rising and old customs gradually dying out, despite of all the reissues of the Statute of Labourers which they obtained from Parliament. It will be remembered that branding with hot irons and outlawry were among the supplementary sanctions which they added to the original terrors of the law of 1351. It does not seem that such punishments were often put in practice, but their very existence was enough to madden the peasant. On the other hand the workers thought every device from petty perjury and chicane up to systematic rioting justifiable against the local tyrant.

On the whole, it would seem that the landless labourer fared better than the villein during this age of strife. He could easily abscond, since he had no precious acres in the common-field to tether him down. If he was harried, held down to the letter of the Statute, and dragged before justices in his native district, he could always move on to another. He therefore, as it seems, enjoyed a very real if a precarious and spasmodic prosperity. He might at any moment fear the descent of a justice upon him, if neighbouring landlords grew desperate, but meanwhile he flourished. Langland's

Piers Plowman, from which so many valuable side-lights on the time can be drawn, describes him as ' waxing fat and kicking '. 'The labourers that have no land and work with their hands deign no longer to dine on the stale vegetables of yesterday; penny-ale will not suit them, nor bacon, but they must have fresh meat or fish, fried or baked, and that hot-and-hotter for the chill of their maw: Unless he be highly paid he will chide, and bewail the time he was made a work-man. . . . Then he curses the king and all the king's justices for making such laws that grieve the labourer.' [1]

So far we have been considering the condition of the land-less worker: but the same economic crisis had also affected the landholding villeins. They were reluctant to abscond and throw up their share of the manorial acres, for only in extremity will the peasant who has once got a grip on the soil consent to let it go. Yet we find that, in the generation which followed the Black Death, even the villeins were beginning to sit more loosely upon the land : the position of the free labourer often seemed more tempting than their own, and those of them whose acres were few, or whose lord was harsh and unreasonable, not unfrequently abandoned all, and fled with their families to seek free service in some distant county or borough. But it would seem that flight was less frequent than attempts to combine against the lord and to worry him into coming to terms. By obstinate perse-verance, the villager hoped in the end to deliver himself from work-days on the demesne, and manorial dues, and to get them commuted for a fixed rent : public opinion among his class had assessed the reasonable rate for such commutation at 4*d.* an

---

[1] *Piers Plowman*, ix, pp. 330-7 and pp. 340-2 :—

'Laboreres that han no londe · to liven on bot here hands
Deyned noght to dyne a-day · night-old wortes.
May no peny ale hem paye · ne a pece of bacon,
Bote hit be freesh fleesch other fysh · fried other ybake,
And that *chaud* and *pluschaud* · for chillyng of here mawe.
Bote he be heylich yhyred · elles wol he chide,
That he was a werkman ywroght · waryen the tyme.

.   .   .   .

And thenne he corseth the kyng · and alle the kynges Iustices
Suche lawes to lere · laborers to greve.'

acre *per annum*. This sum is repeatedly mentioned in many districts during the troubles of 1381 ; where the peasantry obtained the upper hand, they were wont to insert it in the charters which they extorted from their lords. It was undoubtedly too low to represent the real value of land : where free leasing was going on, an acre was worth twice as much.

In the manors where the owner and the villeins could not agree, we find that the very modern phenomena of strikes and agricultural unions were common. The peasants ' confederated themselves in conventicles, and took an oath to resist lord and bailiff, and to refuse their due custom and service '.[1] Weak men yielded, and allowed their serfs to commute. Obstinate men called down the local justice, or even applied directly to the King's Council, and got the strike put down by force. It was sure to break out again after an interval, when the villeins had forgotten the stocks and the heavy fines which were their part in such cases.

One of the most interesting features of these combinations of the peasantry is that in some cases they tried to raise constitutional points against their lords, in the most lawyerly fashion. It is a new thing in English history to find the agricultural classes pleading for that reversion to ancient custom which barons and burgesses had so often demanded when struggling against unpopular kings. The fact is undoubted : in the first parliament of Richard II, a special statute was passed to deal with such attempts. ' In many lordships and parts of the realm of England ', it runs, 'the villeins and holders of land in villeinage refuse their customs and service due to their lords, under colour of certain exemplifications made from Domesday Book concerning the manors in which they dwell ; and by virtue of the said exemplifications, and their bad interpretation of them, they affirm that they are quit and utterly discharged of all manner of serfdom

---

[1] This is the phrase used in the case of Strixton [Northants], a manor of one Thomas Preyers in 1380 : the villeins ' servicia pro tenuriis suis rebellice retraxerunt, ac in conventiculis ad invicem confederati et sacramento interconfederati ad resistendum praefato Thomae et ministris suis, ne huiusmodi consuetudines et servicia facerent, congregati sunt'. See Réville, p. xxxix.

due whether of their bodies or of their tenures, and will not
suffer distresses to be levied on them, or justice done on them,
but menace the servants of their lords in life or members, and
what is more, they draw together in great bands, and bind
themselves by confederation that each shall aid the others
to constrain their lords by the strong hand.'[1] This was
four years before the Peasants' Revolt of 1381, but
the main feature of that revolt is already visible : it was
precisely a gathering in great bands to constrain the landowners and resist by armed violence all attempts to enforce
seignorial dues.

It is to be presumed that the 'exemplifications from
Domesday' were proofs that in particular manors there were
in 1085 free men and socmen, where in 1377 villeins were to
be found, so that some lord in the intervening three centuries
must have advanced his power to the detriment of the
ancient rights of the inhabitants of the place. To find such
archaeological evidence advanced by mere peasants is
astonishing. One can only suppose that they must have
had skilled advisers : probably the growing custom by which
persons of some wealth and status had taken to buying
villein-land explains the phenomenon. Some lawyer who
had invested in acres held on a base tenure, must have hit
on this ingenious idea of appealing to ancient evidence against
the custom of the present day. The real villeins must have
admired and copied him.

It is clear that not only the customary days of service to
be done on the lord's demesne, but also the other incidents
of the manorial system, were very hateful to the peasants of
1381. In all the demands which they made and the charters
which they won, they carefully stipulated for freedom from
such things as the heriot payable at the death of a tenant,
the *merchet* demanded from him when he married his
daughter, the small but tiresome dues exacted when he sold
a cow or a horse. Sometimes the monopoly of the seignorial
mill is made a grievance : sometimes there is a claim for the
abolition of parks and warrens, and the grant of liberty to

---

[1] Statutes of the Realm, ii. 2. 3.

hunt and fish at large. The 'freedom' which was the villein's ideal postulated the destruction of all these restrictions on daily life.

All over England we may trace, in the third quarter of the fourteenth century, local disputes in which one or other of the rural grievances came to the front. The only thing that was new in 1381 was that the troubles were not confined to individual manors, but suddenly spread over half the realm. It is dangerous to conclude, as some writers have done, that this simultaneous action was due to deliberate organization. We have no proof that there was any central committee of malcontents who chose their time and then issued orders for the rising. The leaders who emerged in each region seem to have been the creatures of the moment, selected almost at hazard for their audacity or their ready eloquence. The sole personage among them who had been long known to a large circle was John Ball, 'the mad priest of Kent', and he, so far from starting the actual insurrection, had been for some time in prison when it broke out, and had to be released by his admirers. We shall have to deal presently with his personality and his views. Here it may suffice to say that he was a visionary and a prophet rather than an organizer. He had spread discontent by twenty years of itinerant preaching, but there is not the least proof that he tried to turn it into practical shape by leaguing his hearers into secret societies. We must not be misled by the name of the 'Great Company' (Magna Societas), which occurs sometimes in the annals of the insurrection, and take it to have been a real league, like that of the 'United Irishmen' of 1798. It was a name applied in a few cases by the rebels to themselves, more especially in Norfolk, and no more.[1] There was, of course, much communication between district and district: workmen on the tramp, dodging the 'Statute of Labourers', itinerant craftsmen, religious mendicants, pro-

[1] The best-known case is that of George of Dunsby, a Lincolnshire man, who came to Bury on June 14, saying that he was 'nuncius magnae societatis,' and bidding all men rise in arms. I do not think we can follow Mr. Powell (p. 57) in reading this into a proof there was 'an organization extending so far as the Humber'. Dunsby is in the extreme south of Lincolnshire, near Bourn.

fessional vagrants, outlaws, and broken men of all sorts, were roving freely up and down England, and through them every parish had some knowledge of what was doing elsewhere. But it would be absurd to look upon these wanderers as the regular agents of a definite organization, founded for the purpose of preparing for an insurrection. There were village 'conventicles' and combinations, which must often have been in touch with each other, but no central directing body. The chaotic character of the rising is sufficient proof of this : every district went on its own way of tumult ; and except where men of marked personality (like Wat Tyler in Kent, or Geoffrey Litster in eastern Norfolk) came to the front, there was no definite plan carried out.

The sporadic nature of the insurrection was made still more marked by the fact that it affected many cities and towns, in which the manorial grievances had no part in causing the outburst. We may set in one class places like St. Albans, Dunstable, Bury St. Edmunds, or Lynn, where the insurrection was that of townsmen discontented with their feudal superior, and desirous of wringing a charter out of him, or of adding new clauses to a charter already in existence. We shall have to deal in detail with several of these risings on behalf of municipal liberty : it will be noticed that they all took place in towns where the lord was a churchman : abbots and bishops were notoriously slow in conceding to their vassals the privileges which kings and lay proprietors had been freely granting for the last two centuries. The church was comparatively unaffected by the personal motives which had moved the secular lords to sell civic freedom : a corporation does not suffer so much as an individual from temporary stress of war or dearth, and can carry out a continuous policy in a way that is impossible to a succession of life-tenants of a lordship. Hence there were, in 1381, towns in ecclesiastical lands which had never yet achieved the common municipal liberties, or only enjoyed them in a very restricted form. Such places took advantage of the rising in the country-side to press their own grievances : when anarchy was afoot it was the favourable moment to squeeze charters out of the reluctant monasteries. But there was no logical connexion between such movements and the Peasants' Revolt ; troublous times of any sort suited the townsmen ; Bury had attacked its abbot during Montfort's rebellion, and St. Albans had tried to snatch freedom in the midst of the political chaos that attended the deposition of Edward II ; their chance lay in seizing the opportunity when the laws of the land were in abeyance and violence at a premium.

From risings of this sort we must carefully distinguish another kind of municipal disorders—the numerous cases where insurrections broke out within the towns, not with the object of attacking the external authority of a lord, but with that of overthrowing the power of an oligarchy within the body corporate. Many of the places which had obtained the greatest amount of freedom from the oppressors without, had now new grievances against the oppressors within. The history of the majority of English towns in the fourteenth century, just like that of Italian or German towns during that same period, is in a great measure composed of the struggles of the *inferiores* against the *potentiores*, of the mass of poor inhabitants (whether freemen or unenfranchised aliens) against the small number of wealthy families which had got possession of the corporation or the guild merchant, and ruled for their own profit. When the towns had won their charters under the early Plantagenet kings their population had been comparatively homogeneous, and differences of wealth had been small. But, by the time of Richard II, there was a clear division between the oligarchy and the democracy, the privileged and the common herd. The old theory that the mayor and other officials of the town were the elected representatives of the whole community, and that their resolves ought to be referred, in the last instance, to the approval of the general body of freemen had not been forgotten. But in practice the governing ring often coopted and re-elected itself, without the least regard to the rights of the majority. They raised taxation, undertook public works, contracted debts, as they pleased and laughed the commons to scorn. When they went too far there were disputes, riots, and ruinous lawsuits before the royal courts.[1] Nothing was more natural than that in 1381, when the rural districts were aflame, the lower classes of the towns should seize the opportunity of falling upon their local oligarchies. The numerous cases in which we find the houses of rich townsmen destroyed, and the lesser number of instances in which the owner perished with his tenement, were undoubtedly the results of the desire to pay off old municipal grudges. Wherever the government had been corrupt and unrepresentative, the governing few were attacked in the day of wrath. In some instances the commons of towns far remote from the regions to which the peasant revolt extended, rose upon their rulers, without waiting for the area of general revolt to extend in their direction. This was the case at Winchester, Beverley, and Scarborough.

In London and certain other large towns, the mere division of the inhabitants into an oligarchy and a democracy does not explain all the troubles of 1381. A comparatively new problem of the economic sort was in process of being fought out. This was the struggle of employers and employed within the guilds. A new industrial proletariat was in process of formation, and was striving hard against the conditions which it found existing.[2] In the old days the masters in any trade had been wont to work on a small scale, keeping but two or three apprentices, each of whom aspired to become a master himself in due time. But the growing industrial activity of England, and the multiplication of wealth, was tending to create a class of great employers of labour, and a class of artisans who could never aspire to become masters. These richer and more enterprising members of each craft were now beginning to maintain much greater numbers of workmen. At the same time they deliberately made it more difficult for their employés to start in business for themselves, placing all manner of diffi-

---

[1] For details of such doings by an oligarchy see the case of Beverley, in the documents in Réville, pp. 160-9.

[2] For the details, see chapters ix and x of Mrs. Green's *Town Life in the Fifteenth Century*, and compare Petit-Dutaillis's Preface to Réville.

culties in the way of those who wished to take up the dignity of mastership. Thus many apprentices who had completed their term of years were now forced to continue as hired workers, instead of becoming independent craftsmen. These folks, 'journeymen' as we should call them now, 'valets' or 'yeomen' or 'serving men' in the language of the fourteenth century, were a discontented class. To protect themselves against their masters they formed many leagues and societies, often disguising their true purpose under religious forms, and purporting to meet for the hearing of masses and the discharge of pious duties. As early as 1306 we find a real trades-union of this class formed by the journeymen shoemakers of London : it was suppressed— nominally for the public benefit, really for that of the masters of the trade. But it was only the first of many such combinations : how they worked we may judge from a complaint of the cloth-shearers in 1350 : ' If there is any dispute between a master of our trade and his man, such a man is wont to go to all the men within the city of the same trade, and then by covin and conspiracy between them made, they will order that no one among them shall work or serve his own master, until the aforesaid master and his servant or man have come to an agreement ; by reason whereof the masters of the said trade have been in great trouble, and the public is left unserved '. Such combinations had always been considered illegal, but after the Statute of Labourers the case of the journeymen was apparently more hopeless than ever. Nevertheless they persisted in their endeavours to bring pressure to bear on their masters, and very often, it would seem, with success : in spite of the rates of wages prescribed for artisans in the Statute, the actual sums paid to the hired man continued to rise.[1] In 1381 the struggle between employer and employed was in full swing. The wealthy citizen who tried to keep wages down, as also the mayors and aldermen who helped him by fining strikers and dissolving journeymen's guilds, were not unnaturally detested by the industrial proletariate. A riotous attack on the capitalist and the

[1] See Mrs. Green's *Town Life in the Fifteenth Century*, pp. 122-5.

corporation was certain to occur at the first favourable
opportunity. Such an opportunity occurred when the rural
labourers of England rose in insurrection and marched on
London. They were sure of support from the whole of the
wage-earning class in the city, who were as anxious to get
rid of the Statute of Labourers as the peasants themselves. Nor must it be forgotten that the journeymen and
apprentices were only a part of the discontented class within
the city walls. They represented skilled labour, but there
was also a lower and more miserable stratum of unskilled
labour, always living on the verge of starvation. Already
there had grown up in London and in many of the larger
towns a mass of casually employed hangers-on to the skirts
of trade. These miserable folk, constantly recruited by
fugitive villeins from the countryside and all manner of ne'er-
do-weels, were ready for any change, since they imagined
that nothing could make their status worse than it was at
the moment. They were equally ready to rise against the
corporations that ground down the poor, or against the
King's government which enforced the Statute of Labourers.

We must probably ascribe to this class more than any other
the attack on foreigners which formed such a prominent feature in the insurrection of 1381, not only in London but in
the eastern counties. The foreign resident in those days
was not the destitute alien who now fills the slums of the East
End, but a merchant or less frequently a manufacturer.
The grievance against him was that he was supposed to be
sucking the wealth out of the country, and especially to be
exporting secretly all the gold and silver, for which he gave
in return only useless luxuries.[1] Hence there was no cash
left in the realm, and so, in the ideas of the labouring classes,
money was hard to come at, and wages were low. This was
the guilt of the merchant : that of the manufacturer, nearly
always the woollen manufacturer from Flanders, was that he
was an unfair competitor, who ruined the native artisan by

---

[1] See the evidence of the London Merchants in the Parliament of 1381, as to
the way in which ' all the gold of England, being good and heavy, was gone
beyond the sea, to the great profit of those who exported it ', Shaw, p. 50.

using cheap labour, often that of aliens, women, and children. The Government owed an appreciable part of its unpopularity to the fact that ever since Edward III first tempted the Flemings and Zeelanders to Norfolk, it had encouraged immigration of skilled artisans from abroad. Every journeyman or casually employed labourer in the wide branches of the wool trade who chanced to be out of work, put the blame of his privations on the outlander, whose competition had straitened the demand for native hands. Hence came the sudden fury displayed against the Flemings. It was, no doubt, partly inspired by unreasoning dislike for all strangers, but mainly rested on the economic fallacies that are always rife in an uneducated class living on the edge of starvation.

In London, and not in London alone, we find a few leading and wealthy citizens implicated in the tumults of 1381. Three aldermen of the capital were indicted for taking open part with the insurgents. At York an ex-mayor is found at the head of the rioters who attacked the local oligarchs ; at Winchester a wealthy draper is outlawed after the suppression of the rebellion. The explanation is to be found in the furious jealousies and personal or guild rivalries which sometimes split up the governing classes in the cities. London was at the moment going through the vicious struggle between the victualling guilds and the clothing guilds which continued all through the reign of Richard II, and was at its height during John of Northampton's demagogic career, only a year or two after the rebellion.[1]

We are less well informed as to municipal politics in the provincial towns, but may well suspect that wherever one of the *potentiores* of a town is found implicated in the revolt, he was playing the part of Peisistratus of old, and leading the mob against his own class out of ambition or jealousy, as the result of some personal or guild quarrel. That such men took such a line is only one more indication of the hetero-

[1] For the doings of Alderman Tonge, Sibley and Horne, see pp. 55-6. It is strange to find that all three of them were of the victualling faction, as was Mayor Walworth, and not of the clothing faction.

geneous character of the motives which set England aflame in 1381.

From the list of these motives, however, it seems clear that we must eliminate one which has been made to take a prominent place in the causes of the rising of 1381 by some modern historians.[1] It does not seem that Wycliffe's recent attack on the Pope, the Friars, and the ' Caesarean Clergy ' had any appreciable influence on the origin or the course of the rebellion. Though the celebrated mission of the Reformer's band of ' Poor Preachers ' began several months before the revolt of 1381 broke out, yet it is impossible to discover that the insurgents showed any signs of Wycliffite tendencies. There were no attacks on the clergy *quâ* clergy (though plenty of assaults on them in their capacity of landlords), no religious outrages, no setting forth of doctrinal grievances, no iconoclasm, singularly little church-breaking. The Duke of Lancaster, the reformer's patron, was the person most bitterly inveighed against by the rebels. Indeed, in the midland districts, in which the reformer's influence was strongest in the beginning, e.g. the country between Oxford and Leicester, the rebellion did not come to a head at all. None of the numerous priests who took part in the rising were known followers of Wycliffe:[2] the contemporary chroniclers would have been only too glad to accuse them of it had there been any foundation for such a charge. John Ball had been preaching his peculiar doctrines many years before Wycliffe was known outside Oxford, and never had come

[1] See, for example, Thorold Rogers's *Work and Wages*, pp. 254–5, where the whole rebellion is treated as a revolt against an attempt of the lords to re-introduce commuted corvées, organized by Wycliffe's followers—an entirely imaginative and unhistorical picture. Of course Ball is made ' the most active and outspoken of the "Poor Priests"' (p. 255) as if he was a properly affiliated member of the brotherhood.

[2] Absolutely no credence can be given to the story put about by Walden, a whole generation after Wycliffe's death [Fasc. Ziz. 273], to the effect that Ball, when making his confession before his execution, told Bishop Courtenay that he had been for two years a disciple of Wycliffe, and had learnt from him all the doctrine he had taught—also that the ' Poor Preachers ' were his accomplices, and that ' within two years they had thought to destroy the whole kingdom '. If anything of the kind had been true we should have heard of it from contemporary sources.

into touch with him. It is absurd to call him (as does the Continuator of Knighton) 'Wycliffe's John the Baptist' in any save a purely chronological sense.[1] They had no relation with each other. But the best proof that the 'Poor Preachers' had nothing to do with the rebellion is that their great period of activity lies in the years just after it. For if their teaching had been one of its causes, the Government would have fallen upon them, and silenced them with no gentle hand, quoting their misdeeds as its justification. The attack on Wycliffe and his followers, which began in 1382, was purely one resulting from a general reaction in church and state caused by the excesses of the rebels, not a direct punishment of any part taken by the Reformer and his friends in those excesses. Moreover there was one category of men of religion who were openly accused by contemporary authorities of being responsible for the rebellion, and these were the most bitter enemies of Wycliffe—the mendicant orders.[2] In the curious story of 'Jack Straw's' confession, recorded in the *Chronicon Angliae*, we are told that the only clergy whom the rebels intended to favour in the day of their triumph were the Friars.[3] It is notable that Langland in *Piers Plowman*, accuses them of being preachers of precisely that philosophic communism which the Lollards are credited with having popularized. According to him

'They preche men of Plato and proven it by Seneca
That all things under heaven ought to be in comune.'[4]

In Réville's documents[5] there is a clear case cited of a Franciscan engaged in stirring up the tenants of the monastery of Middleton to combine against their abbot. The Friar's old doctrine of evangelical poverty rather than Wycliffe's theories of 'dominion' is at the bottom of the preaching of John Ball and his allies, and of Wat Tyler's Smithfield demands. The accusation is acknowledged by the Friars themselves, who complain, in their well-known

---

[1] Knighton, ii. 151.
[2] See the curious *Nota* in *Chron. Angl.* p. 312, as to the causes of the revolt. The friar 'seducunt plebem mendaciis et secum in devium pertrahunt'.
[3] pp. 309-10.
[4] *Piers Plowman*, xxiii. 274-5.
[5] Réville, p. lxvii and note.

letter of 1382 to John of Gaunt,[1] that they are being charged by many of their enemies, and especially by the Lollard Nicholas Hereford, with being responsible for the whole rebellion, because of their declamations against wealth and their praises of mendicancy and poverty, as well as for other reasons. They deprecate the charge, but make no attempt to retort it upon Wycliffe and his school.

But though clerks and friars are frequently found among the leaders of the rising, it is clear that religious discontent was one of the least prominent factors among its causes. It was essentially secular in its motives. Religion had nothing to do with the assault of the villein upon his manorial lord, of the unchartered townsman on his suzerain, of the skilled or unskilled labourers of the city upon their employers, of the urban democrats upon the urban oligarchs, of river-side mobs upon the foreign merchants. When the floodgates were opened and the machinery of law and order was swept away in June 1381, it was because the multitude was set on achieving its deliverance from practical grievances, not because it was inspired by fanaticism or disinterested zeal for a spiritual reformation.

[1] See the *Epistula Quatuor Ordinum ad Iohannem ducem Lancastriae*, in Fasc. Zizaniorum, p. 293. They complain that the heretics are so wicked ' ut in ipsis auribus cleri simul et populi clamant et asserant nos et quatuor ordines nostros causam fuisse totius rebellionis populi, anno ultimo, contra dominum regem et dominos proceres tam enormiter insurgentis '.

CHAPTER II

THE PARLIAMENT OF NORTHAMPTON AND THE POLL-TAX

IT was into the midst of an England seething with the complicated grievances that we have described that the ministers and Parliament of Richard II launched their unhappy Poll-tax in the winter of 1380–1. The Chancellor-Archbishop had promised the Houses, when last he met them in the spring, that he would do all in his power to avoid another session till a full year had passed. As early as October he had to confess that his pledge could not be kept, and that he had promised to perform the impossible. The Earl of Buckingham's costly and fruitless expedition to France—the great military event of the year 1380—had drained the Exchequer so far beyond the expectation of the ministers, the financial outlook had grown so utterly hopeless, that it had become necessary to appeal once more to the nation. Very unwillingly the ministers dispatched writs for a Parliament to meet at Northampton on November 5. The place was inconvenient—there was no sufficient housing, we are told, for the members of the two Houses and their retinues, and food and forage ran short. It was a wet winter, floods were out in every direction, and some of the magnates summoned were late at the rendezvous. All met in a most discontented mood. The cause, so it is said, of the choice of Northampton as a place of session, was that the ministers wished to avoid London, as they had in hand a great criminal trial in which the Londoners were deeply interested. A rich Genoese merchant, representing a syndicate of his compatriots, had been negotiating with the Government for a concession to establish a 'staple' for Mediterranean goods at Southampton : this grant would have taken away commerce from London, and the enterprising Italian was murdered by some London traders of whom the chief was a certain John Kirkeby.[1] The ministers were set on making an example of him and his fellows, but there was so much sympathy felt for the assassins in the capital that they did not wish to face the London mob. They had therefore chosen to meet Parliament in a distant county town.

Archbishop Sudbury, from whose virtues and integrity so much had been hoped, was now forced to own himself as great a failure in politics as any of his predecessors in the Chancellorship. He had to report that all the grants made for the sustentation of the war had proved hopelessly inadequate. The tenths and fifteenths were all exhausted, and by an unhappy chance the customs had yielded less in 1380 than in any recent year. Their shrinkage was caused by the outbreak of troubles in Flanders, the first beginnings of the deadly war between Count Louis and his subjects of Ghent, which was to last down to the fatal day of Roosebeke. Distracted by their civil troubles the Flemings had not bought their normal quantity of wool, and the subsidy on exported fleeces, the mainstay of the customs, had therefore fallen off in the most unsatisfactory style. Sudbury reported to the discontented members that he had been forced to borrow on all sides—he had even pledged the King's jewels, which would soon be forfeited if not redeemed. There was three months' pay owing to the garrisons of Calais, Cherbourg, and Brest, and Buckingham's army was in even larger arrears.

It is astonishing to find that the Parliament-men, though they grumbled loud and long, showed no signs of flagging in their determination that the French war should be carried on at all costs. They merely requested Sudbury to name a definite figure for the grants required, and to state it at the lowest possible amount 'because the Commons were poor'. After some hesitation the Chancellor gave them the appalling sum of £160,000 as the smallest contribution that would suffice for the King's needs. The Commons replied that, willing as they were to do their best, they regarded such an

---

[1] See *Chron. Angl.* 281.

estimate as outrageous, and did not see how the money could be raised. They requested the peers and prelates to take counsel in the Upper House, and to suggest some way out of the difficulty. There was a long debate in the Lords on the topic, which resulted in the drawing up of three alternative propositions, which were laid before the Commons. It was first suggested that the money might be raised by a Poll-tax of three groats per head on the whole adult population of England, so arranged, however, that ' the strong might aid the weak ' and the poorest individuals should not pay the whole shilling. Secondly, it might be feasible to collect the money by a ' poundage ' on all mercantile transactions within the kingdom, the seller in every case accounting for the percentage to the King's officials. Or thirdly, the ordinary course of voting ' tenths ' and ' fifteenths ' might be tried, though the number granted would have to be much larger than usual.

The Commons took these three proposals into consideration, and finally chose the Poll-tax as the least objectionable of the three. It seems likely that they were influenced by their own middle-class interests in doing so. They had a strong, and not altogether groundless, idea that the lower strata of society were not contributing their fair share to the defence of the realm, or, as they phrased it themselves ' that all the wealth of England was gone into the hands of the labourers and workmen '.[1] The poundage would have fallen mainly on the merchants, the tenths and fifteenths on landholders in the counties and householders in the boroughs. The Poll-tax would hit every one. Accordingly, the Commons voted that in spite of their great poverty and distress, they would grant £100,000 to be raised by Poll-tax, if the clergy, ' who occupy the third part of the lands of this realm ', would undertake to raise the rest of the money demanded by the Chancellor.

The clergy, anxious in all probability to give no occasion to their enemies for suggesting broad measures of disen-dowment as an easy way of filling the national purse, rose

---

[1] *Continuatio Eulogii Historiarum*, p. 345.

to the occasion with unexpected liberality. They protested
that they would make no grant in Parliament, but promised
that the convocations of the two provinces should vote fifty
thousand marks. On this assurance, which was loyally
carried out,[1] the Commons proceeded to draft their scheme
for the raising of the Poll-tax. It was provided that every
lay person in the realm, above the age of fifteen years, save
beggars, should pay three groats : but that the distribution
of the whole sum of one shilling per head should be so
graduated that in each township the wealthy should aid the
poor, on the scale that the richest person should not pay more
than sixty groats ($£1$) for himself and his wife, nor the poorest
less than one groat for himself and his wife. This was a
very different and much more onerous affair than the two
previous Poll-taxes which the realm had paid. In 1377
the sum raised had been only a single groat all round the
nation. In 1379 the levy had been carefully graduated from
one groat on the ordinary labourer up to £6 13s. 4d. on the
Duke of Lancaster.[2] On neither occasion had more than the
fourpence per head been raised from the poorest classes.
But in 1381 the form of the grant was such that in many
places the whole shilling had to be extracted from the most
indigent persons, and that even in those where some gradua-
tion turned out to be possible, the number of individuals who
got off with a payment of 4d. or 6d. a head was comparatively

[1] The convocation of Canterbury made its vote on Dec. 1 ; that of York on
Jan. 10. They chose the same method of Poll-tax that their lay brethren had
favoured. Every priest, monk or nun paid half a mark.

[2] The scale had been—

(a) The Duke of Lancaster, and the Duke of Brittany for his English
estates, £6 13s. 4d.

(b) The Chief Justices of the King's Bench and Common Pleas, and the
Chief Baron of the Exchequer, £5 each.

(c) Earls, Countesses, and the Mayor of London, £4 each.

(d) Barons, Banneretts, the Prior of the Hospitallers, Aldermen of London,
Mayors of large towns, Sergeants-at-law, Advocates, Notaries, and Proctors of
senior standing, £2 each.

(e) Knights-Bachelors, Knights and Commanders of the Hospital, Mayors
of small towns, jurors and merchants of large towns, Advocates and Notaries of
junior standing, from £1 down to 3s. 4d.

(f) All other persons a groat.

small. How this inequality of pressure between place and place worked out with grave injustice we shall explain a little later. It is probable that the legislators had not in the least realized how inequitable their arrangement would prove.

In addition to granting the Poll-tax the Commons continued the existing subsidy on wool, though owing to the troubles in Flanders it was likely to prove less productive than usual. They suggested to the Government that all alien priories should be dissolved, and foreign monks living in them be forced to return to their own country. But this was not done, and it was left for Archbishop Chichele to take up the scheme half a century later, and to found with the revenue of many alien priories his college of All Souls.

Shortly after the two Houses had dispersed [1] and gone home through the flooded midland shires, the Treasurer, Bishop Brantingham of Exeter, resigned. He had probably had enough of his invidious task of endeavouring to make two ends meet : perhaps he was clear-sighted enough to foresee something of the trouble that was at hand, and to resolve that he at least would have no share in it. Undoubtedly he saved his own neck by throwing up his appointment. In his place Sir Robert Hales, Prior of the Knights Hospitallers, was placed over the treasury. By accepting this office he brought upon himself a dreadful death six months later.

After the new year the ministers set to work to collect the Poll-tax, which was raised in January and February 'non sine diris maledictionibus '. The method adopted was to appoint a small body of collectors for each shire, who were to deal by means of a more numerous body of sub-collectors with the constables of townships and the mayors or bailiffs of towns, and to see that from each place as many shillings were paid as there were adults over fifteen years of age. The grievance which at once leapt into sight was that this form of levy bore most hardly on the poorest places. Wher-

---

[1] *Post festa Natalis Domini celebrata,* presumably between Christmas and the New Year, Walsingham, i. p. 449.

ever there were rich residents, as in large towns, or manors where a great landowner chanced to reside, the poorest classes got off cheaply ; because the wealthy households gave many groats, and so the labourers paid no more than fourpence or sixpence a head, as Parliament had provided. But in poor villages, where there was no moneyed resident, every villein and cottager had to pay the full shilling, because there was no 'sufficient person' to help him out.[1]

The remedy for this inequitable taxation which seems to have occurred simultaneously to every villager over the greater part of England, was to make false returns to the commissioners of the Poll-tax. The constables must either have been willing parties to the fraud, or have been coaxed or forced into it by their neighbours. The result was that every shire of England returned an incredibly small number of adult inhabitants liable to the impost. This can be proved with absolute certainty by comparing the returns of the earlier one-groat Poll-tax of 1377 with those of this one-shilling Poll-tax of 1381. To the former all persons over *fourteen* had to contribute, to the latter all persons over *fifteen*, so that there should have been a small, but still perceptible, falling off in the returns. But instead of the slight diminution in taxable persons expected, the commissioners of the Poll-tax reported that there were only two-thirds as many contributaries in 1381 as in 1377. The adult population of the realm had ostensibly fallen from 1,355,201 to 896,481 persons.[2] These figures were monstrous and incredible—in five years, during which the realm, though

---

[1] The case may be made clear by comparing two Suffolk villages from the Poll-tax returns of that county. In Brockley, in Thingoe hundred, a place with seventy adult inhabitants, there were resident an esquire, who paid 6s. for himself and wife, and five wealthy farmers who each paid 2s. 6d. The consequence of this was that the poorest persons in the place got off with paying 4d. or 6d. each, representing the value of a day and a half or two days' unskilled labour. But in the neighbouring village of Chevington there was no resident landowner and only one farmer of substance. The result was that every one of the resident villeins and labourers had to pay the full three groats, to make up a shilling a head on the seventy-eight adult inhabitants. Thus the poor man in Chevington had to pay just thrice as much as the poor man in Brockley, which he naturally conceived to be an abominable grievance.

[2] Excluding in both cases the Palatinates of Durham and Chester.

far from being in a flourishing condition, had yet been visited
neither by pestilence, famine, nor foreign invasion, the ministers were invited to believe that its population had fallen off
in some districts more than 50 per cent.,[1] in none less than
20 per cent.

A glance at the details of the township-returns, of which
a considerable number survive, though no single county list
is complete and some are altogether lost, reveals the simple
form of evasion which the villagers had practised when sending in their schedules. They had suppressed the existence of
their unmarried female dependants, widowed mothers and
aunts, sisters, young daughters, &c., in a wholesale fashion.
The result is that most villages show an enormous and impossible predominance of males in their population, and an
equally incredible want of unmarried females. Nothing is
better known than the fact that in an old agricultural community the females tend to be in an excess. Only in new
settlements, or in lands where female infanticide prevails, is
the opposite case to be found. When therefore we find Essex
or Suffolk or Staffordshire townships returning, one after
another, a population working out in the proportion of five
or four males to four or three females, we know what to
conclude.[2] Some of these communities refuse to acknowledge
any unmarried females at all in their midst, and send in a roll
consisting solely of a symmetrical list of men and wives, with

---

[1] The figures of a few shires are sufficient to explain the situation :—

	1377	1381		1377	1381
Kent . . .	56557	43838	Suffolk . .	58610	44635
Norfolk . .	88797	66719	Berks. . . .	22723	14895
Northants .	40225	27997	Devon . . .	45635	20656
Salop . . .	23574	13041	Dorset . .	34241	19507
Somerset . .	54604	30384	Essex . . .	47962	30748

For the whole set of figures and some comments thereon see the Table in
Appendix II of this book.

[2] For the figures of a typical Essex hundred in detail see my Appendix, No.
III, 167–82. I worked out in the Record Office many villages from scattered
counties, with results such as this :—Cam, 18 males, 11 females ; Beauchamp
Oton, 44 males, 30 females; Shillingford, 45 males, 36 females ; Snareshill,
18 males, 15 females ; Lapley, 58 males, 52 females ; Pentlow, 29 males,
22 females ; Hammerwych, 9 males, 5 females, &c., &c. In the whole hundred
of Thingoe, Suffolk, we get 487 males to 383 females, and so on through the
hundreds.

no dependants of either sex.[1] In a certain amount of cases, apparently where a very honest or a very simple-minded constable made the return, we find households such as we should expect to have existed in reality, with a due proportion of aged widows, and of sisters or daughters who are living with their brothers and fathers, but this is quite exceptional. In the majority of the townships we find an unnatural want of dependants male and female, but more especially female. In short the main body of the returns bear witness to a colossal and deliberate attempt to defraud the Government of its odious tax-money by a general falsification of figures. It failed because it was overdone : the numbers given defied belief, and drove the ministers into an inquisitorial research into the details of the returns, with the object of discovering and punishing the persons who had endeavoured to deceive them.

The collectors had been charged to pay in two-thirds of their receipts in January, and the rest in June, 1381. They appear, however, to have set to work to raise not a part but the whole of the exigible groats at once. The moment that their accounts began to come in the Government took the alarm. On February 22, 1381, the Council issued a writ to the Barons of the Exchequer, in the King's name, stating that instant efforts must be made to collect the whole of the Poll-tax, as the sum received had fallen lamentably short of what should have been forthcoming. On March 16 they issued an additional mandate, declaring that they had ample evidence that the collectors and constables had behaved with shameless negligence and corruption, and creating a fresh body of commissioners, who were to travel round the shires to compare the list of inhabitants returned in the first schedules with the actual population of the townships, to compel payment from all persons who had evaded the impost, and to imprison all who resisted their authority.[2] It is said that this commission was suggested to the ministers by John

---

[1] Woodbaston (Staffs.) is a case of this. Northwood (Glos.) returned only one unmarried woman in a population of 34 souls.

[2] See the writ in my Appendix IV, p.183-5.

Legge, one of the King's sergeants-at-arms. The reputation
of having done so cost him his life.[1] For reasons which we
cannot discover, the commissioners were directed to set to
work on fifteen shires only, including all those of the south-
east, and, in addition, Somerset, Devon, Cornwall, Gloucestershire, and the West Riding of Yorkshire. Some of the counties
left unscheduled had produced returns as bad as any of these.
The second roll of commissioners for the survey of the Poll-
tax was drawn up in March, not without difficulty, for many
of the persons designated to serve excused themselves, fore-
seeing, no doubt, the unpopularity which they would incur.
There must have been in many districts hardly a family
which had not sent in a false return, and thereby rendered
itself liable not only to the payment for the concealed
members but also to punishment for having concealed them.

Nevertheless the commissioners were at last got together,
and in many districts had begun to work in April and May.
So far as their activity had gone, it sufficed to show at once
that the ministers had been right, and that wholesale fraud
had been practised against the Government during the first
levy of the Poll-tax. In Norwich town 600 persons were
discovered to have evaded the original collectors, in Norfolk
about 8,000, but still more striking was the case of the county
of Suffolk, where no less than 13,000 suppressed names were
collected in a few weeks.[2] But the revision had not gone
far when an explosion of popular wrath occurred on a scale
that not even the gloomiest prophet had foreseen.

The explanation of the outburst is simply that the countryside was seething with discontent ere ever the Poll-tax was
imposed, that the Poll-tax itself was monstrously heavy for
the poorest classes, that these classes had—with wonderful
unanimity—tried to defend themselves by the simple device
of false returns, and that they had been 'found out', and
were in process of being mulcted. The Government had
taken in hand the chastisement of tens of thousands of

[1] Knighton's Continuator, ii. 130.
[2] First return of Norwich, 3,268 adults, revised return of May, 3,833; first
return of Suffolk, 31,734 adults, revised return, 44,635; first return of
Norfolk, 58,714, revised return, 66,719. See Powell, p. 6.

offenders, and had entrusted it to commissioners who were backed by no armed force, but descended on the offending districts accompanied by half a dozen clerks and sergeants only. Their task was so odious, their compelling power so weak, that it is only surprising that they were not stoned out of the very first villages that they took in hand. Yet it was only after a month of friction, and when thousands of shillings had been extorted from the needy evaders of the tax, that the trouble commenced.

CHAPTER III

THE OUTBREAK IN KENT AND ESSEX

THE actual outbreak of violence began in Essex, on the last day but one of May. Thomas Bampton, one of the new commissioners, had ridden down to Brentwood to revise the taxation-returns of the hundred of Barstaple. Not suspecting in the least that he was likely to meet with resistance, he brought with him only his three clerks and two of the King's sergeants-at-arms. He opened his inquiry with the examination of the three marshland villages of Fobbing, Corringham, and Stanford. The peasants and fishermen of these little places came prepared to resist.[1] The Fobbing men were cited before him; as the chronicler tells us, they informed him that they did not intend to pay a penny more than they had already contributed,[2] and used such contumacious language that Bampton bade his sergeants arrest the spokesman.[3] This gave the signal for violence, which had obviously been premeditated : the peasants, about 100 strong, fell upon the party from London, beat them, and stoned them out of the town.[4]

Bampton, bruised and frightened, returned to the Council, and reported his misadventure. Thereupon the Government, still misconceiving the aspect of affairs, sent down to Brentwood Robert Belknap, Chief Justice of the Common Pleas, on a commission of Trailbaston, with orders to seek out and

[1] All this comes from the excellent chronicle published by Mr. George Trevelyan in *Hist. Rev.* vol. xiii.

[2] 'Ilz ne voderont nulle denier paier, pur cause que ils avoient un acquitance pur celle subsidie. Sur lequel le dit Thomas les manassa fortement', &c., ibid. p. 510.

[3] Probably the Thomas Baker of Fobbing who is mentioned by the Continuator of Knighton as the first leader of sedition, Knighton, ii. p. 131.

[4] 'Fueront en purpose de occire le dit Thomas et lesditz seriantes', says the chronicle, perhaps somewhat exaggerating their fury.

punish the rioters.   But meanwhile the men of Fobbing and
Corringham had sent messages all round southern Essex, to
call out their neighbours.   We learn from the judicial
records of the rebellion that these emissaries, some of them
local men, others strangers from London, were riding up
and down on June 1, rousing all malcontents and bidding
them be ready to offer armed resistance when the judge
should appear.   It would seem that confident assurances
were made to the effect that Kent and London were prepared to rise, the moment that the signal should be given.[1]
When, therefore, Belknap came down to Brentwood on June 2
and opened his commission, he and his clerks were suddenly
set upon by an armed multitude.   It was inexcusable folly
on the part of the Council to have sent them forth without an
escort.   Belknap was seized, and forced to swear on the
Bible that he would never hold another such session ;   his
papers were destroyed, yet he was finally allowed to escape.
But the mob beat to death and then beheaded three of the
local jurors who had been called up to ' present ' the original
rioters before the chief justice, and then killed three unfortunate clerks.   Their heads were set on poles, and paraded
round Brentwood and the neighbouring villages.   After this
bloodshed there could be no turning back :   the men of south
Essex would be forced in self-preservation to defend themselves from the vengeance that they had called down upon
their own heads.   Accordingly, the murders at Brentwood
were promptly followed by a general outbreak of plunder and
riot, which spread through the county, eastward and northward, during the first week of June.

It might have been expected that the Council, now at last,
after such a desperate defiance of its power had been made,
would collect every armed man in London that could be

---

[1] For example, Roger of South Ockendon, and John Smith of Rainham,
'equitaverunt vi armata et compulerunt homines earundem villarum cum iis ire,
in conventiculis et congregationibus huiusmodi ' ; while the two London butchers,
Adam Attewell and Roger Harry, both of whom were afterwards prominent in
the troubles in the capital, are said to have been raising the Essex peasantry
fourteen days before they entered London, i. e. about May 31 or June 1.   See
Essex indictments and the Sheriff's reports of Nov. 20, 1382, in Réville, p. 196.

trusted, and send a force—however small—to occupy Brentwood on the day after the outbreak.   But this was
impossible : for already Kent was following the example
of Essex, and even in the capital itself the King's ministers
felt the ground quaking beneath their feet

As early as June 2 a small armed band, headed by one
Abel Ker of Erith, had set the example of rebellion in Kent.
They burst into the monastery of Lesness, and frightened the
Abbot into swearing an oath to support them.   Then they took
boat across the Thames estuary, conferred with the men of
the villages about Barking, and returned on June 4, bringing
with them a band of about 100 auxiliaries from beyond the
river.   On the following day this small mob entered the town
of Dartford, and 'traitorously moved the men of the said
town to insurrection, making divers assemblies and con-
gregations against the King's peace '.

It was apparently about this moment [1] that the Council
sent down into Kent a judge with a commission of Trailbaston
just as they had done in Essex a few days before.   He proposed to ride to Canterbury to open proceedings, but was
intercepted and driven back to London by an angry mob ;
unlike Belknap, however, he and his party got off scot free
as far as their persons were concerned.[2]   All the central
parts of the shire were now in a disturbed state.   We hear
no more of Abel Ker ; but one Robert Cave, a baker of Dartford, now appears for a few days as the ringleader of the
rioters.   He led a multitude collected from Dartford, Erith,
Lesness, Bexley, and all the small places in their neighbourhood, towards Rochester, on the morning of June 6.   It was on
this day that the Kentishmen first began to do serious mischief ; hitherto nothing more than riotous assembly had been

---

[1] So at least we should gather from the sequence of events in the chronicle
in *Hist. Rev.* xiii, p. 511.

[2] 'En celle temps une justice fust assigné par le roy et son counciel et maundé en
Kent pour sere illonques de Trailbaston, en mannere comme fust en Excesse, et
ovesque luy un seriant d'armes du roy Johne Legge per nome, portant ovesque
lui graunde nombre de enditements . . . et voyderont avoir assis en Kanterburye,
mais ilz furent rebotés par les commons ', ibid. p. 511.   I do not think that this
means that they ever got near Canterbury ; probably they were intercepted and
turned back as early as Dartford.

laid to their charge. But now they beset the castle of Rochester, and, after making several ineffective assaults on the old Norman keep, finally terrified the constable, Sir John Newton, into capitulating. They broke open the dungeons, delivered a certain prisoner named John Belling,[1] and plundered the castle. After this success the doings of the rebels became much more outrageous. The whole mob, now several thousands strong, marched up the Medway to Maidstone, and on entering that town murdered a burgess named John Southall—how he had offended them we do not know—and plundered his house and that of a certain William Topcliffe, who must have been a person of great wealth, as goods to the value of no less than 1,000 marks were taken from him.

It is on the next day, June 7, that we are first confronted with that famous but enigmatic personage Wat Tyler. ' There at Maidstone ', says the most detailed and trustworthy of the chronicles, ' they chose as chief Wat Teghler of that place, to maintain them and act as their counsellor.' His origin and his earlier career are entirely unknown : the legends which make him an artisan of Dartford, whose daughter had been insulted by one of the collectors of the Poll-tax, may be safely neglected.[2] If he had been a Dartford man, his name would certainly appear among those of the companions of Robert Cave during his riotous proceedings

---

[1] In the indictment of Robert Cave it is stated that the captive objected to being released. ' Robertum Belling, prisonem in eodem castro detentum, contra voluntatem ipsius prisonis cepit [idem Robertus Cave] et cum eo abduxit.' It is clear that this man must be identical with a person mentioned in the chronicle of the Peasants' Revolt printed in the *Historical Review*, xiii. pp. 509-22. This document states that Sir Simon Burley had on June 3 caused much anger at Gravesend by arresting there an escaped villein of his own. He seized the man, and took him off to Rochester Castle, where he placed him in custody. Apparently the purpose of Cave's assault on the castle was the deliverance of this prisoner, whose capture had caused much excitement and sympathy. Burley was very unpopular, as being one of the knot of courtiers about the King whose responsibility for the misgovernment of the realm was being loudly asserted.

[2] The story of a Tyler of Dartford, who slew the tax-collector, is only found in the Elizabethan annalist Stow, and he calls the man *John*, not Walter. The tale, however, that some of the poll-tax men had behaved indecently in Kent —without details given—comes from the better authority of the Continuator of Knighton, ii. 130.

on June 5–7. But though seven or eight of these rioters are registered in the legal proceedings against these insurgents there is no Walter and no Tyler among them. It even seems doubtful whether he was really domiciled at Maidstone : the rolls of Parliament simply call him, 'Wauter Tyler del countée de Kent ', while the juries of the hundreds of Faversham and Downhamford, which lie only a few miles east of Maidstone, style the great rebel 'Walterum Teghler *de Essex*' in their presentations.[1] A Maidstone document calls him Walter Tyler of Colchester : if so, he was a compatriot of John Ball. The continuer of the *Eulogium Historiarum*, a good contemporary authority, also makes him appear as *unus tegulator de Estsex*. It is probable that he was an adventurer of unknown antecedents, and we may well believe the Kentishman who declared that he was a well-known rogue and highwayman.[2] The authority of Froissart for English domestic events is not very great, but it is tempting to follow him in this case, and to credit the tale that Wat (like his successor Jack Cade) was a discharged soldier returned from the French wars. We are told that he had been overseas in the service of Richard Lyons (the swindling financier against whom the Good Parliament had raged) when the latter was one of the sergeants-at-arms of Edward III. Froissart adds that Lyons lost his life in the riots of June 14, because of his old subordinate's rancorous remembrance of a thrashing received many years before. The way in which Tyler established his authority over the disorderly multitude, his power of enforcing discipline, and his evident capacity for command, all tend to make us suspect that he won his supremacy over the insurgents because he was a man with military experience. There must have been a very considerable sprinkling of old soldiers among the mob : a large proportion of the able-bodied men of the realm had been serving as bills or bows in one or another of the expeditions sent out in the later years of

---

[1] See *Archaeologia Cantiana*, iii. 92–3.

[2] 'Un valet de Kent, estant entre les gentz du roi, pria pur vier le dit Watt cheftaine de les commons, et quant il luy vist il dist apertement que fust le plus grand robbare et larron de toute Kent.' Chronicle in *Hist. Rev.* xviii. p. 519.

Edward III, and it would be among them that chiefs would naturally be sought. But whatever may have been Tyler's antecedents, we know that he was a quick-witted, self-reliant, ambitious fellow, with an insolent tongue, and the gift of magniloquence, which a mob orator needs.[1] That he was anything more than a bold and ready demagogue there is no proof whatever. There is no reason to believe either that he had been the organizer of the revolt, or that when he had talked or pushed himself to the front he had elaborated any definite plan for the reformation of the body politic of England. Who can say what ideas may have flashed through the brain of an adventurer who suddenly found himself in command of a host of ten or fifteen thousand angry, reckless, and ignorant insurgents ? He may have been dreaming of no more than his own personal aggrandizement : he may have had some vague notion of changing the framework of society, perhaps he may even have conceived the machiavellian plan of using the King's name to destroy the governing classes, and then making away with the King himself, which is attributed to him by some contemporary writers.[2] It is probable, however, that he was a mere opportunist, whose designs expanded with the unexpected growth of his short-lived empire over the multitude. Originally he was but the nominee of the Kentish mob, whose desires were firstly to destroy the ' traitors ' about the King—the men responsible for the Poll-tax, the general misgovernment, and the disasters of the French war, such as the Duke of Lancaster, Archbishop Sudbury and Treasurer Hales—and secondly, to do away with the tiresome incidents of the manorial system. When the

---

[1] He was ' vir versutus, et magno sensu preditus ', says the *Chron. Angl.* p. 294. For his magniloquence see his speeches to the Hertfordshire insurgents in ibid. 300, and elsewhere. For his insolence his conduct at the Smithfield interview is sufficient evidence. His capacity for maintaining discipline is shown by the fact that he executed thieves among his own followers, and his authority seems never to have been questioned by any rival.

[2] See mainly the celebrated confession of Jack Straw in *Chron. Angl.* p. 309. It is impossible to say how far it can be trusted. It embodies the fears of the ruling classes, but it may also embody the real design of the more desperate of the leaders of the insurgents. Certainly, however, the bulk of them had no such intentions : they were perfectly loyal to the King.

rebels found themselves undisputed masters of the countryside, and still more when they had entered London in triumph
and slain their enemies, the leaders at least—whatever the
multitude thought—must have had a glimpse of the greatness of their opportunity. Tyler's assumption of dictatorial
authority, and his ruthless exercise of the power to slay
during the two days of his domination in the city, together
with his gratuitous insolence in the presence of the King,
indicate that he had no intention of going home when the
redress of grievances had been promised, but was intending
to maintain himself as a power in the realm. A landless
adventurer who had pushed his way to the front in the crisis,
and who had bathed his hands in blood, was not the sort of
person to be satisfied with the King's concessions, or to retire
content into his former obscurity. But whatever visions
of greatness may have hovered before him on June 15, he
was on June 7 merely the casually chosen captain of the
unruly mob that thronged the streets of Maidstone. The
first use that he made of his influence would seem to have
been to direct the march of his followers on Canterbury.

On the 8th and 9th the rising was extending itself in all
directions, and bands of recruits from every village between
the Weald and the estuary of the Thames were flocking in to
join the main body. On these two days a good deal of mischief seems to have been done in the countryside. The anger
of the insurgents would appear to have been directed mainly
against four classes—royal officials, lawyers, adherents of
John of Gaunt, and unpopular landlords.[1] We learn that
they seized great quantities of official documents in the
houses of Thomas Shardelow of Dartford, the coroner of
Kent, and of Elias Raynor of Strood, which they 'traitorously burnt and consumed in the midst of the streets
of the aforesaid towns'.[2] They levelled to the ground the
great manor house of Nicholas Herring at North Cray,
pillaged his goods, and drove off his cattle. They seized as

---

[1] For murders of lawyers see *Chron. Angl* p. 287. For attack on retainers
of Lancaster, see Chronicle in *Hist. Rev.* p. 512.

[2] See the Indictments in Réville, pp. 185-6.

hostages four prominent country gentlemen—Sir Thomas Cobham, Sir Thomas Tryvet, John de Freningham, and James Peacham, and held them as hostages, after making them swear an oath of fealty to ' King Richard and the Commons of England '. They broke open all the gaols and released their inmates, to whose deliverance we may probably attribute the epidemic of burglary in the houses of private persons which accompanied the second stage of the rebellion.

All this sporadic mischief seems to display no fixed plan of campaign ; but at last, on the 10th, a definite movement was made. On that day Tyler moved off to Canterbury at the head of the main body of his horde. They entered the city without opposition, and were joined by a large number of the citizens. They then proceeded to sack the palace of the Archbishop. It was clearly against Sudbury as chancellor and politician, and not against churchmen at large, that they were enraged, for they spared the great monastic establishments of Canterbury. They made, it is true, a riotous entry into the Cathedral during service time, but it was only with the object of shouting to the monks of the chapter that they would soon have to elect a new primate, for Sudbury was a traitor and was doomed to a traitor's death : they were going to seek him in London, and to deliver the King from his hands. Next to the Archbishop, Sir William Septvans the sheriff, as the main instrument of the local government, was the best hated man in Kent : but he was lucky enough to escape with his life, though he was hustled, maltreated, and forced to give up all his store of official documents. The judicial and financial records of the county—a hoard that would have been invaluable to the historians of to-day— were burned in the street. Moreover, the castle was sacked, and the gaol, as usual during the rising, was broken open and emptied.

The arrival of the insurgents seems to have been the signal for the settling of many old grudges among the citizens of Canterbury. ' Have you not some traitors here ? ' the newcomers are said to have asked : whereupon three unfortunate persons were pointed out by the local mob. They were

dragged into the street and beheaded : [1] moreover the houses
of several other ' suspects ' were broken open and sacked,
though they themselves escaped with their lives. There
was an immense destruction of legal documents, leases, bonds,
and suchlike, belonging to private individuals of no importance.[2] This must have been the work of their personal
enemies, who turned the mob against them, in order to get
the chance of burning inconvenient papers. Housebreaking
and wanton pillage of this kind went on for several days after
the main body of the rioters had departed, and was so outrageous that the city of Canterbury was one of the places
excepted from the general amnesty, in the first list drawn
up by Parliament after the suppression of the revolt. The
Mayor and bailiffs had not been deposed by the mob, though
they had been forced to take the oath to ' King Richard and
the Commons ', which was now the watchword of the insurgents. But it is clear that they were wholly impotent, and
could do nothing to preserve peace and order in the city.

It is notable that on the very day of the entry of the bands
of West Kent into Canterbury outbreaks of plunder and riot
are chronicled not only in the villages close to the metro-
politan city, but in places so remote as Sandwich, Tenterden,
and Appledore. Evidently the emissaries of the rising had
penetrated in all directions, far ahead of the main body, and
had succeeded in raising the local malcontents even before
the news of the capture of Canterbury could have reached
them. On this day and the two following all eastern Kent
was in an uproar. Everywhere the houses of unpopular
landlords were sacked, and manor rolls were burnt. But it
is a notable feature of the whole movement that very few
murders were committed : there seems to have been comparatively little of that ferocious hatred for the whole of the
upper classes which had been displayed in France twenty-
three years before, during the horrors of the Jacquerie. The

---

[1] See the *Hist. Rev.*, Chronicle, p. 512.

[2] See, for example, the documents 7 and 8 of Réville's Appendix, p. 189,
where Agnes Tebbe and John Spicer plead that all their documents had been
destroyed by the rebels.

doings of the insurgents are much more like those of the peasants of South Germany during the *Bauernkrieg* of 1525, where (as in England) bloodshed was the exception and not the rule. Many of the gentry of Kent deserted their homes, and rode off with their families and their retainers to undisturbed districts : others, as we are told, took to the woods and lay hid for many days : others locked themselves up in their dwellings and waited for the worst. The worst, when it came, took the shape of pillage and insult; but, in Kent at least, it only fell to the lot of the minority. The larger number of the landowners had only to pay blackmail, under the name of contributions to ' the Cause ', and to consent to take the oath of fidelity to ' King and Commons '. Moreover their court-rolls were usually taken from them and made into a bonfire before the unwelcome visitors departed. Occasionally, but only occasionally, a man of importance was carried off as a hostage and compelled to accompany the rebel host, as Cobham and his three companions had been during the first days of the rising. But we have no clear instance of the murder of any one of the Kentish squirearchy : what little bloodshed there was took place in the towns.

On the very next morning after the capture of Canterbury, Tyler led off his horde toward London. This, from his and their point of view, was undoubtedly the right policy : it was only by seizing the capital and the person of the King that they could attain their ends. No amount of local riot and plunder would help them, and if they dallied long the Government would have time to organize an army and defend itself. Long ere the whole of the bands of eastern Kent had flocked in to the muster in the cathedral city, the van of the rebel host was in full march westward. On the 11th it passed through Maidstone on its return journey, and there renewed the scenes of riot that had taken place on June 8.

It is said to have been at Maidstone [1] that the host was joined by the personage who was to be its most notable figure after Tyler, the celebrated John Ball, the ' mad priest of Kent ' whom we have already had occasion to mention.

---

[1] So the Continuator of Knighton, ii. p. 131.

He had been delivered by the mob from the Archbishop's prison, where he had been confined since April. Ball was a familiar figure all over southern England: originally a secular priest, he had ministered first in York and then in Colchester; but he had after a time thrown up regular clerical work for the life of an itinerant preacher. He had been for twenty years on the tramp, and was a well-known agitator long ere Wycliffe—on whom his doctrines have been so wrongly fathered—was anything more than an orthodox lecturer on theology at Oxford. Ball was a prophet in the ancient Hebrew style—a denouncer of the wickedness of the times, and more especially of the wickedness of the higher clergy. His inspiring idea was the 'evangelical poverty' which had been preached by the Franciscans in the previous century: his butts were the political bishops and pluralist dignitaries in whose hands so much of the wealth of the Church was accumulated. The Papacy too had come in for a share of his abuse—in the day of the Great Schism, the spectacle of the rival pontiffs waging war with swords as well as curses provoked much milder men to use violent language. But evil secular lords and their oppressions were not omitted in his objurgatory sermons. He was a kind of modern Jeremiah, hateful to the Pashurs and Zedekiahs of 1381.

Though he was always a very half-hearted persecutor, the primate had twice felt himself obliged to put Ball in ward. After his first release, as Sudbury complained, 'he had slunk back to our diocese, like the fox that evades the hunter, and feared not to preach and argue both in churches and churchyards (without the leave or against the will of the parochial authorities) and also in markets and other profane places, there beguiling the ears of the laity by his invectives, and putting about scandals concerning our own person, and those of other prelates and clergy, and (what is worse) using concerning the Holy Father himself dreadful language such as shocked the ears of good Christians.'[1] For three months Ball had been constrained to silence in his dungeon, and when he was liberated by the rioters he had a fund of suppressed

[1] *Conc. Brit.* iii. 153.

eloquence to vent. Now for the first time he could preach without fear of arrest or punishment, and was certain of an audience far larger than he had ever before addressed, an audience, too, which was in entire sympathy with his views. Hence it came about that his daily harangues grew more and more confident ; he thought that he saw the actual commencement of that reign of Christian democracy of which he had so long dreamed. All social inequalities were to be redressed, there were no longer to be rich and poor, nor lords and serfs. Spiritual wickedness in high places, evil living, covetousness, and pride were all to be chastised and ended. It was presumably in the first days of his triumph that Ball wrote and sent abroad the strange rhyming letters which the Continuator of Knighton and the author of the *Chronicon Angliae* have preserved :

'John Ball greeteth you well all, and doth you to understand that he hath rungen your bell. Now right and might, will and skill. Now God haste you in every thing. Time it is that Our Lady help you with Jesus her son, and the Son with the Father, to make in the name of the Holy Trinity a good end to what has been begun. Amen, Amen, for charity Amen.'[1]

And again : 'John Ball, priest of St. Mary's, greets well all manner of men, and bids them in the name of the Trinity, Father, Son, and Holy Ghost, to stand together manfully in truth. Maintain the truth and the truth will maintain you.

> Now reigneith Pride in price,
> And Covetise is holden wise,
> And Lechery withouten shame,
> And Gluttony withouten blame,
> Envye reigneth with treason,
> And Sloath is take in grete season.

God give aid, for now is the time. Amen.'[2]

Still more interesting is a third effusion, which seems to bear a more definite and more political character. 'John Schepe, some time St. Mary's priest of York, and now of Colchester, greeteth well John Nameless, and John the Miller, and John the Carter, and biddeth them that they beware of

---

[1] Knighton, ii. 139. [2] Ibid. ii. 140.

guile in borough,[1] and stand together in God's name, and biddeth Piers Plowman go to his work, and chastise well Hobbe the Robber [i.e. Robert Hales the treasurer], and take with you John Trueman and all his fellows, and no mo, and look that ye shape you to one head and no mo.'[2]

The point of this epistle is evidently to urge the multitude to give implicit obedience to their one head, i. e. Tyler—discipline being all important; to bid them beware of being turned from their designs by the townsfolk (who had their own separate ends to seek); and above all to warn them not to take into partnership false brethren who would turn aside to pillage and self-seeking, but only honest partisans of the cause. It is curious that Sudbury's name is not bracketed with that of ' Hobbe the Robber ' : was Ball perhaps grateful to the primate for having dealt no harder with him in spite of their repeated collisions ?

Of Ball we have a very full knowledge : of Tyler we catch a glimpse long enough to enable us to form some conception of the man. But their lieutenants are mere names to us : of John Hales of Malling, Alan Threder, William Hawke, and John Ferrour, and other leaders named in Kentish documents we have no personal knowledge whatever : we have only a list of the outrages laid to their charge. Even Jack Straw, the most notable of them, is a vague figure who flits across Essex no less than Kent, and though he is mentioned, we seldom or never detect him actually at work till the entry of the rebels into London. He is probably identical with the John Rackstraw mentioned in some of the chronicles and in the judicial proceedings which followed the insurrection.[3]

---

[1] Does this mean to avoid being tricked when they get to London, or to avoid being drawn by designing persons into taking sides in town quarrels, such as those then raging in Canterbury ?

[2] *Chron. Angl.* p. 322.

[3] An article, more ingenious than convincing, in the *Hist. Rev.* for January, 1906, by Doctor F. W. Brie, will have it that Jack Straw is no real person at all, but a mere nickname of Wat Tyler. It is quite true that the Continuator of Knighton held this view [' proprio nomine Watte Tyler sed jam mutato nomine vocatus est Jakke Straw '], and that two or three ballads and several fifteenth-century chroniclers (e. g. Adam of Usk, Harding, and Gregory) speak of Jakke

A glance through the roll of the Kentishmen implicated in the rising shows only one person of gentle birth, a certain squire named Bertram Wilmington who raised a band at Wye;[1] in the eastern counties, as we shall see, the proportion of chiefs drawn from the upper classes was much larger. In Kent there is a sprinkling of wealthy yeomen and priests,[2] but the great majority are artisans and peasants of the poorest class, whose goods the escheators valued at a few shillings.

On June 11 and June 12 the insurgent host executed in wonderfully rapid time their march from Canterbury to the outskirts of London. They were growing in numbers every moment, as the numerous contingents from the villages of western Kent joined them. Hurried as was the movement, they yet found leisure to break open manor houses and burn court-rolls on their way. It is said—but trustworthy details are wanting—that they caught and slew several lawyers. As they drew near London, they met the King's mother, the Princess of Wales, who was hastily returning from a pilgrimage to the shrines of Kent, to put herself in safety behind the walls of the Tower. She and her attendants gave themselves up for lost, but to their surprise suffered no more than a short arrest : after passing some ribald jokes upon the trembling ladies, the leaders of the insurgents gave orders that they were to be allowed to proceed, unplundered and unmolested. They wished, no doubt, to show that they were not thieves or murderers ; moreover they hoped to get the King upon their side, and could not hope to win his favour if they started by mal-treating his mother.

Straw being killed by Walworth at Smithfield. But the Rolls of the Parliament of 1381, the most primary authority of all, most carefully distinguish Tyler and Straw as two separate persons. So does the *Chron. Angliae,* whose account of the whole business is excellent ; there is no possibility of confusing the Wat Tyler killed at Smithfield with the Jack Straw who is arrested and tried before the commissioners some days later, and who makes the curious and elaborate confession concerning the ultimate designs of the rebels. This latter, no doubt, was that same John Rakestraw who made proclamation to the people of the Isle of Thanet. See *Archaeologia Cantiana,* iii. p. 76.

[1] For his doings see the document in *Arch. Cant.* iii. 81, 82.

[2] Such as John Coveshurst of Lamberhurst, one of the decapitated leaders, who owned a freehold farm of 120 acres. See Réville's documents, p. 233.

On the night of the 12th, the main body of the Kentishmen encamped on Blackheath, but those of them who were not tired out by their long march pushed as far as Southwark and Lambeth ; there they were met by a mob of malcontents belonging to the suburbs and even by numerous sympathizers from the city itself, who had been obliged to take boat across the river to join them, for the drawbridge in the midst of London Bridge had been raised on the news of their approach. The advanced guard of rebellion broke open the two prisons in Southwark, those of the Marshalsea and King's Bench, and let loose the captives.   They pushed on two miles further to sack the Archbishop's palace in Lambeth, and then burnt the house of John Imworth, the Warden of the Marshalsea : its flames flared up all night in the sight of the King and his councillors in the Tower, and of the citizens of London, who watched from their wharves and windows the signs of approaching trouble. ,

It was not only on the southern side that the city was now threatened.   The progress of affairs in Essex had been exactly parallel to that in Kent ; indeed there is no doubt that the insurgents of the two counties had been in close touch with each other : Essex men (as we have already seen), had crossed the Thames to join the original band of rioters which commenced the trouble at Dartford. Between the 2nd and the 12th of June the rising which had started at Brentwood had spread in every direction.   It was a little more agrarian and less political in character than the Kentish insurrection, just because Essex was a more purely rural county than Kent, and suffered more from feudal grievances. But that the political element in the troubles was not absent is shown by the fact that a systematic attack was made on the King's officers.   John Ewell, the escheator of the county, was murdered at Langdon-hills ; the manor-house of the sheriff, John Sewall, at Coggeshall, was plundered (though he himself escaped), as was also that of John Guilsborough, one of the justices. Special fury was shown in destroying the dwelling of the treasurer, Sir Robert Hales, at Cressing Temple (June 10). This might have been expected, as, with the possible exception of Archbishop Sudbury, 'Hobbe the Robber' was undoubtedly the most unpopular man in the realm. The Admiral Edmund de la Mare was also a victim of the rioters : his manor of Peldon was sacked, and a bundle of Admiralty papers stuck on a pitchfork was borne before the local band of rioters when they marched on London[1].

Colchester, the county town of Essex, fell into the hands of the insurgents without making resistance. Its capture was celebrated by the massacre of several Flemings, which we may suspect to have been the work of the urban mob rather than of the peasantry. We also hear of the murder of a Fleming at Manningtree. But the main object of the bands in every direction seems to have been the destruction of court-rolls, and the forcible extraction of leases or charters from the landowners who could be caught. The religious houses suffered quite as much as the laity, and the great abbey of Waltham in especial saw every document that it possessed consigned to the flames. In the general anarchy which prevailed we learn that many persons enlisted the services of parties of rioters, to instal them in manors or lands on which they had old claims of doubtful validity, after expelling the present occupants by force.

On June 11, no doubt in strict concert with the men of Kent, the Essex bands began to gather in a mass, and moved off towards London. On the 12th their main body lay encamped in the fields by Mile End, outside the north-eastern corner of the walls of the city. Their leaders seem to have been very obscure persons—Thomas Farringdon, a Londoner,[2] is the only one of whom we know much ; Henry Baker of Manningtree, Adam Michel, and John Starling are mere names to us. It would seem that some of the local clergy must have been implicated, as we are told that many of them, both

---

[1] For all these details see the indictments of the Essex men in the Appendices to Réville, pp. 216–39.

[2] According to the report of the sheriffs this Thomas was the most prominent person in the Essex mob. We are told that 'ivit ex proprio suo capite, ad malefactores de comitatu Essexiae ... et cum praedictis insurrectoribus ut unus eorum capitaneus, venit Londonias ducens retro se magnam turbam'. Réville, p. 194.

chaplains and parish priests, had to fly and go into hiding when the insurrection was over.[1]   But none of them, it is clear, took such a prominent part in the troubles as did John Ball in Kent, or Wraw and Sampson in Suffolk.

On the evening of June 12, therefore, the King's Council in the Tower, and the Mayor Walworth and his aldermen at the Guildhall, gathered together in no small perturbation of mind, to face the situation, and to see how the joint advance of the Kentish and Essex insurgents could be met.   It is astonishing that the ministers had not yet succeeded in gathering an armed force with which to take the field against the rebels.   They had now had thirteen days since the outbreak at Brentwood, in which they might have made their preparations.   But absolutely nothing had been done: an attempt had (it would seem) been made to stop the expedition under the Earl of Cambridge which was starting for Portugal : but it turned out that his squadron had already put to sea before the orders of recall came to hand.   Preparations had also been in progress for the sending of a small reinforcement to the English garrisons in Brittany.   The Council countermanded their voyage and bade them muster in London; but it would seem that only the old *condottiere* Sir Robert Knolles, and some few scores of men-at-arms and archers whom he had enlisted, were available.   Their head quarters were at his house in the city.   It is impossible to make out why the ministers had not called out the whole of the gentry of the home counties, and also put under arms all the trustworthy elements in the London militia : there were thousands of citizens (as later events showed) who were ready to take the field for the suppression of a rising which meant plunder and anarchy.   Probably a military head was wanting at the council board: of the King's uncles John of Gaunt was away on a mission to Edinburgh ; Thomas of Woodstock was somewhere in the Welsh March ; Edmund

---

[1] In Réville's documents, on p. 225, we find the King ordering the collectors of the clerical subsidy not to press for the contributions due from those who 'timent se occasione insurrectionis in comitatu Essexie faciliter posse impetiri, unde capellani et clerici isti forte culpabiles existunt '.

of Cambridge had just sailed for Portugal. The main responsibility lay on the chancellor-archbishop and the treasurer Hales, neither of whom rose to the occasion. So far was Sudbury from thinking of self-defence that on June 12, the day of the appearance of the rebels at Blackheath, he laid down the Great Seal and begged for leave to retire from the conduct of public affairs. The other notables present in the Tower were the King's half-brothers, the Earl of Kent and Sir John Holland, his cousin Henry of Bolingbroke, the heir of John of Gaunt, and the Earls of Salisbury, Warwick, and Oxford. Bolingbroke and Oxford were mere lads of fifteen and seventeen years respectively, but Salisbury and Warwick were middle-aged men, who had seen service in the wars of France : the first-named earl had commanded one of the wings at Poitiers, with great credit to himself. It is astonishing that neither of them came forward to take upon himself the responsibility of urging prompt action at all costs, during the first twelve days of June. It would certainly have been possible to gather in a considerable force from the districts of the midlands where no troubles had yet broken out—for, as we shall see, it was only after Tyler's arrival at London that the rebellion spread into those regions. But no attempt to collect the loyalists of the home counties was made : contemporary chroniclers noted with wonder the extraordinary panic or apathy which had struck the governing classes during the first fortnight of that memorable June. The only guard which lay about the person of the King, when the rebels appeared at Blackheath, consisted of about 600 men-at-arms and archers, retainers of the royal household, or of the members of the Council, who had followed their masters into the Tower.

A large force could have been raised in London, where the Mayor, William Walworth, and the majority of the aldermen were perfectly loyal, and viewed the insurrection with horror. The wealthier citizens quite understood the perils that were involved in the collection of a great body of ignorant peasants led by adventurers and fanatics. If the horde entered their gates, it would almost inevitably get to

the liquor and fall to riot and plundering.   But the difficulty
which lay before the city fathers was that they were fully
conscious that the proletariate of London was no less discontented than the country folk of the home counties.   Their
grievances were different, but their spirit was the same : if
the lower classes of the city had not manorial customs and
feudal dues to resent, they had grudges of their own—against
the foreigners whom they believed to be making undue profits, against the royal officers who represented to them the
misgovernment of the time, most of all against the municipal
oligarchy.   The Mayor and his fellows knew that the artisans and unskilled labourers of London regarded them as
selfish, unscrupulous, and oppressive rulers, and were only
waiting for an opportunity to burst out into rebellion.   Nor
could they trust the whole of their own body—there was
a bitter and unscrupulous minority, even in the council,
which was ready to stir up trouble in order to get rid of the
existing office-holders, and instal itself in their places.   The
events of the next two days were to show the lengths to
which these persons were ready to proceed.   In the earlier
days of June the opposition contented itself with protesting
against the adoption of vigorous measures, and extenuating
the doings of the insurgents—probably representing them
as harmless men driven into a righteous protest against the
corrupt and incapable rule of the King's present ministers.
However this may be, the Mayor and his colleagues made
no vigorous attempt to call to arms the classes who had
something to lose, still less did they go out of their way to
offer the support of the London militia to the Council.   Yet
if they had chosen they might have called out 4,000 or 5,000
well-equipped and trustworthy fighting-men.   But it was
only three days later, after they had seen and recognized the
methods of the insurgents, that they showed their power.
Meanwhile the discontented section was displaying a very
different activity : on June 11–12 there were already many
Londoners present with the insurgents in Kent and Essex,
others had gone far afield, even to Cambridge and Suffolk,
to spread the news of the rising and organize local tumults.

On the evening of June 12, Walworth, as we have already seen, had raised the drawbridge in the midst of London Bridge, had closed the gates on all sides of the city, and had commissioned the aldermen of the various wards to set guards upon the portions of the defences committed to their charge. He also sent out some of his council—Adam Carlisle, John Fresch, and John Horne—all three aldermen—to visit the insurgent camp, warn the rebels to approach no nearer to the city, and bid them respect the King's commands and retire to their homes. Carlisle and Fresch seem to have delivered their message; but Horne, separating himself from his companions, sought a secret interview with Tyler and the other chiefs. He told them that the whole of London was ready to rise in their aid, and urged them to demonstrate against the bridge and the gates, promising them help from within. When night fell he took back with him to his house three of Tyler's lieutenants, and put them in touch with the malcontents of the city, for the purpose of concerting a tumult on the following morning. Horne then had the effrontery to go to the Mayor, and assure him that the insurgents were honest folks and that he would wager his head that if they were admitted within the walls they would not do a pennyworth of damage.[1]

On the morning of June 13, therefore, the rebels were in high spirits, and confident that they would soon be admitted into the city. It was apparently early on this day that John Ball preached his famous sermon on Blackheath to the assembled multitude, using as his text his famous jingling couplet—

> Whan Adam dalf, and Eve span,
> Who was then a gentilman?

The version of his discourse that the chroniclers[2] have preserved for us is no doubt drawn in the most lurid colours, but the main thesis is probably correct:—'In the beginning all men were created equal : servitude of man to man was introduced

---

[1] See the Sheriff's report on the doings of the rebel aldermen in Réville's documents, pp. 190-8.

[2] See especially *Chron. Angliae*, p. 321, for a full account of the sermon.

by the unjust dealings of the wicked, and contrary to God's will.   For if God had intended some to be serfs and others lords, He would have made a distinction between them at the beginning.   Englishmen had now an opportunity given them, if they chose to take it, of casting off the yoke they had borne so long, and winning the freedom that they had always desired.   Wherefore they should take good courage, and behave like the wise husbandman of scripture, who gathered the wheat into his barn, but uprooted and burned the tares that had half-choked the good grain.   The tares of England were her oppressive rulers, and harvest-time had come, in which it was their duty to pluck up and make away with them all—evil lords, unjust judges, lawyers, every man who was dangerous to the common good.   Then they would have peace for the present and security for the future; for when the great ones had been cut off, all men would enjoy equal freedom, all would have the same nobility, rank, and power.'

We may suspect that the horrified chronicler has exaggerated the preacher's incentives to a general massacre, but otherwise his thesis must, from the nature of things, have been much what the chronicler puts into his mouth.   It is notable that Ball is made to preach democracy and not communism— the insurgents wanted to become freeholders, not to form phalansteries and hold all things in common.   When the sermon was over, the multitude (as we are told) cried with a loud and unanimous voice that they would make him both archbishop and chancellor, for the present primate was a traitor to the commons and the realm, and should be slain as soon as they could lay hands on him.

It was probably while Ball's sermon was in the course of delivery that the leaders of the insurgents learnt that the King was coming out to meet them.   They had received a message from him on the previous afternoon, asking their intent, and had replied by protesting that they were his loyal subjects, and zealous for the honour of England, and wished only to lay before him their grievances against his uncles and his ministers, who had so long misgoverned the realm. It is said that the bearer of their answer was Sir John

Newton, the constable of Rochester Castle, who had been
kept as hostage ever since his capture on June 6.[1]   In spite
of the protests of the Archbishop and the Treasurer, Richard
determined to give the Kentishmen a hearing.   He sent
the answer that he would come to meet them on the shore
below Blackheath, and listen to what they had to say.   The
morning was still young when the royal barge, followed by
four other boats, was seen to leave the Tower, and drop
down the river to the Greenwich shore.   It had on board
the King, the Chancellor-archbishop, and the Earls of Warwick, Salisbury, and Oxford, besides several others of the
Council.   They found the sloping bank covered with a vast
crowd of insurgents, 10,000 or more, arrayed under two great
banners with St. George's cross and more than forty pennons.
All burst out into a medley of shouts and yells as the barge
drew in to land.   There was no show of discipline or order
among them, some were giving loyal cheers for the King,
others were howling for the heads of John of Gaunt and
Sudbury, others brandishing their weapons and shrieking
like men possessed.[2]   It was clear from the first that it
would be impossible to allow the King to land in the midst
of this frantic crowd.   The rowers were ordered to lie
upon their oars a score of yards from the shore, and in
a moment of comparative silence Richard raised his voice
to open the parley.   ' Sirs,' he is said to have shouted,
' what do you want ?   Tell me, now that I have come to talk
with you.'   But the whole multitude began to roar that he
must disembark, they had many things to say, and could not

[1] So Froissart, and though he is not supported by any other chronicler, yet
Sir J. Newton would have been exactly the sort of person whom the rebels
were likely to send.   Froissart says that they had secured his faithful delivery
of the message and return to their camp, by swearing to kill his two sons, also
prisoners, if he did not bring back the King's reply.   In the documents the only
person mentioned as being sent to the rebels on the morning of June 13 is
a certain John Blydon.   But there were three separate interchanges of messages
on the Tuesday and the Wednesday, as shown in the *Hist. Rev.*, Chron. p. 513.

[2] ' Ils commencaient tous a huer et a donner un si grand cri, qu'il sembla
proprement que tous les diables d'enfer fussent venus en leur compaignie ', says
Froissart, in his graphic (and probably accurate) account of the scene.   x. 106.
His description is borne out by the Chronicle in *Hist. Rev.* ' ils furent gentz sans
reason, et ne avoient sceu de bien fair ' [p. 513].

easily confer with him at a distance.   To have permitted
the King to land would have meant to surrender him into the
hands of the rebels without hope of escape.   It would also
probably have involved the death of several of the unpopular
councillors who attended him.   Wherefore the Chancellor,
according to one version, or the Earl of Salisbury, according
to another,[1] bade the bargemen push off and return to the
Tower.   The rebels thereupon burst out into curses and
wild shouts of 'treason! treason!' but did not, as might
have been expected, salute the departing boats with a volley
of arrows.   The first minute of the rowing, however, must
have been one of deadly terror to the royal party—they
might every one of them have been riddled with shafts before
the barge had got out of range—for the longbow would carry
far.   That nothing of the kind happened is a clear proof that
there was a very real loyalty to the King's person prevalent
among the rank and file rebels.

[1] The Chronicle in *Hist. Rev.* says that the Chancellor and the Treasurer both
protested, and that the boats turned back (p. 513).   The *Chronicon Angliae*
makes them even prevent the King from leaving the Tower, which is clearly
wrong (p. 287).   Froissart agrees with the Chronicle in *Hist. Rev.*, but makes
Salisbury dissuade the King from landing, x. 106.

CHAPTER IV

The Rebels in London : King Richard and Wat Tyler

THE attempt to open negotiations with the King having failed, the only course remaining to the insurgents was to endeavour to obtain an entry into London, either by force or by fair words. They were by now beginning to suffer from hunger, for they had already eaten up both the scanty supplies of food that they had brought with them and all the provisions that they could obtain in the suburban villages south of the Thames. Observers, wise after the event, maintained that if they could have been kept out of London for another twenty-four hours, the bulk of them would have dispersed from mere starvation.[1] But the party of malcontents inside the city saved them from this danger.

As the multitude thronged down from Blackheath towards Southwark and London Bridge, they were met by John Horne, the alderman who had encouraged them on the preceding day. He was on horseback, and waving in his hand a standard with the royal arms, which he had obtained by false pretences from the town-clerk.[2] He harangued the Kentishmen, telling them to press on, for they would find none but friends in London, the citizens were ready to join them in their designs, and would give them any succour that they might need. There was good foundation for what he said, for another of the malcontents, Walter Sibley [or Sybyle], the alderman of Billingsgate, was preparing to admit them. He had taken post at the drawbridge with a very few armed men, and sent away all the burgesses who came to offer him aid to resist

---

[1] The Sheriffs of London, in their report, say that the rebels at this moment ' in proposito fuerunt ad hospicia sua revertendi ' (Réville, p. 190).

[2] For the details of Horne's double-faced conduct see the documents in Réville, pp. 190–5.

the rebels, angrily bidding these volunteers to mind their own business, and leave him to do his duty in his own ward.[1] When the mob came surging on to the southern arches of the bridge, he exclaimed to those about him that it was useless to resist, and lowered the drawbridge : the Kentishmen at once streamed into the city. As if this was not enough, there was treachery displayed on the other side of the city also. Alderman William Tonge opened Aldgate to the Essex rebels, ' but whether because he was in agreement with the aforesaid John Horne and Walter Sibley, or because he was terrified by the threats of the Kentish rebels who had already entered the city, no man knows to this day '.[2] By the afternoon of Thursday, June 13, the rebels were in possession of London, without having had to strike a single blow. The leading loyalists barricaded themselves in their houses, or retired to join the King in the Tower. The bulk of the well-to-do citizens tried to make the best of the situation, by offering food to the newcomers and broaching for them great barrels of ale. The last at least was a very short-sighted measure on the part of these worthy householders ! But at first the men of Kent and of Essex behaved far better than might have been expected : it is recorded that many of them paid for their meals, and that they did no damage to private property that afternoon. Their chiefs had them well in hand, and kept reminding them of their political duty, the obligation to chastise John of Gaunt, the Archbishop, the Treasurer, and the rest of the ' traitors '. The ministers were

[1] ' Ubi Thomas Cornwallis, dicto die Iovis, venit cum magna armatorum comitiva et obtulit se ad succurrendum eidem Waltero, et ad custodiendum introitum pontis . . . idem Walterus Sybele felonie et proditorie illud adiuvamen recusavit, . . . dicens "Quid facitis hic ? Redite ad proprias vestras wardas vel domus custodiendas, quia nemo intromittet se hic in mea warda nisi ego et socii mei.". . . . Et non permisit aliquam custodiam contra praedictos malefactores, sed sine custodia reliquit portas civitatis apertas ' (Réville, documents 193 and 197, from the Sheriffs' report).

[2] On Tonge see ibid. pp. 197-8. But there is an error in the date, as the document says that Tonge let in the Essex rebels on the night of June 12-13 (Wednesday), the Kentishmen being already in the city, while earlier in the same narrative the Sheriffs say that Sibley only let in the Kentishmen on the morning of Thursday, June 13. I suppose, therefore, that we must place Tonge's treachery on the later day.

in the Tower, safe for the moment, and the Duke of Lancaster was far away at Edinburgh, but at least their houses could be sacked. Lambeth Palace had already been pillaged on the preceding night,[1] but there was a still prouder dwelling open to assault, John of Gaunt's great mansion, the Savoy, the most magnificent private residence in the whole of England. It was but lately finished, but was already stored with all manner of valuables—tapestry, furniture, armour, plate, and ornaments, the gifts of his father, Edward III, and the spoil of France. The moment that the insurgents had filled their empty stomachs they moved off in mass towards the Strand, guided by their London friends, and shouting in union, 'To the Savoy!'[2] It was about four o'clock in the afternoon when the mob, swollen by thousands of the apprentices, artisans, labourers, and professional criminals of the city, reached their goal. They went very methodically to work, the leaders repeatedly reminding them that they were come to destroy, not to steal; that they were executing vengeance, not seeking profit. The doors of the palace were broken open, the caretakers having fled without offering resistance. Everything in the Savoy capable of destruction was then destroyed. The furniture was thrown out of the windows and hacked to pieces in the street; the rich hangings, the clothes, and carpets were torn up; the plate and ornaments were broken into small fragments and cast into the river; the jewels, it is said, were smashed with hammers or brayed in a mortar. When the whole dwelling had been gutted it was set on fire and burnt to the ground: its destruction was completed by the explosion of three barrels of gunpowder from the duke's armoury.[3] So anxious were the rioters to show their disinterested motives, that when a man was caught making off with a silver goblet, he was seized and put to death. But a party of reprobates made their way

[1] See p. 46.

[2] So Malverne's *Chronicle*, p. 2. The Chronicle in *Hist. Rev.* (p. 514) says that the Londoners attacked the Savoy before the country folk had come up; but we have good proof in the Indictments that Kentishmen were in the forefront of the mischief.

[3] *Hist. Rev.*, Chron. p. 515.

to the cellars, and there swilled the rich wines till they were overcome with bestial intoxication ; they could not escape when the palace was fired, and so were smothered or burnt.[1] An indictment of the year 1382 shows that a small party of Rochester men found and stole the duke's strongbox, containing £1,000 in cash, smuggled it into a boat at the watergate in rear of the palace, and took it over to Southwark, where they hastily divided it and then escaped. Evidently they were in fear of being detected and lynched by their more scrupulous comrades.[2]

In rushing on to the Savoy, the greater part of the insurgents had passed by the Temple without turning aside,[3] but in the late afternoon they returned to attack this ancient group of buildings. Their object was twofold : the Temple now belonged to the Knights of St. John, and the Treasurer, Robert Hales, the head of that order in England, was, next to John of Gaunt and Simon of Sudbury, the most prominent of the ' traitors ' of the King's ministry. But this was not all : already theTemple had become the head quarters of the lawyers of England ; here were their Inns, their schools, and their library. Of all classes obnoxious to the insurgents the legal profession was the most hated ; it was they who were the tools of the manorial lords in binding the chains of the serf : from them were chosen the judges and officials who descended on the shires at assize time to gloze might into right. It was their cursed parchments which were the ruin of honest men. Nothing, therefore, was more natural than that the mob should make a general assault on the Temple. They burst into the church and there broke open the chests full of books, which they tore up and burnt in the street.[4]

[1] Knighton's Continuator, ii. p. 135, says that they were ' iocis et canticis et aliis illecebris ebrietatibus vacantes, donec ostium obturatum fuit igne '.

[2] Indictment of John Ferrour, of Rochester, and Joanna, his wife, in Réville, pp. 196–7.

[3] But it would seem from the *Hist. Rev.*, Chron. p. 515, that some of them turned off to attack the lawyers, though the greater portion went on to the Savoy.

[4] Apparently the libraries were kept in the Temple Church, just as at Oxford the University books were kept in St. Mary's. ' Cistas in ecclesia sive in cameris apprenticiorum inventas fregerunt et libros inventos securibus scindebant et in cibum ignis dederunt ' (Knighton's Continuator, ii. p. 135). The *Hist. Rev.*

They sacked the Inns and dwellings of the lawyers, destroying an enormous quantity of charters, muniments, and records. The book-chests and furniture supplied materials for the bonfire in which the documents were consumed. The lawyers and students had fled at the first irruption of the mob ; ' it was marvellous to see', says one chronicler, ' how even the most aged and infirm of them scrambled off, with the agility of rats or evil spirits '.

It was now dark, but the work of the insurgents was not yet done. From the Temple they hurried off to another of Treasurer Hales's official abodes—the priory of St. John's, Clerkenwell, the head quarters of the Knights Hospitallers in England. They were guided by Thomas Farringdon, the London malcontent who had put himself at the head of the Essex rioters, who rode at their head shouting threats against the unfortunate prior. The church, hospital, and mansion of the Hospitallers were sacked and burnt, and seven Flemings who had taken sanctuary at the altar were dragged out and murdered. This was the first sign of the length to which the hatred of the Londoner against aliens was to be carried.

Other exploits of the rioters during the evening hours of June 13 were the destruction of the prisons of the Fleet and of Newgate, and of several private houses in Holborn. All the felons were released, and eagerly joined in the arson and housebreaking which was afoot. There were nine or ten murderers committed that night, beside the slaughter of the Flemings. The best-known victim was a 'questmonger' named Roger Legett, who was torn from the altar of St. Martin's-le-Grand, and beheaded in Cheapside. At last, tired with their day of excitement, the multitude lay down to rest, some taking lodgings with their London friends, but the majority encamping on the open spaces of Tower Hill and St. Catherine's Wharf, where they slept round great watch-fires, blockading the King and his Council in the old Norman fortress, for they were determined that their enemies should not escape them.

Chronicle says 'Allerent en Esglise et pristeremt livres et rolles et remem-brances, et porteront en le haut chemine et les arderent'

Only the leaders were still alert ; it is said that they met in the house of that Thomas Farringdon[1] whom we have already had occasion to mention, and occupied themselves in drawing up plans for the morrow, and in compiling a proscription list of all those whom they intended to put to death. It is said that the catalogue of 'traitors' drawn up by the men of Kent embraced the names of John of Gaunt, Archbishop Sudbury, Treasurer Hales, Courtenay Bishop of London, John Fordham, Clerk of the Privy Seal and Bishop-Elect of Durham, Chief Justice Belknap, Chief Baron Plessington, Sir Ralph Ferrers, John Legge, the King's sergeant who was supposed to have advised the sending out of the Poll-tax commissioners, Thomas Bampton, and Sir Thomas Orgrave, Sub-Treasurer of England.[2]

The King and his Council meanwhile were holding a conclave within the Tower in a very different frame of mind. The flames of the Savoy and of Clerkenwell were reddening the horizon, while close at hand the rebels kept up a din far into the night, clamouring for the heads of ' the traitors ' and shouting that they would storm the fortress next morning. This, of course, was mere ' windy folly '—the Tower could have held out for an indefinite time against any enemy unprovided with a battering-train. Nevertheless the situation was very grave, since the King and the ministry had allowed themselves to be shut up in a place from which they could not easily escape, and there was no one outside to organize an army for their relief. If they could have guessed that London was about to fall into the hands of the insurgents without a blow being struck, the ministers would certainly have retired with the King into the Midlands before the Kentishmen arrived at Blackheath.

Facing the present crisis the magnates beleaguered in the Tower fell into two parties.[3] One held that desperate

---

[1] ' Recepit secum noctanter [idem Thomas] plures principales insurrectores, Robertum Warde et alios, imaginando illa nocte cum aliis sociis suis conspirando nomina diversorum civium, quae fecit scribi in quadam schedula, quos vellet decapitare.' (The grammar is peculiar !) Sheriffs' indictment, Réville, p. 195.

[2] See *Hist. Rev.*, Chron. pp. 512, 513.

[3] The general course of the discussion in the Tower is given by several

measures were the only way to safety, that it would be wise
to make a midnight sally upon the rebels and endeavour to
destroy them before they could put themselves in a posture
of defence. The disorderly mass bivouacked around the
fortress absolutely invited an attack. Walworth, the Mayor,
who was a strong partisan of vigorous action, declared that
he would guarantee that 6,000 or 7,000 armed men, all the
wealthier citizens and their households, would readily strike
in on the side of law and order if only the garrison of the
Tower opened the attack. Sir Robert Knolles, with the 120
men-at-arms who were garrisoning his mansion, would provide the nucleus around which the loyalists could rally.
But while the energetic Mayor pleaded for a resort to arms,
the Earl of Salisbury, the most experienced soldier present,
maintained the opposite opinion. He held that a sally
against the unsuspecting besiegers might begin well, but that
if they rallied and were joined by the whole of the lower
classes of London, the battle would develop into street fighting
and no one could foresee how that might end. The loyalists
might not be able to unite and combine, and might be annihilated piecemeal.—'If we begin what we cannot carry through
we should never be able to repair matters. It will be all
over with us and our heirs, and England will be a desert.' [1]
Salisbury, therefore, urged that negotiations should be tried
before the final resort to arms was made. The one thing
necessary was to disperse the multitude ; if this could be
done by any reasonable concessions the situation might be
saved. His arguments carried the day.

The first attempt to open up negotiations failed. The
King sent out two knights with a letter directing the commons to formulate their grievances in writing, to dispatch
them to him by the hands of a deputation, and then to
betake themselves to their homes. This offer was made to
the assembly on St. Catherine's Wharf by one of the knights,

chroniclers. The advice of Walworth and Salisbury by Froissart only. But
the tenor of their speeches is so probable that I venture to follow Froissart in
this point, despite his well-known capacities for going wrong.

[1] These details are from Froissart, but must be reasonably correct.

who stood on an old chair and read the epistle by torch-light. The rebels cried out that 'all this was trifles and mockery',[1] and bade the messenger return and bring back a better proposition. The Council, after a short debate, resolved that the King should grant the insurgents on Friday morning the interview which he had refused to them at Blackheath twenty-four hours before. His position had been so much changed by the fall of London, that he was now forced to take the risk of being imprisoned or even murdered by the rebels, which had seemed unnecessary on the previous day. Richard fully understood his danger, but surprised all the followers by the eager courage with which he resolved to face it. Apparently, the boy was agreeably excited at the prospect of putting himself forward and of showing that he could assert his personal influence over the multitude.

In his second message to the commons Richard bade them all muster in the meadows at Mile End—a favourite suburban promenade of the citizens of London, some way outside the north-eastern angle of the walls. It is said that the Council had their secret reasons for naming this rendez-vous. If the rebels evacuated the city in order to attend the conference, a chance would be given to the loyalist party to rise and shut them outside the gates. Even if this happy consummation did not occur, yet when the besiegers moved off from round the Tower, Sudbury and Hales would be given a way of escape, when the exits of the fortress were no longer beset by so many thousand watchful enemies.[2]

The insurgent chiefs sent back word to the King that his offer was accepted. But though the mass moved off to the

---

[1] *Hist. Rev.*, Chron. 516.

[2] Knighton and the anonymous chronicle in the *Historical Review*, p. 517, both lay stress on the fact that the interview was intended to give Sudbury a chance of absconding. Walsingham's venomous suggestion that Richard quitted the Tower in order to let the insurgents enter and slay the scapegoats, the Archbishop and Hales, may safely be disregarded. He says 'Rex igitur in arcto constitutus, permisit eis in Turrim intrare, et loca secretissima pro sua voluntate nequissima perscrutare, quia nihil negare tute potuit quod petebant'. It is incredible that Richard should have left his mother in the Tower if he had intended it to be sacked during his absence.

place of conference, Tyler left a small but compact body of picked men to watch the Tower. When Sudbury tried to escape by boat during the morning, he was sighted and forced to turn back to the water-gate from which he had emerged.

About seven o'clock on the Friday morning Richard and his *cortège* rode out of the Tower : he was followed by all his Council save Sudbury and Hales, who dared not show themselves, but by a small escort only. The bulk of the garrison of the fortress remained behind. The magnates who accompanied the King included the Earls of Warwick, Oxford, and Kent, Sir Thomas Holland, Sir Thomas Percy, Sir Robert Knolles, and the Mayor Walworth; Aubrey de Vere, uncle of the Earl of Oxford, bore the sword of state before the King.[1]

The ride to Mile End was perilous : at any moment the crowd might have broken loose, and the King and all his party might have perished. On Tower Hill the notorious Thomas Farringdon seized the King's bridle-rein, and began clamouring for the instant execution of Treasurer Hales. ' Avenge me ', he shouted, ' on that false traitor the Prior, who has deprived me of my tenements by fraud ; do me right justice and give me back my own, for if you do not, I am now strong enough to take justice into my own hands.' Richard answered that he should have all that was just, whereupon Farringdon dropped his rein, but instead of accompanying the *cortège* to Mile End, slipped back with a band to the Tower to look for the unfortunate Hales.[2] A little further on a certain William Trewman stopped the horse of Nicholas Bramber, late Mayor of London, loaded him with insults, and was with difficulty prevented from assaulting him. Nevertheless, though surrounded all the way by a noisy and boisterous multitude, Richard and his

---

[1] The *Hist. Rev.*, Chron. is clearly wrong in stating that Buckingham was also there. He was in Wales. Also in stating that the King's mother accompanied him in a *whirlecote*. *Chron. Angl.* 191 and other authorities prove that she was left in the Tower.

[2] All this is taken from the Sheriffs' report, so often quoted already, printed in Réville, pp. 195-6.

party ultimately reached Mile End. On the way the Earl of Kent and Sir John Holland, taking advantage of a casual thinning of the crowd, edged their horses out of the procession and galloped off over the fields beyond Whitechapel. It was an infamous act to abandon their half-brother in the hour of need, and one wonders that Richard ever forgave them. They were the only members of the royal party who thus betrayed their master.

The conference occupied some time, and was noisy in the extreme.[1] But the King had come prepared to grant almost anything, and the leaders of the insurgents found, to their surprise, that their demands were granted one after another. Tyler himself was the spokesman : the topics which he brought forward on this day were mainly connected with manorial grievances. Richard consented that serfdom should be abolished all over the realm, that all feudal services should disappear, and that all holders in villeinage should become free tenants, paying the moderate rent of 4*d.* an acre per year to the lord. In addition all restrictions on free buying and selling were to be swept away, and the market monopolies of all favoured places were to disappear. Finally, a general amnesty was to be given for all irregularities committed during the rising. The King promised to give his banner to the chosen representatives of each county present, as a token that he had taken them under his protection. As a sign of the honesty of his intentions he engaged to set thirty clerks to draw up charters bestowing the freedom and amnesty on the inhabitants of such districts as came forward to claim them. A great number of such documents were issued that day, and the formulae have been preserved in more than one copy.[2]

There remained one question—the punishment of the ministers whom the insurgents regarded as ' traitors '. Tyler pressed the King on this point. ' The commons ', he said, ' will that you suffer them to take and deal with all the

---

[1] One person at least, a certain John French, was killed at Mile End. See Réville, lxxxviii, and *Archaeologia Cantiana*, iii. 95.

[2] One may be found in *Chron. Angl.* pp. 298-9.

traitors who have sinned against you and the law.' Richard replied, in a temporizing fashion, that they should have for due punishment such persons as could be properly proved by process of law to be traitors. Indeed, all traitors throughout the realm of England should be arrested and brought before him, and justice should be done on them as the law directed.

But justice, after due trial and legal process, was not what Tyler and his friends intended to secure for their enemies. While the King was still at Mile End, distributing promises and banners, he went off with a chosen band of his personal following, and made a dash for the gate of the Tower.[1] Either by mere mismanagement, or to show an ostentatious confidence in the people, the drawbridge had not been raised, nor the portcullis lowered after the King's departure. When, therefore, a solid mass of several hundred[2] determined rebels made a dash for the open entry, the men-at-arms on guard had to make instant decision whether they would keep the intruders out by violence, and so provoke an affray, or suffer them to pass. It probably flashed through the brain of the captain at the gate that if he resisted and shed blood, the King and his retinue, who were still in the power of the mob, would perish. At any rate, he gave no order to strike, and the mob rushed in. The rebels did not molest the soldiers; indeed, they showed a jocular friendliness, shaking hands with the men-at-arms, stroking their beards with uncouth familiarity, and telling them for the future they were all brothers and equals. Tyler had come not to fight the garrison, but to slay the ' traitors '.[3]

[1] That the invasion of the Tower took place after the Mile End interview had reached its culminating point, and the King's promise had been given, is proved by Tyler's presence at both. The Chron. in *Hist. Rev.* gives the sequence exactly. From some of the other chroniclers (e. g. Malverne and Knighton) we might have supposed that the rush into the Tower took place soon after the King's departure.

[2] It is said that only 400 rioters took part in the actual murders, but this is probably far too small a number.

[3] 'Quorundam militum barbas suis incultissimis et sordidis manibus contrectare, demulcere, et verba familiaria serere modo de societate cum eisdem habenda de cetero, modo de fide servanda ipsis ribaldis ', &c. *Chron. Angl.* 291.

Separating into a number of bands, they ran through the wards and towers hunting for their victims. Tyler and Thomas Farringdon are recorded as being at the head of the hunt. The men-at-arms looked on helplessly, while the King's private chamber was invaded, and his bed turned up to see if there was not a ' traitor ' hiding under it. The rebels also searched the Princess of Wales's room; one ruffian, it is said, wanted to kiss the terrified lady,[1] who fainted and was carried off by her pages, put into a boat, and taken round to the 'Queen's Wardrobe' near St. Paul's. Not one of the garrison drew his sword ; the chroniclers unite in pouring scorn on the knights and squires who allowed a half-armed mob of a few hundred men to run riot through every corner of the fortress.

The victims whom Tyler and his gang sought were found without much trouble. The Archbishop, when his abortive attempt to escape in the early morning was foiled, had apparently realized the full danger of his position. When the hazardous experiment of letting the King go forth to Mile End had been decided upon, he retired to the chapel of the Tower, and prepared for the end that was only too likely to come. ' He sang his mass devoutly ', and then confessed and communicated his colleague the prior-treasurer, the other minister whose death was certain if the mob should break loose. While the King and his retinue were making ready to depart, and while they were on the first stage of their ride, the unhappy Sudbury and Hales had to endure a long and agonizing time of waiting. ' They heard two masses, or three, and then the Archbishop chanted the *commendacione* and the *placebo*, and the *dirige*, and the seven penitential psalms, and last of all the litany, and when he was at the words *omnes sancti orate pro nobis*, the murderers burst in upon him.' There was a general howl of triumph—the traitor, the spoiler of the people, was run to earth. Sudbury boldly stood forward and faced the horde : 'here am I, your Archbishop', he is said to have replied, 'no traitor nor spoiler am I '. But the insurgents rushed in upon him, cruelly

---

[1] *Chron. Angl.* 191. Froissart tells the tale at greater length.

buffeted him, and dragged him out of the chapel and across the courts of the Tower to the hill outside, where they beheaded him upon a log of wood. The headsman's work was so badly done that eight strokes were spent in hacking through the unhappy prelate's neck. His companion, the treasurer Hales, was executed immediately after. Only two other persons seem to have perished [1] : the first was William Appleton, a Franciscan friar, who was the physician of John of Gaunt, and passed for one of his chief political advisers ; the other was John Legge, whose advice concerning the Poll-tax had made his obscure name notorious in every corner of the realm. The heads of all the four victims of Tyler were mounted on piles and borne round the city, that of the Archbishop having his mitre fixed to the skull by a large nail. They were then set over the gate of London Bridge.

It is impossible not to regret Simon of Sudbury's dreadful end. He was made the scapegoat not merely of the ministry but of the whole nation : for it was the nation's wrong-headed determination to persist in the unrighteous French war which necessitated the grinding taxation that was the cause of the outbreak. Personally, the Archbishop seems to have been an honest, pious, and charitable man. All that we know of him is to his credit, save that he does not seem to have been clever enough to realize that the policy of the realm required alteration. Assuredly he had sought no personal advantage when he accepted the Chancellorship, nor had he profited in any way by his tenure of the office. But in times of revolution the multitude looks for individuals on whom to fix the responsibility for all that has gone wrong—and it is the highest head that falls first. If Sudbury regarded the late policy of the Council as correct and inevitable, he should have taken measures to defend it by force. A fighting chancellor might perhaps have nipped the rebellion in the bud. But to watch the growth of the rising with helpless

---

[1] Possibly three other victims suffered on Tower Hill, if we may trust Knighton, ii. 134, who calls the three unknown sufferers 'socii' of John Legge. The *Hist. Rev. Chron.* adds not three but *one* person more, 'un juror', p. 517.

dismay, and then to lay down the Great Seal on the day when the rebels entered London, was feeble in the last degree. It was not personal courage that Sudbury lacked : he died like an honest man, nay even like a martyr, but he was no statesman. It is curious to find that his contemporaries did not make a saint of him, in spite of his many virtues and his dreadful end ; but the reason is not far to seek : he had refused to be a persecutor in his day of power, and the priestly caste bitterly resented his mild treatment of the Lollards. If only he had set himself to root up Wycliffe and his followers, his name might be standing beside that of Peter Martyr in the Calendar of the canonized defenders of the mediaeval church.[1]

After the execution of Sudbury, Hales, and their fellows, the section of the insurgents under Wat Tyler's immediate command appear to have evacuated the Tower, and to have allowed the garrison to close its gates. The King, however, did not return thither ; probably the news which he received at Aldgate, while riding back from Mile End, made him imagine that it was still in the hands of the frantic crowd which had wrought the murders. He turned aside, and joined his mother in the Wardrobe, near St. Paul's. There his clerks and secretaries spent the afternoon in copying out the charters exacted at the late conference, and in distributing them to the representatives of the Essex peasantry. Satisfied with these tokens of the King's submission, many thousands of the insurgents went home. ' The simple and the honest folk, and the beginners in treason departed ', remarks Froissart.[2] But the rising was far from being at an end—the demagogues and the criminals and the fanatics were not to be pacified by the mere abolition of serfdom and feudal dues—they had ambitions of their own which were still far from satisfied. Tyler and his friends, indeed, were far more busy on Friday than they had been on the preceding day, and still had

[1] Walsingham notes that public opinion in his own class held ' Archiepiscopum, quanquam credibile est eum martyrio finisse vitam, tamen propter teporem curae quam adhibuisse debuerat in hac parte [persecution] horrenda mortis passione puniri '.

[2] ' Les simples, et les boines gens, et les novices.'

about them ' thirty thousand men who were in no hurry to get their seals and charters from the King '.

The murders in the Tower indeed were only the commencement of the outburst of slaughter and arson to which the more sinister members of the insurgent host had been looking forward. The whole of June 14, from morning to midnight, was a carnival of anarchy. We have only space to record some of its more prominent and typical features. The most notable was a general assault on aliens : ' The commons made proclamation that every one who could lay hands on Flemings or any other strangers of other nations might cut off their heads.' [1] Nor was this an empty cry : some 150 or 160 unhappy foreigners were murdered in various places— thirty-five Flemings in one batch were dragged out of the church of St. Martin in the Vintry, and beheaded on the same block. Popular tradition records that every man suspected of Flemish birth was seized, and asked to pronounce the shibboleth ' bread and cheese ' ; if he answered ' brod and case ' he lost his head.[2] The Lombards also suffered, and their houses yielded much valuable plunder. But the aliens were not the only sufferers : all manner of unpopular Londoners met their death. Tyler himself, it is said, went in search of Richard Lyons, the old enemy of the Good Parliament, and cut off his head—whether in revenge for the ancient chastisements recorded by Froissart or on general grounds we are unable to say. One John Greenfield was killed in Cheapside merely because he had said that Appleton (the Franciscan beheaded on Tower Hill) was a good man and suffered unjustly.[3] Disorderly bands, as we are told, went about putting to passers-by the watchword ' With whom hold you ? ' and if the person interrogated refused to say ' with King Richard and the true commons ', they tore off his hood, and raised the hue and cry upon him, and dragged him to one of the blocks, which they had set up at street corners, to be beheaded. It is recorded that they killed no one save by the axe, and that the larger proportion of the

[1] Chron. in *Hist. Rev.* p. 518.   [2] *London Chronicle*, ed. Kingsford, p. 15.
[3] Chron. in *Hist. Rev.* p. 518.

victims were either lawyers, jurymen of the city, persons connected with the levying of taxes, or known adherents of the Duke of Lancaster. But many perished, not because they had given any public offence, but merely because their personal enemies had the craft to turn the rioters against them by some vamped-up tale.

Beside murder, the streets of London and even the scattered suburbs round about it were rife with arson, plunder, and blackmail. Jack Straw led a gang several miles beyond the walls to burn the manor-house of the Prior of St. John at Highbury:[1] another party went out to destroy the dwelling of John Butterwick, under-sheriff of Middlesex, in the village of Knightsbridge. Within the city, John Horne, the alderman who had played the traitor on the preceding day, went up and down with a great crowd at his heels, bidding any man who wanted swift and speedy justice to apply to him : he turned citizens out of houses to which he said that they had no right, forced creditors to give their debtors bonds of release, and levied fines on persons whom he chose to regard as swindlers or usurers ; ' thereby taking upon himself the royal prerogative of justice ', as his indictment somewhat superfluously proceeds to add. The legal proceedings which followed the suppression of the rebellion show us that every form of villany was in full swing on that dreadful Friday, from open murder down to the extorting of shillings, by dreadful threats, from clergymen and old ladies.[2]

The young King, no longer sheltered by the walls of the Tower, but lying with his small retinue in the unfortified Wardrobe, must have felt that all his diplomacy at Mile End had been wasted. The state of London on Friday night was far worse than it had been even on Thursday. Yet the

[1] The Indictments in Réville, pp. 210–12, show that the Highbury fire was on Friday, not (as several of the chroniclers assert) on Thursday. The same proofs show that the Knightsbridge fire was also on the second day. The otherwise accurate Chron. in *Hist. Rev.* goes wrong here. Note that the St. Albans deputies, journeying to the Mile End meeting, found Jack Straw at work at Highbury. *Chron. Angl.* p. 300.

[2] How Simon Gerard and John Fawkes extorted twelve pence from Robert, vicar of Clapham, and how Theobald Ellis threatened to kill Elizabeth, widow of Sir Ralph Spigornell, may be read in Réville, Indictments, pp. 210–15.

evil was beginning to cure itself : the conduct of the insurgents had grown so intolerable, that every man who had anything to lose saw that he must prepare to defend his life and his property by armed force. Already some small attempt at resistance had been made : a riotous band which had presented itself at the Guildhall, brandishing torches and proposing to burn 'the book which is called the Jubilee', and all the muniments of the city of London, had been refused entry and turned back without difficulty.[1] All the wealthier citizens must have been asking themselves whether it was necessary to wait till they were cut off in detail by the drunken bands which were parading the streets. Apprentices were murdering their masters, debtors murdering their creditors ; at all risks the anarchy must be stopped. Yet no attempt to combine against the terror was made, and it was not till the following day that the party of order turned out in force.

Saturday morning opened as gloomily as ever : the sacking of houses continued,[2] and one more notable murder was wrought before the day was many hours old. John Imworth, the Marshal of the Marshalsea, had taken sanctuary in Westminster Abbey. A body of rioters entered the church, passed the altar rails, and tore the unhappy man away from the very shrine of Edward the Confessor,[3] one of whose marble pillars he was embracing in the vain hope that the sanctity of the spot would protect him. He was dragged along to Cheapside, and there decapitated.

The state of mind of the King and his Council is sufficiently shown by the fact that instead of endeavouring to call out the loyal citizens and the garrison of the Tower for an open attack on the rebels, they merely tried to resume the negotiations which had been opened at Mile End. A messenger[4] was sent out to the leaders of the rebels to invite them to a second

[1] This curious fact may be found in the indictment of Walter Atte Keye, in Réville, p. 206.

[2] It lasted even till the afternoon, and some rioters were arrested in the very act of housebreaking when the reaction began, after Tyler's death. See Réville, Indictments, p. 195.

[3] Chronicle in *Hist. Rev.* p. 518.

[4] Sir John Newton, according to *Chron. Angl.* 296. It will be remembered that this knight is said to have carried messages on June 12 also.

conference, as it seemed, from their refusal to depart, that they had still something to crave of the King. Richard invited them to meet him outside Aldersgate, in the open place of Smithfield, a square partly surrounded by houses, where the cattle-market of the city was held even down to the second half of the nineteenth century. The meeting was likely to be even more perilous than that which had taken place on the previous day, for the rebels were now more certain of their own strength, and had waded so far in massacre during the last twenty-four hours that they can have had but few scruples left. Moreover, the greater part of the simple peasantry had gone home with their charters ; those who remained were the extremists, the politicians, and the criminals. Tyler himself, as his conduct was to show, was beside himself in the insolent pride of success : we get a glimpse of him on the Friday night declaring that he would go wherever he pleased at the head of 20,000 men, and ' shave the beards' of all who dared oppose him—' by which', adds the simple annalist, ' he meant that he would cut off their heads '.[1] He is also said to have boasted that within four days there should be no laws in England save those which proceeded out of his own mouth.[2] It is certain that he and his subordinate demagogues had no intention of letting the insurrection die down. But, whatever were his ultimate intentions, he did not refuse the conference offered by the King. Did he intend to utilize it for the capture of Richard, or perhaps for the massacre of the nobles and councillors of the royal suite ?

Fully conscious that they were very possibly going to their death, but yet resolved to try this last experiment, Richard and his followers made ready for the interview by riding down to Westminster, and taking the sacrament before the high-altar from which Imworth had been torn only an hour before. The King shut himself up for a space with an anchorite, confessed to him, and received absolution.[3] His

---

[1] *Chron. Angl.* p. 300.   [2] Ibid. p. 296.

[3] ' Et apres le roi parla avesque le ankre, et luy confessa, et fust par longe temps avecque lui ', *Hist. Rev.*, Chron. p. 518. Who was this anchorite ?

retinue pressed round the shrine of the Confessor in long and devout prayers. At last they rode off together toward Smithfield, a body of about 200 men in all, most of them in the robes of peace, but with armour hidden under their long gowns. It is noteworthy that, when once at Westminster, Richard and his party might have made a dash for the open country to the west,[1] and have got away to Windsor. The fact that they made no such attempt shows that the wish to secure their personal safety was not the guiding motive of the moment : they were determined at all costs to pacify London, if only it were possible.

At Smithfield the King found the insurgents prepared to meet him. He and his party drew rein on the east side of the square, in front of St. Bartholomew's : all along the western side was the array of the rebels drawn out in ' battles ' in a very orderly fashion. The mid space was clear. Presently Richard ordered the Mayor Walworth to proclaim to the multitude that he wished to hear their demands by the mouth of their chief. Thereupon Tyler rode out to him on a little hackney, with a single mounted follower bearing his banner at his heels, but no other companion. He leapt down from his saddle, made a reverence to the King, and then seized his hand and shook it heartily, telling him ' to be of good cheer, for within a fortnight he would have thanks from the commons even more than he had at the present hour '. Richard then inquired why he and his fellows had not gone home, since all that had been asked at Mile End had been conceded to them.[2]

Of what followed we have several accounts varying in their details, though showing a general similarity. Tyler, it would seem, answered that there were many additional points which required to be settled over and above the mere abolition of serfdom and manorial dues. According to one

[1] This is pointed out and commented upon with much sagacity by Mr. Trevelyan in his *Wicliffe*, p. 241.

[2] All this is from the Chronicle in *Hist. Rev.*, which gives both the most detailed and the most probable of all the narratives. I follow it for most of the incidents of Smithfield.

narrative he required that the game laws should be abolished,[1] according to another that the charters concerning serfdom given on the previous day should be revised ; but the most precise and detailed of our chronicles makes him touch on much higher matters—' there should be no law save the law of Winchester,[2] no man for the future should be outlawed as the result of any legal proceedings ; lords should no longer hold lordship except civilly (whatever exactly that may mean) :[3] the estates of the church should be confiscated, after provision made for the present holders, and divided up among the laity : the bishoprics should be abolished all save one ; all men should be equally free and no legal status should differentiate one man from another, save the King alone '.   Such a programme could not be settled offhand in Smithfield : if Tyler really broached it, it must have been with the object of provoking opposition, or at least in the hope that the King and Council would ask for delay and discussion.   Either would suit him equally well, since he wished to have an excuse for keeping his bands together, if not for seizing on the person of his master.

Richard, as might have been expected, replied that the commons should have all that he could legally grant ' saving the regalities of his crown '.   This was practically no answer at all—and much of what the demagogue had demanded most certainly could not be granted by the royal fiat and without the consent of Parliament.

There was a pause : no one said a word more, ' for no lord or councillor dared to open his mouth and give an answer to the commons in such a situation '.   Tyler, apparently taking the King's reply as a practical refusal, began to grow un-mannerly.[4]   He called for a flagon of beer, which was

[1] This comes from Knighton, ii. 137, and is not mentioned in the Chronicle in *Hist. Rev.*, where the other points are rehearsed.

[2] Apparently a confused reference to the police-provisions of Edward I's Statute of Winchester.

[3] ' Et que nul seigneur averoit seigneurie fors sivelment ester proportioné entre tous genz, fors tant solement le seigneur le roi.'   *Hist. Rev.*, Chron. p. 519.

[4] According to *Hist. Rev.* Chron. he called for a mug of water and ' rincha sa bouche laidement et villaineusement avant le roi, pour le grand chaleur que il avoit ', before drinking his beer.

brought him by one of his followers, drained it at a draught—
it was a hot day and he had made a long harangue—and then
clambered upon his horse. At this moment a Kentish
retainer, who was riding behind the King and who had been
intently gazing on the demagogue, remarked in audible tones
that he had recognized the man, and knew him for the most
notorious highwayman and thief in the county. Tyler
caught the words, looked round on the speaker and bade
him come out from among the others, ' wagging his head at
him in his malice '. When the Kentishman refused to stir,
Wat turned to the fellow who was bearing his banner, and
bade him draw his sword and cut down the varlet. At this
the other answered that he had spoken the truth and done
nothing to deserve death ; whereupon the rebel unsheathed
a dagger which he had been holding in his hand throughout
the debate, and pushed his horse in among the royal retinue,
apparently with the intent of taking justice into his own
hands.[1] Then Walworth the Mayor thrust himself across
the demagogue's path, and cried that he would arrest him
for drawing his weapon before the King's face. Tyler replied
by stabbing at his stomach, but the Mayor was wearing a
coat of mail under his gown and took no harm. Whipping
out a short cutlass, he struck back and wounded the rebel in
the shoulder, beating him down on to his horse's neck. A
second after one of the King's squires, a certain John
Standwick,[2] ran him twice through the body with his
sword. Tyler was mortally wounded, but had just strength
enough to turn his horse out of the press ; he rode half
across the square, cried ' Treason ! ' and then fell from his
saddle in the empty space in sight of the whole assembly.

[1] The *Hist. Rev.* Chronicle says that Tyler ' porta un dragge en sa main quel il
avoit pris d'un autre homme'. This seems to refer to the incident described by
Chron. Angl. p. 297, and Froissart, who says that the rebel on first meeting
the King insisted on being presented with a fine dagger that he had noticed in
the possession of one of the King's followers,—Sir John Newton, according to
Chron. Angl. Richard ordered his knight to give it up, and Tyler continued
playing with it all through the time of his speech and the altercation which
followed.

[2] Or Ralph Standyche according to Knighton, ii. 138.

This was the most critical moment of the whole rebellion :
there seemed every probability that Richard and all his followers would be massacred. A confused cry ran round the
ranks of the insurgents as they saw their leader fall ; they
bent their bows, untrussed their sheaves of arrows, and in
ten seconds more would have been shooting into the royal
cortège massed in front of the gate of St. Bartholomew's.
But the young King rose to the occasion, with a cool courage
and presence of mind which showed that he was the true son
of the Black Prince. Spurring his steed right out into the
open, he cantered towards the rebels, throwing up his right
hand to wave them back, and crying, ' Sirs, will you shoot
your King ? I will be your chief and captain, you shall have
from me that which you seek. Only follow me into the fields
without '.[1] So saying he pointed to the open fields about
St. John's, Clerkenwell, which lay to the north of Smithfield,
and rode forth into them at a slow walk. After a moment's
hesitation the insurgents began to stream out in his wake.
Part of the royal retinue, lost in the crowd, followed as best
they could.[2] But Walworth, the Mayor, turned back hastily
to the city, to bring up all the loyalists that he could find and
rescue the King from his perilous position. For the danger
was not yet over: Richard was absolutely at the mercy of the
insurgents, and nothing was more likely than that an affray
might be provoked by some angry admirer of Tyler.

The Mayor rode in at Aldersgate, and began to send messages to the aldermen and officers of the twenty-four wards,
bidding them turn out every armed man that could be
trusted, and come to save the King. There was a stir all
through the city, and in a few moments the party of order were
beginning to draw together in Westcheap and St. Martin's-
le-Grand. It was in vain that the traitor-alderman Walter
Sibley, who had been present at Smithfield, strove to disperse

[1] There are as many versions of the King's words as there are descriptions of
the scene in the Chroniclers. I give the common element, partly in the phrase
of *Chron. Angl.* 297. But this version is too long, Richard had only time for
a hurried sentence or two.

[2] But many shirked off ' pur doubt que ils avoient d'un affray ', *Hist. Rev.*,
Chron. p. 520.

the loyalists, swearing that he had seen the King slain, and
warning the burgesses to man their walls and close their gates,
since no more could be done. He and his ally Horne were
swept aside, 'after they had done all that in them lay to prevent men from succouring the King and the Mayor when they
lay in such peril'.[1] No one would listen to them: Walworth
within half an hour was able to open Aldersgate and send out
the van of a considerable army. The loyalists had appeared
in numbers far greater than any one had expected : the atrocities of the last two days had converted many citizens who
had been lukewarm or even hostile to the Government, into
friends of order. Whatever their discontents had been, they
could not tolerate the anarchy that was on foot, or allow
London to be burnt and sacked piecemeal. The misgovernment of the Council was, at any rate, better than Tyler's
'hurling time'.[2] When, therefore, the banners of the more
distant wards, each surrounded by its clump of bills and bows,
had come into line at the foot of St. Martin's Street, Walworth
found that not less than 6,000 or 7,000 men had been collected. There was a stiffening of trained soldiers from the
garrison of the Tower and the mercenaries of Sir Robert
Knolles. The Mayor begged that old *condottiere* to take
military charge of the sortie, and march at once.

When the head of the column reached the fields that surrounded the blackened ruins of Clerkenwell, they found the
King still safe, and engaged in parleying with the ring of
insurgents who surround him. What he had said or promised
during the last three-quarters of an hour we do not know.
He must have been ' talking against time ', and arguing with
strange interlocutors, for John Ball and other wild extremists
were in the press. But at last, overlooking the crowd from
his saddle, he saw the banners of the wards pressing forward
from Smithfield, and noted that Knolles had deployed his
force to right and left, and was pushing forward on each flank
so as to encircle the mass of rebels. Presently a band of
lances pushed through the throng, and ranged itself behind

---

[1] Sheriff's Inquest in Réville's Documents, p. 194.

[2] 'And thys was called "the Hurlyng Tyme"',' Gregory's *Chronicle*, p. 91.

the King, and Knolles reported to him that 7,000 men were at his disposition. It is said that some of these at Richard's side whispered to him that he could now avenge himself, by ordering his army to fall upon the insurgents, and make an end of them. The King refused to listen to the proposal : the mob had spared him when they had their chance, and he had not the heart to reply to their confidence by a massacre. We are told that he answered to his evil counsellors, ' three-fourths of them have been brought here by fear and threats ; I will not let the innocent suffer with the guilty '.[1] He simply proclaimed to the multitude that he gave them leave to depart : many of them, as we read, fell on their knees in the trampled wheat of the fields and thanked him for his clemency.[2] A great swarm of Essex and Hertfordshire men dispersed devious to north and east, and hurried home. The London roughs slunk back to their garrets and cellars. Only a solid mass of Kentishmen remained : the royal army blocked their way home. But Richard formed them into a column, gave them two knights as guides and escort, and bade them march back through the city and over London Bridge, nothing doubting ; this they did, neither molesting nor molested, and went off from Southwark down the Old Kent Road.

While Richard sat triumphant on his charger, watching the multitude disperse, the Mayor brought him the head of Tyler, the only one of the rebels who perished on that memorable day. When Walworth went to seek him in Smithfield, the rebel could not be found at first. His friends had carried him, three-quarters dead, into St. Bartholomew's hospital ; there the Mayor had him sought out, and dragged into the square, where, unconscious or perhaps already dead, he suffered the decapitation that he had inflicted on so many others. Richard ordered his head to be taken to London

---

[1] For this we have only Froissart's authority, but it probably expresses the King's views.

[2] 'Ils chayeront al terre en my les bleés, comme genz discomfitées, criant al roy de mercye pour lour mesfaytz, et le roy benignement les granta mercye', says *Hist. Rev.*, Chron. 520.

Bridge, to replace that of the unfortunate Archbishop Sudbury. Before leaving the Clerkenwell fields, he knighted Walworth, and with him two other Londoners of the loyal party, the Aldermen Nicolas Bramber and John Philpott, as well as the squire John Standwick.

That afternoon, while the watch was engaged in arresting local London malefactors who were still at the work of plunder and blackmail,[1] not realizing what had happened, the King rode back to the Wardrobe 'to ease him of his heavy day's work'. His mother met him, crying, as we are told, 'Ah, fair son, what pain and anguish have I had for you this day!' To which he made reply, 'Certes, Madam, I know it well. But now rejoice and praise God, for to-day I have recovered my heritage that was lost, and the realm of England also'. And well might he make the boast, for his own courage and presence of mind alone had saved the situation and turned the perilous conference of Smithfield into a triumph. What might not have been hoped from a boy of fourteen capable of such an achievement, and who could have guessed that this gifted but wayward king was to wreck his own career and end as the miserable starved prisoner of Pontefract?

---

[1] e. g. the celebrated Thomas Farringdon was 'captus et prisonae deliberatus quo tempore idem Thomas fuit circa prostrationem tenementi Iohannis Knot, in Stayning Lane'. Réville, Indictments, p. 195.

CHAPTER V

THE REPRESSION OF THE REBELLION IN LONDON AND THE ADJACENT DISTRICT

THE Kentishmen had tramped home, half cowed, half tricked, and wholly sullen. The peasants of Essex had dispersed with their charters, elated for the moment, yet doubting, rightly enough, if those hardly won documents were worth the parchment on which they were engrossed. In short, the initiative had passed out of the hands of the rebels, and was now in that of the King and his councillors. Surrounded by the mass of armed London burghers, and with reinforcements dropping in every day, as the squires of the home counties came flocking in to the capital, the Government might at last feel itself safe, and begin to devise measures for the repression of the tumults which still raged all around. It would seem that the advisers who had most weight round the royal person at the moment were the Earl of Arundel, who had hastily taken over the Great Seal in Sudbury's place, and the Earls of Salisbury and Warwick. A few days later they were joined by the King's uncle, Thomas of Woodstock, who came hurrying in from the Welsh March, and by the Earl of Suffolk who (as we shall see) had escaped with some difficulty from the rebels of East Anglia. But Richard himself, elated at the triumph which he had won at Smithfield by his personal ascendancy over the multitude, was no longer the mere boy that he had been down to this moment, and was for the future a factor of importance in the government of the realm. Like his father, the Black Prince, he had 'won his spurs' early, though in the unhappy field of civil strife and not on the downs of Northern France.

The first necessity was to stamp out in London the last flickerings of the fire of insurrection. On the night of that same June 15 which had seen Tyler's death, we find the

King granting a dictatorial authority over the city to Walworth the Mayor, with whom were associated the old *condottiere* Robert Knolles, and the aldermen Philpott and Bramber. They were charged with the duty of guarding the King's peace, and given power to proceed against all malefactors not only by the law of the land, but if necessary ' by other ways and means '. If it pleased them they might go so far as beheading and mutilation.[1]

In pursuance of this commission, Walworth and his colleagues arrested on that night and the following day a considerable number of insurgents, Londoners and others, some of whom were actually seized while they were still at work on the task of riot and plunder.[2] A certain proportion of these prisoners were beheaded, without being granted a jury or a formal trial. Among them were John Kirkeby and Alan Threder, notable leaders of the Kentishmen, and Jack Straw, who had been Tyler's principal lieutenant. This last-named rebel left a curious confession behind him, which may or may not have contained an element of truth in it. When he had been condemned, Walworth offered to have masses said for his soul during the next three years, if he would give some account of what the designs of his friends had been. After some hesitation, Straw spoke out,[3] and answered that Tyler had intended to keep the King as a hostage, and to take him about through the shires, using the royal name as a cloak for all his doings. Under this pretended authority he intended to arrest and execute the leading magnates of the land, and to seize on all church property. The rebels would have made an end altogether of bishops, canons, rectors, abbots, and monks, and would have left no clergy in the land save the mendicant orders. Finally they

[1] 'Ad castigandum omnes qui huiusmodi insurrectiones et congregationes contra pacem nostrum fecerunt, iuxta eorum demerita, vel secundum legem Angliae, vel aliis viis et modis, per decollationes et membrorum mutilationes, prout melius et celerius iuxta discretiones vestras vobis videbitur faciendum.' Commission to Walworth, &c., of June 15, 1381.

[2] As for example Thomas Farringdon, see p. 79, who was actually pillaging a house when arrested, Réville, Documents, p. 193.

[3] For his alleged revelations see *Chron. Angl.* pp. 309-10.

would have killed the King himself, 'and when there was no one greater or stronger or more learned than ourselves surviving, we would have made such laws as pleased us'. Tyler would have been made ruler of Kent, and other chiefs were to have governed other counties. He added that if the scene at Smithfield had had another end, the insurgents were intending on that same evening to set fire to London in four places, and to have sacked the houses of all the wealthier citizens. How much of this was the bravado of despair, how much a serious revelation of the plans of the rebel leaders, it is wholly impossible to determine. We may at least believe that the projected atrocities lost nothing in the mouths of the horrified auditors who reported them to the chronicler.

Another of the victims of Walworth's court-martial was John Starling, an Essex man, who said that he had been the actual executioner of the Archbishop. He had made himself notorious by going about with a drawn sword hanging from his neck in front, and a dagger dangling on his back to match it. He owned to the murder before the Mayor, and gloried in it even at the gallows.[1]

The executions, in spite of the magniloquent language of some of the chroniclers, do not seem to have been very numerous. Even persons who had taken such a prominent part in the insurrections, as Thomas Farringdon, and the aldermen Horne and Sibley, were imprisoned, but not put to death under martial law. After long detention they and many others escaped the extreme penalty, and were released in 1382 or 1383 on bail and finally allowed to get off scot free.[2]

---

[1] Was Starling one of the class of lunatics who claim to have done any great murder that is occupying public attention ? Such folks crop up frequently in our own day. His actions, as reputed by the *Chron. Angl.* (p. 313), were not those of a sane man, for he walked about London, after the restoration of order, saying that he had killed Sudbury and expected the reward of his meritorious deed.

[2] Horne, Sibley, and Tonge were let out on bail in April 1383, finding personal security for £300, and providing each four guarantors who undertake on a penalty of £200 to produce them if called upon. In 1384 they are finally discharged, and 'eant quieti'. See documents in Réville, pp. 198-9. Farringdon, whose guilt was even greater, since he had been in the Tower at the moment of

After the first hour of wrath was over the Government (as we shall see) showed itself far less vindictive than might have been expected. We can hardly credit a story of the chronicler Malverne to the effect that certain insurgents, who had taken part in the slaughter of the Flemish merchants, were handed over to the private vengeance of the relatives of those whom they had murdered, and that some of them were beheaded by the very hands of the widows of the unfortunate merchants.[1] There is no trace of any such extraordinary measures of retaliation in the official documents relating to the rebellion.

The peace of London having been provided for, and a considerable army having been mustered and reviewed on the rebels' old camping-ground of Blackheath, the Government could now take in hand vigorous measures for the repression of the rebellion in the shires. On June 18, a general proclamation to all sheriffs, mayors, bailiffs, &c., was issued, charging them with the duty of dispersing and arresting malefactors in their respective spheres of action.[2] This was followed by more specific commissions two days later : on June 20, the sheriff of Kent, the constable of Dover Castle, Sir Thomas Trivet, the old *condottiere*, and two others, are directed to take in hand the pacification of Kent, where many rebels were still hanging together, and where pillage and charter-burning was still in progress.[3] On the same day, apparently, the Earl of Suffolk was sent down with 500 lances to establish law and order in the county from which he drew his title.[4] But the region in which the insurrection seemed least inclined to die down, and where the bands were most numerous, was Essex, and it was thither that on June 22 the King directed his march at the head of the main body of his army. On the following day he was at Waltham, and there published a

---

the Archbishop's murder, was imprisoned for a time in Devizes Castle, but pardoned as early as Feb. 25, 1382.

[1] Malverne, p. 8.

[2] There is a copy of this document in *Chron. Angl.* p. 314.

[3] The text may be found in Réville, p. 236.

[4] The Earl had already reached Sudbury on June 23 with his corps, so probably started from London on the twentieth or at latest on the twenty-first.

curious proclamation, warning all his subjects against rumours put about by the rebels to the effect that he approved of their doings and that they were acting in obedience to his orders. Richard in no measured language declares that he has not, and never had, any sympathy for their riotous and treasonable conduct, and that he regards their rising as highly prejudicial to his kingdom and crown. All true men are to resist, arrest, and punish any bands found under arms, as rebels against their sovereign lord.

This proclamation was perhaps provoked by the arrival at Waltham of a deputation sent by the Essex insurgents, with a demand for the ratification of the promises made at Mile End on June 14, and a request that they might be granted the additional privilege of freedom from the duty of attending the King's courts, save for the view of frankpledge once a year.[1] Richard spoke out roundly to this embassy; he told them that the pledges made during Tyler's reign counted for nothing, having been extorted by force. ' Villeins ye are still, and villeins ye shall remain ', he added, ending with a threat that armed resistance would draw down dreadful vengeance. It is clear that the sentimental sympathy for the oppressed peasantry attributed to the young King by some modern authors had no real existence. He was incensed at the duress which he had suffered on June 14–15, and anxious to revenge himself.

The Essex rebels, or at least a large section of them, were not prepared to submit without trying the chances of war. The Government and the insurrection had not yet been matched against each other in the open field, and in the vain hope of maintaining their newly-won liberties by force the local leaders sent out the summons for a general mobilization at Great Baddow and Rettenden, not far south of Chelmsford. They threatened to burn the house of every able-bodied man who failed to come to the rendezvous.[2] A great host was thus got together, and the rebels stockaded themselves in a strong position upon the edge of a wood near

---

[1] See *Chron. Angl.* p. 316.
[2] See Réville, p. cxvi, and *Chron. Angl.* p. 316.

Billericay, covering their flanks and rear with ditches and rows of carts [1] chained together, after the fashion that the English had been wont to employ in the French wars.

Hearing of this muster, the King dispatched against it the vanguard of his army, under his uncle, Thomas of Woodstock, and Sir Thomas Percy, the brother of the Earl of Northumberland. There was a sharp fight, but the entrenchments of the rebels were carried at the first charge, and a great number of them—as many as 500, if the chronicles can be trusted— were cut down [June 28]. The rest escaped under the cover of the forest in their rear, but the victors captured their camp, in which were found no less than 800 horses.

The majority of the insurgents dispersed after this unfortunate appeal to arms, but the more compromised among the leaders kept a considerable band together, and, retiring on Colchester, tried to persuade the townsmen of that place to continue the struggle. Meeting with little encouragement there, they continued their flight northward, and reached Sudbury in Suffolk, where they hoped to recruit new levies, as the insurrection had been very violent in that region ten days before. But Suffolk had already been pacified, and instead of meeting with reinforcements, the rebels were attacked by a body of local loyalists under Lord Fitz-Walter and Sir John Harleston. They were routed, many captured, and the rest scattered to the winds.

Another band, also, as it would appear, composed of Essex men, fled in another direction about this same time, and tried to escape northward in the direction of Huntingdon, but the burghers turned out and drove them off. The wrecks of this party escaped to the abbey of Ramsey, whither they were pursued by the victors. They were surprised, some twenty-five slain, and the rest dispersed.[2] For this loyal act the men of Huntingdon received the King's thanks.

Meanwhile Richard advanced by slow stages to Chelmsford, in the rear of his uncle and the vanguard. He reached the

---

[1] 'Se munierant in fossatis palis et cariagio, praeterquam fruebantur maiori silvarum et nemorum tutamento', ibid. 317.

[2] *Hist. Rev.*, Chron. p. 521.

place on July 2, and there issued a proclamation which formally revoked all the charters issued at Mile End, both those of manumission and those of amnesty for crimes done during the first days of the revolt.   The ground was thus cleared for a judicial inquiry into all the proceedings of the rebels from the first moment of their assembly.   The chief part in this great session was taken by Sir Robert Tresilian, who had been named Chief Justice, in the room of the murdered Cavendish.   He sat in many places, mostly in Essex and Hertfordshire, while Belknap and other of his colleagues were busy in Kent and elsewhere.

The restoration of peace and order in Kent, we may remark, was not accomplished by the march of a great army, like that of Essex, nor was there any single decisive combat such as that which took place at Billericay. The Constable of Dover, Sir Thomas Trivet, and after a time Thomas Holland, the Earl of the shire, seem to have gone round at the head of small bodies of local levies, trampling out the last embers of revolt and arresting great numbers of insurgents.   They met with little or no resistance, yet the rising had been so widespread that July was far spent before they had visited every township and restored the machinery of government in each.

It has not unfrequently been stated that the months of July and August were a veritable reign of terror in London and the south-eastern counties, that the executions were numbered not by scores but by hundreds.   Froissart's estimate of 1,500 rebels hanged or beheaded does not suffice for some modern historians, and even Bishop Stubbs thought it worth while to quote the monk of Evesham's wild estimate that seven thousand persons perished.   It is satisfactory for the credit of the English nation to find, from the original records of the inquests, trials, and escheats, that these figures are as gross exaggerations as most other estimates of the mediaeval chronicles.   We cannot, owing to unfortunate *lacunae* in our documents, reconstitute anything like a complete list of the victims of the reaction.   But we have enough evidence to show that it cannot have been very large.   The praiseworthy and painstaking efforts of André Réville in exploring the rolls of the Record Office resulted in the compiling of a list of 110 persons who had suffered capital punishment for their doings in the insurrection.[1]   Of course this total is incomplete, but by comparing the rolls of persons indicted or delated with those of the executed, we cannot fail to come to the conclusion that the larger proportion of those who perished have been identified.

On the whole the proceedings of the justices seem to have been far more moderate, and the observation of forms of law more complete than we should have expected. The only persons put to death without a proper trial were Jack Straw and a few other leaders who fell into the hands of the Government at the very commencement of the repression. But the number of these was very small, as is clearly shown by the passage in the Rolls of the next Parliament, which specially speaks of them as a few 'capitaines, hastiment descolléz sans processe de ley '.[2]

When the Government had recovered from its panic, every prisoner without exception was proceeded against under the normal processes of law, with the co-operation of a jury. Even such a notorious offender as John Ball was no exception. He had fled from London after Tyler's death, but was caught in hiding at Coventry, whence he was taken to St. Albans to be tried before Chief Justice Tresilian.   On July 13 he met his accusers, fearlessly avowed that he was guilty of taking a leading part in the insurrection, and acknowledged that the incendiary letters dispersed in Kent were of his writing. He denied that any of his doings were blameworthy, and refused to ask for a pardon from the King. Considering that he had not only fomented the rising, but apparently was present in the Tower during Sudbury's murder, it is not astonishing that he was condemned to be hanged, drawn, and quartered. What does provoke surprise is that, at the special request of Courtenay, Bishop of London, he was given two days

[1] See Petit-Dutaillis's remarks of Réville's figures on p. cxxi of his introduction to the latter's book.
[2] Rolls of Parliament, iii. 175.

respite to make his peace with God, and only executed on July 15.[1]

No doubt there must have been a certain amount of judicial errors committed during the trials of the rebels in July-August 1381.   We are told that in many cases the juries of presentment allowed themselves to be carried away by old grudges and personal enmities, and delated individuals who were comparatively innocent as guilty of the graver offences. In other instances the jurors, conscious that their own conduct would not bear examination, pandered to the desires of the judges by denouncing such persons as they knew that the Government would gladly see indicted.   Tresilian occasionally hectored juries, and frightened them into giving up the names of local leaders, by warning them that their own necks would not be safe if they shielded the guilty.[2]

But on the other hand there are numerous signs of a merciful spirit on the part of the Government.   There were many reprieves and pardons from the very first, and on August 30, Richard was advised to issue orders that all further arrests and executions were to cease, and that the consideration of the cases of all rebels still in prison and untried should be transferred from the local courts to the King's Bench.   This practically brought the hangings to an end, for one after another the surviving insurgents were pardoned and released. An amnesty for all save certain specified offenders was published on December 14, 1381 ; the larger number of these 247 excepted persons were fugitives, who had not fallen into the hands of the law, and never did.   Of those who were unlucky enough to be caught and imprisoned there is a fairly long list.   We shall see, when dealing with the annals of the Parliament that met in November 1381, that it was at first proposed to exclude from the amnesty the towns of Canterbury, Cambridge, Bridgewater, Bury St. Edmunds, Beverley, and Scarborough, in each of which the majority of the townsfolk had been implicated in the rising.   But after consideration Bury alone was excepted from the general pardon, for reasons

---

[1] *Chron. Angl.* p. 320.   [2] See for example *Chron. Angl.* p. 323.

which we shall easily comprehend when we come to deal with the events that took place in that turbulent town.

After the amnesty had been proclaimed a great number of persons whose names were not on the list of the excluded thought it worth while to procure from the Chancery letters *de non molestando*, protecting them against any further inquiry by the sheriffs and justices. They were then quit of all further trouble. Not so the excepted men, actually in the hands of the law, who had to stand their trials : yet it is surprising to find how lightly these latter were dealt with. The Government, when the first spasm of revenge had passed, was extraordinarily merciful, and seems to have considered that anything was better than waking anew the memories of the rebellion by belated executions. Among persons who escaped with their lives after shorter or longer terms of durance we may quote not only the London offenders already spoken of—Farringdon, Horne, and Sibley—but Thomas Sampson, the leader of revolt about Ipswich, Robert Westbroun, who had been saluted ' King of the Commons ' at Bury, and Sir Roger Bacon, a great offender (as we shall see) in Eastern Norfolk. These three were released at various dates between December 1381 and April 1385.[1] The only man who seems to have endured a really long term of imprisonment was Robert Cave of Dartford, the leader of the first assembly in Kent. He must be considered very fortunate for having escaped the first burst of vengeance : but having done so was simply left in prison, and kept there till 1392, when he was turned loose.[2] Considering the sanitary condition of mediaeval prisons, we must conclude that he possessed a wonderful constitution.

[1] Bacon was amnestied on December 18, 1381, Sampson in January 1383, Westbroun in April 1385. See Réville's notes and appendices, pp. 158, 172.

[2] See document 3, p. 180, in Réville's Appendix.

CHAPTER VI

The Rebellion in the Home Counties and the South

In following up the fate of the insurgents of London, Kent, and Essex, whose doings form the main thread of the history of the Great Rebellion of 1381, we have been drawn on beyond the strict sequence of events. While Tyler was running riot in the capital, troubles were beginning to break out in regions of which we have hitherto hardly spoken. While the Government was already commencing its measures of repression in the Home Counties, the rebellion was only just reaching high-water mark in districts remote from the centre of affairs. For the rising in the outlying shires only began when the news of the successes of the first insurgents was bruited abroad, and so came to a head some days after Tyler's march on London, and continued for some time after his death. It was long before the full import of the dramatic scene at Smithfield on Saturday, June 15, became known in the remoter centres of disturbance.

Though all the counties of Eastern and South-Eastern England were affected by the insurrection, we shall see that the only district where the troubles broke out with an intensity similar to that seen in Kent and Essex, was East Anglia, i.e. the counties of Norfolk, Suffolk, and Cambridge. There we find a reign of anarchy of the most complete kind with marked local peculiarities of its own. But outside this focus the troubles were no more than the ground-swell moving outward from the central disturbance which had burst so tempestuously upon London. In Surrey, Sussex or Hertfordshire, and still more in the remote counties, the riots and outrages were sporadic and short-lived; they only broke out where there was some pre-existing provocative cause, or where detachments from the main body of the insurgent horde were actually present or close at hand.

Northern Surrey, Middlesex, and Hertfordshire were in actual contact with Tyler's hordes after they had marched on London. In all these the troubles broke out only after the arrival of the Kentishmen at Blackheath : emboldened by the sight of these successful insurgents, the inhabitants of the villages for a ring of ten miles round the capital copied their doings ; they burnt the local manor rolls, and often the manors with them, and sometimes blackmailed or hunted away unpopular residents. We can trace serious disturbances at Clapham, Croydon, Kennington, Kingston-on-Thames, Harrow, Barnet. Inhabitants of almost every parish of Middlesex and Northern Surrey are to be found among the list of persons excluded from the general pardon issued by the King, at the end of the measures of repression which followed the revolt. Hendon, Hounslow, Ruislip, Twickenham, Chiswick, Carshalton, Sutton, Mitcham [1]—the list would be endless if complete—each supply their contingent ; some of the outlawed men had been to London, and taken a prominent part in the arson and murder started by Tyler's gangs : others had done local mischief. In the main the inhabitants of the suburban region had merely their rural grievances to avenge, and struck out no line of their own ; they simply followed the lead of the Kentishmen.

In Hertfordshire the tale is more interesting, all the more so that we have elaborate narratives of the proceedings of the rebels by monks of St. Albans and Dunstable, so that we can follow the progress of events with a minuteness of detail that is wanting in most other regions. Though there was a good deal of the ordinary revolt against serfdom and manorial customs in the county, yet in the main centre of trouble, at St. Albans, a very different cause was at the bottom of the disturbance. Here the rising of 1381 was but an incident in a long and venomous struggle between the abbots and the townsfolk : it is exactly parallel to the similar feud at Bury St. Edmunds, which we shall have to mention when dealing with East Anglia. St. Albans, like Bury, was a considerable market town which had grown up around the

---

[1] See the documents in Réville, pp. 214-33.

abbey ; if it had been on royal demesne, or had belonged to some lay lord, it would long ago have obtained a charter of incorporation, and have achieved some measure of local autonomy. But the wealthy and powerful abbots, free from the political necessities which affected kings, and the financial stress which often lay heavy on earls and barons, had never sold or given municipal freedom to their vassals. The town of St. Albans remained a mere manor, governed autocratically by the monks, and for two hundred years had been chafing against the yoke. The leading inhabitants bitterly resented the pressure of the dead hand of the church, which kept them in the same subjection as the serfs of a rural hamlet, and carefully maintained every petty restraint that dated back to the twelfth or eleventh century. They were always on the look-out for a chance of upsetting the dominion of the abbots and winning their liberty.[1] They had even invented a legend that the town had received a charter from King Offa, which the monks had stolen away and suppressed. In 1274 and again in 1314 and 1326 they had risen against their lords and freed themselves for a moment, only to be put down by the interference of the royal authority.

Hence the insurrection of 1381 seemed to the townsfolk of St. Albans an admirable opportunity for making one more dash for liberty. They were neither rural serfs oppressed with boonwork, nor politicians anxious to remove ' traitors ' from the ministry, but they saw the advantage of throwing in their lot with the rebels of Kent and Essex. Moreover they had a very able and determined leader in the person of a certain William Grindcobbe, one of the few popular chiefs of the day of whom we possess a detailed knowledge.

The troubles began at St. Albans only on June 14, the day after Tyler entered London ;[2] but it is clear that the leaders of the townsfolk had been watching the face of affairs for some days before. On that morning a deputation presented itself to the abbot Thomas de la Mare, a hard-handed and litigious priest much hated by his vassals,[3] and informed him that

---

[1] *Gesta Abbatum*, III. p. 329.   [2] *Chron. Angl.* p. 289.
[3] For a sketch of his character see Riley's Preface to *Gesta Abbatum*, III. x.

they had received a summons from the chief of the Kentishmen.   They were bidden to come to him in arms and pledge
their loyalty to the true Commons of England : if they de-
layed, Tyler had sworn that he would come in person to
St. Albans and lay the town waste.   This pretence of com-
pulsion can hardly have deceived the abbot, more especially
as Grindcobbe, the leader of the deputation, was a noted
enemy of the monastery, and had been excommunicated and
forced to do penance for violent assaults on certain of the
brethren.

The band of townsfolk started for London at dawn on
June 14, and passed Highbury just as the manor was being
burnt by Jack Straw ; [1] they fraternized with his band, took
the oath to 'King and Commons', and pressed on their way.
They were in time for the end of the conference at Mile End,
slipped in among the representatives of the Essex hundreds,
and were promised one of the numerous charters which the
King's clerks were distributing that day.   While it was being
written, Grindcobbe and some of his associates stole away
and interviewed Wat Tyler, who made them swear a solemn
oath recognizing him as their captain and chief : he promised them his aid, gave them a set of instructions as to the
line of conduct they were to pursue with the abbot, and vowed
that they should have the aid of 20,000 of his men to ' shave
the monks' beards ' if they met with any resistance.[2]

Without waiting for the King's letter, the leaders of the
St. Albans townsmen hastened back that same afternoon
to their houses—they must have gone more than thirty miles
that day—and proclaimed to their friends that the King
had abolished serfdom and all manorial rights.   As a token
of their new freedom they broke down, before retiring to
rest, the gates of the abbot's home-park, and destroyed the
house of one of his officials in the town.

Next morning the whole of the townsfolk set to work to
make an end of the outward and visible signs of the abbot's
seignorial authority over them.   They drained his fish-pond,
broke down the hedges of his preserves, killed his game, and

[1] *Chron. Angl.* p. 290.   [2] Ibid. p. 300.

cut up and divided among themselves certain plots of his domain-ground. They hung a rabbit at the end of a pole on the town pillory, as a token that the game-laws were abolished. But it was not only rabbits that were killed that day : the mob entered the abbot's prison, and held a sort of informal session on its inmates. They acquitted and dismissed all the captives save one, a notorious malefactor, whom they condemned and executed, fixing up his head alongside of the dead rabbit.

Presently those of the deputation who had remained behind in London arrived with the King's letter, which they had duly received. Armed with this all-important document they interviewed the abbot, and after a long debate, in which the wily ecclesiastic tried all possible methods of turning them from their end, obtained all the old regal charters on which his manorial rights were based, and burnt them in the market-place. They then tried to get from him the imaginary charter of King Offa, granting borough rights to their ancestors ; this, of course, could not be found[1] ; in default of it the abbot was told to draw up a new document emancipating the townsmen. He did so, but it failed to satisfy them, and they resolved to construct one for themselves, and to force him to seal and sign it. Meanwhile this same Saturday saw the sacking of the houses of the abbey officials, and an irruption into the monastery buildings to tear up some famous stones in the floor of one of the rooms. These were ancient millstones, a trophy of the victory of a former abbot, who had prevented the inhabitants from establishing private mills of their own, and had confiscated their querns to pave his parlour.[2] No other damage of importance was done to the abbey buildings.

On Sunday morning the scenes of Smithfield and the death of Tyler were known in St. Albans. But neither abbot nor townsfolk knew exactly how much was implied by the King's success. The news, however, rendered the rioters

[1] *Gesta Abbatum*, III. 291-2.

[2] This had been the work of Abbot Roger Norton in 1274. See *Gesta Abbatum*, I. 453 and III. 309.

cautious, and they drew up a very moderate charter for themselves. By it their liege lord was made (a) to grant them wide rights of pasturage on his waste ; (b) to give them leave to hunt and fish in his woods and ponds ; (c) to abolish the monopoly of the seignorial mill ; (d) to concede to the town municipal freedom, the right to govern itself by its own elected magistrates without any interference on the part of the bailiff and other officials of the monastery.[1]

When the men of St. Albans had worked their will on the abbot, his troubles were by no means at an end. Between Saturday, June 15, and the following Wednesday, June 19, he was visited by more or less turbulent deputations from all the minor manors belonging to the abbey, who, by more or less violent harangues and threats, forced him to ratify the King's general abolition of serfdom, by drawing up a charter for each village. He was made to resign his rights over all his serfs, and often to grant free hunting and fishing, and exemption from tolls and dues, to them. Except that they killed the game and broke the closes in the abbatial preserves in their neighbourhood, they seem to have conducted themselves with moderation. No murder and little pillage or blackmailing is reported.

The Abbot of St. Albans was the greatest landowner, but by no means the only one in Hertfordshire. The rising was, of course, not confined to the boundaries of his scattered estates. At Tring, which belonged to the 'traitor' Archbishop of Canterbury, there was a bonfire of local manorial archives. The houses of two justices of the peace, John Lodewick of Digswell and John Kymperle of Watford, were broken open. The indictments drawn up after the rebellion was over, give us many more instances of roll-burning and of violent seizure of lands in various corners of the county. The Priors of Redbourne and Dunstable were forced to draw up charters emancipating their servile tenants, just as their wealthier neighbour at St. Albans had been.[2] But on the whole, the doings of the Hertfordshire men compare very

---

[1] For the text see *Gesta Abbatum*, III. 317-20.
[2] See *Annals of Dunstable*, pp. 417-18.

favourably with those of their neighbours. Only two murders are reported from the county, both of persons of no importance : but one of them (that of an unpopular bailiff at Cublecote) deserves mention, because it was committed by a band headed by a priest, 'Hugh, the Parson of Puttenham'.[1] In every shire there was a proportion of the lower clergy implicated in the most violent episodes of the rising.

When the day of repression and punishment arrived, there was no attempt at armed resistance in Hertfordshire, as there had been in Kent, Essex, and East Anglia. This was due partly to the cautious behaviour of the King's ministers, who acted by negotiation instead of by open attack, and partly to the fact that the insurgents, conscious that they had no long list of atrocities to their discredit, did not feel so desperate as the Kentishmen or the East Anglians. After much haggling with the abbot, the St. Albans men surrendered their charter, and bound themselves to pay a fine of £200 for the damage that they had done to the monastic property, while their lord engaged, on his part, not to delate them to the King, nor to press for their punishment. Richard arrived in person at St. Albans on July 12, after having made an end of the Essex rebels. The whole population of the county did homage to him, assembled in the great court of the abbey, acknowledged their guilt, and swore never again to rise in arms. In return, the King pledged his word that none should suffer except ringleaders in definite acts of rebellion or murder, who should be dealt with by regular process of law.[2]

About eighty persons were arrested in the county ; they were tried by Robert Tresilian, the Chief Justice of the King's Bench. All were regularly ' presented ' by local juries : indeed, Tresilian took the precaution of summoning three separate bodies of jurors one after another, each of which was made to go through the list of suspects, so that no prisoner was brought to trial who had not been delated by thirty-six of his neighbours.[3] In all, fifteen insurgents were

[1] The victim's name was William Bragg. See Réville, p. 40.
[2] Chron. Angl. p. 325.
[3] Chron. Angl. p. 320 ; Gesta Abbatum, III. 347.

condemned and executed, three of whom were prominent
inhabitants of St. Albans ; the rest were persons concerned
in the two murders that had taken place in the shire, or in
other acts of violence.   Thus it cannot be said that the vengeance of the Government was ruthless or indiscriminate ;
the remainder of the rebels, including several leaders who had
laid themselves open to severe punishment, were released
after a few weeks or months of imprisonment.[1]   The most
notable victim of Tresilian's sessions was the chief organizer
of the St. Albans rising, William Grindcobbe, a man whose
courageous bearing and evident disinterestedness might have
moved a sentiment of pity and admiration in any one but
the monastic chronicler, who has told his tale.[2]   This 'son
of Belial ' was liberated on bail in the early days of repression,
under the expectation that he would use his influence with
the townsfolk to procure their speedy submission.   He disap-
pointed the abbot's hopes.   The harangue which he made
to his neighbours rings finely even when reproduced by
the monk's unsympathetic pen.   'Friends, who after so
long an age of oppression, have at last won yourselves a short
breath of freedom, hold firm while you can, and have no
thought for me or what I may suffer.   For if I die for the
cause of the liberty that we have won, I shall think myself
happy to end my life as a martyr.   Act now as you would
have acted supposing that I had been beheaded at Hertford
yesterday.'   He returned to prison, and was one of the first
to suffer.   St. Albans had to wait till the Reformation
before it achieved the liberty of which he had dreamed.

About the troubles of Sussex and Hants we are much less

[1] See Réville, pp. 152-3, and the corresponding documents in the list of
indictments.

[2] The most odious paragraphs in the St. Albans Chronicle are those which
tell the story of what happened to the bodies of Grindcobbe and his fellows.
Their friends stole them away and buried them ; but they were compelled
to dig them up, when far gone in corruption, and to hang them up again with
their own hands.   'Et quidem merito', says the chronicler, 'hoc erat foedum
officium virorum usurpantium minus iuste nomen "civium", ut apte vocarentur,
et essent, suspensores hominum.   Compulsi sunt propriis manibus suos concives
resuspendere catenis ferreis, quorum iam corpora tabe fluentia, putrida et
foetentia, odorem intolerabilem refundebant', &c.   Chron. Angl. 326.

well-informed than about those of the East Midlands. We know that in the former county the villeins of the Earl of Arundel were up in arms during the days that followed Tyler's entry into London : one chronicler tells us in vague terms that many murders were committed in the shire,[1] and the less doubtful evidence of the royal escheators shows us that at least two rebels were executed in Sussex, while eight more who had escaped the gallows by flight were outlawed. In Hampshire it would seem that the centre of revolt lay among the urban malcontents of Winchester, rather than among the peasantry. Apparently the lower class of craftsmen rose against the burgess-oligarchy of mayor and aldermen, as had happened in London. At any rate, the list of the confiscated property of local rebels condemned to death or outlawed, shows that we are dealing with small tradesmen and artisans—skinners, tailors, hosiers, fullers, &c. There is only one exception, a wealthy draper, named William Wigge, whose goods were valued at £81, and who got a pardon in February 1383, though three knights of the Parliament of 1381–2 had protested against his being included in the list of pardons, because he had been a leader in ' treasons and felonies '.[2] No doubt, like Horne and Sibley in London, he had gone against his own class owing to some old municipal grudge.

[1] The Continuator of the *Eulogium Historiarum*, p. 354.
[2] See the Winchester documents in Réville, pp. 278–9, especially no. 192.

CHAPTER VII

THE REBELLION IN NORFOLK AND SUFFOLK

WHEN we cast our eyes northward, and turn from Wessex to East Anglia we find a very different state of affairs. The rebellion in Norfolk, Suffolk, and Cambridgeshire was not sporadic and partial, but universal and violent in the extreme. There was as much disorder and even more arson and murder than had prevailed in Kent and Essex. The urban and the rural districts were equally affected; though the motives were diverse, the action of peasants and townsfolk was similar in its reckless and misdirected energy. The movement received its original impulse from London and Essex, yet its history was not intimately connected with that of the main rebellion. It came to a head after Tyler's death, and was at its height when the insurgents of the south had already been dispersed. Its leaders seem to have had no ambition beyond that of dominating their own districts, and made no attempt to march on the capital, or to rekindle the smouldering embers of revolt in Essex and Kent. Finally, the main rising was quelled, not by force sent from the capital, but by local magnates. The whole story of the eastern revolt can be treated as an independent episode.

Our authorities give us no reason for supposing that any trouble broke out in East Anglia before June 12, the day when the Kentishmen reached Blackheath. On that day the most prominent of the chiefs of the rising, John Wraw, made his appearance at Liston, on the Stour, just outside the shire-line of Suffolk, at the head of a band of rioters, mostly drawn from Essex. There he made proclamation that he was come to right the grievances of all men, and called the 'true commons' to his banner, sending a special message to the neighbouring town of Sudbury, from which he expected to raise a large contingent of allies. When a few scores of rioters had rallied round him, he opened his proceedings by sacking the manor of Richard Lyons, that same dishonest financier whom the 'Good Parliament' had impeached five years before, and whom the London mob was to murder next day. Evidently the name of Lyons so stank in the nostrils of all Englishmen, that an assault on his property was a good advertisement for an insurgent chief just about to open his career. On the following morning Wraw was already at the head of a great horde of followers, and able to take serious enterprises in hand.

Rebellions do not flare up in this sudden fashion unless the ground has been prepared. What were the special circumstances which made Norfolk and Suffolk so ready and eager to rise ? They were the most thickly peopled counties in England, and Norfolk at least (Suffolk was poorer) stood at the head of the list in wealth also.[1] They were not purely rural and agricultural : besides the towns such as Norwich, Lynn, Bury St. Edmunds, Ipswich, and Yarmouth, which were noted for their commerce, they were full of minor centres of industry : even small villages had a considerable proportion of artisans among their population. It would seem that the economic condition of the countryside compared favourably with that of any other part of the realm. But nowhere else was there a greater and more flagrant diversity between the status of different sections of the people. Side by side there were towns which enjoyed the best possible charters, such as Norwich and Yarmouth, and others, like Bury, which had been gripped in the dead hand of the church, and had never been able to win their municipal independence. So among the rural districts there were villages where the old preponderance of the free man (so prominent in the Norfolk of Domesday Book) had never disappeared, where there was no demesne land, or where at least the inhabitants owed nothing to the demesne.[2] But on the other hand, there were

---

[1] Norfolk, with 97,817 inhabitants, stands in the Poll Tax returns of 1377 at the head of all the counties, save the vast shire of York with 131,040; Suffolk comes fourth in the list, being beaten only by the far larger county of Lincoln, which runs Norfolk close with 95,119 inhabitants.

[2] See Vinogradoff's *Villeinage in England*, p. 316.

other places where the manorial system reigned in its ex-
tremest form, and where every due and service was stringently
exacted.   It is notable that many East Anglian landowners
had already despaired of the old system, and let out all their
estates on farm, since it was no longer possible to work them
profitably by the labour of the villeins.[1]   Wherever this had
happened, the peasants of the neighbouring manors must have
chafed more than ever at their own servitude.   It has been
noted that peasant-revolts all over Europe were wont to
spring up, not in the regions where the serf was in the deepest
oppression, but in those in which he was comparatively well
off, where he was strong enough to aspire to greater liberty,
and to dream of getting it by force. This was a marked feature
of the great German rising of 1525, where the regions on which
feudalism pressed heaviest were precisely those which took
no part in the insurrection.   It would seem that the same
rule held in England, and that the violence of the outburst
in East Anglia was due to the fact that it was the most advanced of all the sections of rural England.   Freedom was
almost in sight, and therefore seemed worth striving for.
We may add to this general cause all the particular causes
that we have noted in other parts of England—hatred of
hard-handed landlords, clerical or lay, in some parts, grievances
in the towns felt by the small folk against the local oligarchy,
political discontent with the misgovernment of the land.
It would be rash, however, to add the possible influence of
Wycliffite doctrines which some have suspected in these
counties.   Though afterwards a great focus of Lollardy they
showed in 1381 no signs of being actuated by religious motives.[2]
If clerical landlords were attacked, it was because they were
landlords, not because they were clerics.   If an unusual
number of poor parsons appear among the rebel leaders,
it was because they were poor and discontented, not because
they were fanatical reformers.   In East Anglia, as in Herts

---

[1] See Petit-Dutaillis's note on p. 56 of Réville, to the effect that the letting
of manors in farms was far more common in Norfolk than in e. g. Kent,
Middlesex, or any other county.

[2] See Réville, pp. 123-4, most convincing pages.

or Kent or Essex, we find no sign whatever of a tendency to church-breaking or other sacrilege. It is one of the most notable features of the rebellion throughout the whole of England.

The leaders of the East Anglian rising were drawn from many and divers ranks of life. In Kent and Essex the insurgent chiefs, with the exception of John Ball, were peasants and artisans ; in London a few citizens of wealth and good position, like the aldermen Horne and Sibley, and Thomas Farringdon, had been drawn into the revolution either by personal grievances or by bitter municipal quarrels. In Norfolk and Suffolk we find not only, as has been already pointed out, an extraordinary number of priests among the organizers of the troubles, but also a fair sprinkling of men drawn from the governing classes. Two local squires were deeply implicated in the disturbances at Bury, a knight, bearing the honoured name of Roger Bacon, directed the sack of Yarmouth, another, Sir Thomas Cornerd, is recorded as having gone about levying blackmail at the head of a band. In addition, members of well-known county families of Norfolk and Suffolk, such as Richard and John Talmache, James Bedingfield, Thomas de Monchensey, Thomas Gissing, William Lacy, are found taking an active part in deeds of murder and pillage : it is clear from the details that they were willing agents, and had not been forced by threats to place themselves at the head of the hordes which followed them. After studying the crimes laid to their account, we are driven to believe that they were unquiet spirits, who took advantage of the sudden outbreak of anarchy in order to revenge old grudges or to plunder their weaker neighbours. It is impossible to recognize in them ' liberal ' members of the governing class, honestly endeavouring to guide the revolt into channels of constitutional reform.[1] Their deeds betray their real character : the genuine reformer does not

[1] I therefore cannot agree with Mr. Powell in his *East Anglian Revolt* when he says that ' A genuine sympathy for the working-classes, combined with the strong aversion which they held, in common with them, to the Poll Tax, may possibly account for these members of the better class giving their active assistance to the revolutionary party ', [p. 3].

occupy himself in compelling his neighbours to sell him their land at a nominal price, or in extorting money by threats from those who are too weak to defend themselves.[1]   But it is clear, from the way in which these East Anglian knights and squires behaved, that the insurrection was not socialistic in its general bent, nor purely a rising of the poor against the rich.   If that had been the case, the rebels would never have chosen landed gentry for their leaders.

It seems, in short, that the rising in the eastern counties was caused by a general explosion of the suppressed grievances of every class :   villeins who disliked manorial customs, townsfolk who wanted a charter, artisans oppressed by municipal oligarchs, clergy who felt the sting of poverty, discontented knights and squires, all took part in it, with the most diverse ends in view.   Hence came the chaotic and ineffective character which, from first to last, it displayed.

But it is time to return to the detailed history of this sudden outburst of wrath.   It was on June 12, as we have already seen, that John Wraw gave the signal by unfurling his banner at Liston, and sacking the house of Richard Lyons, the financier.   Wraw was a priest ;   he was, or had been, vicar of Ringsfield near Beccles.   Of his earlier life we know nothing more ;   but it is evident that he was poor[2], discontented, and ambitious.   His acts during the insurrection were those of a vain, cruel, and greedy man ;   he was filling his privy purse (as his own confession shows) throughout his short tenure of power.   When it was over he displayed despicable cowardice, and tried to save his life by

---

[1] e. g., Sir Roger Bacon took prisoner William Clere, who owned the Manor of Autingham, forced him to sell it to him, and then sold it himself at a profit, three days later, to William Wychingham. [Réville, pp. 111–12.] He also levied ten marks of blackmail from John Curteys by horrible threats. Sir Thomas Cornerd, a still meaner scoundrel, went as the lieutenant of Wraw to a certain John Rookwood, and took from him by threats ten marks in gold. He came back to Wraw, swore that he had only got eight, and begged for a percentage 'pro labore suo' : Wraw gave him 40s., so that Cornerd got off with 66s. 8d. out of the whole 133s. 4d. extorted—50 per cent. [Wraw's confession in Réville, p. 181.]

[2] At his trial it was deposed that he had no property, real or personal, whatever.   Réville, p. 59.

turning King's evidence. He laid depositions against all his own lieutenants, and furnished the Government with sufficient information to hang many of them, though (as we are glad to see) he did not thereby save his own miserable neck. Of the qualities that an insurgent leader should own, Wraw seems to have possessed only unscrupulousness and a loud and ready tongue. He was neither a fighter nor an organizer, and collapsed the moment that he met with opposition.

It would seem that this turbulent priest had come straight from London to raise the peasantry of his native county. There he had been conferring with the leading malcontents, though the *Chronicon Angliae* must be wrong when it says that he had met Tyler, for the latter reached Blackheath only on the same day on which the Suffolk rising commenced [June 12].[1] But Wraw knew all that had happened in Kent, and the way for him had been prepared by emissaries from Essex, who had been carrying the news of the revolt northward for some days before the actual call to arms.[2]

It was on the Wednesday that Wraw sacked Lyons's manor and raised the men of Sudbury. On the next morning he was at the head of a large following, whose leaders were a squire, Thomas Monchensey of Edwardston, and three priests from Sudbury—probably old friends and allies of the insurgent chief. They commenced their march into the heart of the county by visiting the manor of Overhall, which belonged to the Chief Justice of the King's Bench, Sir John Cavendish. The judge was unpopular, not only as being a prominent member of the governing clique at London, but as having lately taken over the invidious task of enforcing the Statute

[1] The chronicle says that Wraw conferred with Tyler in London, and got orders from him on the day before he raised his standard. But Wraw rose on June 12, and Tyler only entered London on June 13. Therefore the priest cannot have seen the Kentishman, unless he had crossed the Thames and met him on the ninth, or tenth at Canterbury or Maidstone. This is unlikely, as it is more than fifty miles from London to Liston, and therefore Wraw must have started from London on the tenth. Probably he conferred with London malcontents only.

[2] Such as Adam Worth, and Thomas Sweyn of Coggeshall, who appear in the indictments as having come out of Essex to stir up Suffolk early in June. See Réville, pp. 58, 59.

of Labourers in Suffolk and Essex.[1]   It would seem that he had been warned of the approach of the insurgents, for he stowed all his valuables in the church tower of Cavendish, and escaped in a north-westerly direction, perhaps intending to seek refuge at Ely.   Wraw's gang pillaged his manor, and not finding his plate and other precious goods in the house, went to seek them in the church.   They broke open its doors, and distributed the silver among themselves, but did no further damage to the sacred edifice.

In the afternoon Wraw marched for Bury St. Edmunds, the largest place in Suffolk,[2] though not its county town.   He knew that he was eagerly expected there, and would meet with much support from the inhabitants.   For Bury, like St. Albans, was one of those unhappy towns which owned a monastery for its lord, and had hitherto failed to secure municipal rights and liberties.   It was not for want of trying : the townsfolk had risen against the abbots on four or five separate occasions during the last sixty years.   In 1327 they had extorted a charter by violence, only to see it torn up a few months later, when the sheriff of Norfolk came down on the town with his men-at-arms and hanged several ringleaders. On another occasion they had kidnapped their abbot, and spirited him away to Brabant, a freak for which they had to pay 2,000 marks in fines.   Now matters were again ripe : the title of abbot was disputed between two rivals, Edmund Brounfield, a papal ' provisor ', and John Tymworth, who had been elected by the majority of the monks.   Pending the settlement of their claims by litigation, the management of the monastery was in the hands of the Prior, John Cambridge. The townsfolk were strong partisans of Brounfield, who was a local man with relatives in their midst, and had given them secret promises of a favourable charter ; but their candidate was at this moment in prison.   He had been arrested under the Statute of Provisors, and was expiating in durance vile his presumption in introducing the papal

[1] See Powell's *East Anglian Rising*, pp. 13, 14.
[2] In the census of persons liable to the Poll-tax (i. e. over 15 years of age), in 1377, Bury St. Edmunds shows 2,445 adults, and Ipswich only 1,507.

bull into England. The men of Bury were full of wrath against the monks in general, and against Prior Cambridge, the chief opponent of Brounfield, in particular.

The time of insurrection seemed favourable for the humbling of the monastery and the winning of a charter. Accordingly, the townsfolk sent messages to Wraw and his horde, inviting them to come to Bury and set matters right. On the evening of June 13 the rebels appeared in great force, and were welcomed with open glee by the poorer classes, many of whom joined them. The wealthier burgesses affected to hold themselves aloof from the movement, but secretly gave both encouragement and advice to the invaders. For good consideration received, Wraw undertook to bring the monks to reason in his own way. His band started operations by plundering the houses belonging to the abbey officials, as also the town residence of Sir John Cavendish. That night Prior Cambridge fled, having heard that it was the intention of the rebels to kill him on the following morning. But he only gained himself thirty-six hours of life by thus absconding. Parties of Wraw's followers, guided by men of Bury, sought for him in every direction. On the afternoon of June 14, he was betrayed by a treacherous guide, and captured in a wood three miles from Newmarket, as he strove to make his way to Ely. His captors dragged him to Mildenhall; there he was subjected to a mock trial before John Wraw and certain of the Bury men,[1] and beheaded on the morning of June 15. His body was left lying for five days unburied on Mildenhall Heath ; his head, fixed on a pike, was borne back to Bury. The monastic chroniclers unite in deploring the fate of one who was a faithful servant of his abbey, and who, moreover, 'excelled Orpheus the Thracian, Nero the Roman, and Belgabred of Britain in the sweetness of his voice and in his musical skill '.[2]

The Prior's head was not the only trophy that was carried

[1] Wraw delated his own lieutenant, Robert Westbroun, and two Bury squires named Denham and Halesworth, as the main agents of the Prior's trial and death. But he could not disguise the fact that he participated himself in the affair. Réville, Documents, p. 177.

[2] *Chron. Angl.* p. 301.

in triumph to Bury that afternoon. Another band of the insurgents had got upon the track of Sir John Cavendish, and caught him up at Lakenheath, a place on the border of the fenland, not many miles from Mildenhall. Seeing that he was pursued, the unfortunate Chief Justice made for the ferry over the river Brandon. He had nearly reached it when a certain Katharine Gamen pushed off the boat into mid-stream, so that he was apprehended at the water's edge. He was promptly beheaded by the pursuing mob, who were under the leadership of two local men, John Pedder of Fordham, and John Potter of Somerton [June 14]. They had taken his head to Bury, and fixed it on the town pillory, when Wraw's party, bearing that of the Prior, arrived. Cavendish and Cambridge had been intimate personal friends during their lifetime, wherefore it seemed an excellent jest to the mob to parade the two heads side by side, sometimes placing the Judge's mouth to the Prior's ear, as if he was making his confession, at others pressing the dead lips together for a kiss.[1] When tired of this ghoulish pleasantry, the rebels fixed the two heads on the pillory. A few hours later, they added to its adornments a third trophy, the head of John Lakenheath, a monk who, bearing the office of *custos baroniae* in the abbey, had been charged with the unpopular duty of exacting manorial dues and fines. Three other brethren, designated for a similar fate, escaped, one by concealing himself, the other two by taking sanctuary at the altar, where (by some inexplicable chance) the mob did not seek them.[2] On Sunday, one more head, that of a local notable, who was considered too friendly to the abbey, was set with the others.[3]

Wraw was in full possession of Bury and its neighbourhood for eight days. His armed men aided the townsfolk to impose hard terms on the surviving monks. They were made to surrender their deeds and muniments into the hands

[1] See *Chron. Angl.* p. 303, and Gosford's narrative in Powell, pp. 140, 141.
[2] See Gosford and Walsingham, as above.
[3] 'Quendam valentem de patria, eo quod amicus fuit ecclesiae, occiderunt, et caput eius super collistrigium suspenderunt.' Gosford, in Powell, p. 142.

of a committee of burgesses ; their jewels and plate were taken from them, to be held as a pledge for their good behaviour, and a great charter of liberties for the town was drawn up, which the sub-prior was forced to seal, pending the release of the townsmen's candidate for the post of abbot—for Edmund Brounfield still lay a prisoner in Nottingham Castle. All through these proceedings, we are told, the Bury men carefully held back from the actual slaying and plundering, which they deputed to their rural allies, and confined themselves to intimidation and bargaining ; but on the principle of *cui bono* it was easy to see that their responsibility for the outrages was no less than that of the actual murderers.

Wraw seems to have remained at Bury for the greater part of his short day of power. He sent out his lieutenants to spread the revolt, and to exact blackmail where it was to be got. Thus his two clerical friends, Godfrey Parfeye and Adam Bray of Sudbury, extorted twenty marks in gold from the mayor and corporation of Thetford, who thereby bought off a visit from Wraw himself. Sir Thomas Cornerd, one of the renegade knights who joined the rising, got ten marks out of John Rookwood of Stanfield in a similar fashion, but cheated his employer of part of his gains, by pretending that he had only obtained eight. But on at least one occasion Wraw went forth himself, to conduct a particularly lucrative tour in the north-eastern corner of Suffolk. His first exploit was the sack of Mettingham Castle near Bungay. He led thither a strong detachment of his followers, over 500 men, and got possession of £40 in cash and £20 worth of chattels [June 18[1]]. On the following day he held a sort of assize in the neighbouring town of Beccles, and presided at the execution of Geoffrey Southgate, an unpopular resident, who was delated to him by three of his neighbours. On the same afternoon he employed himself more profitably in sacking the manor of Hugh Fastolf at Bradwell, from which his followers are said to have carried off goods to the value of no less than £400. The offence of

---

[1] See Réville, p. 75, and Powell, p. 24.

the owner was that he had been one of the commissioners for the collection of the Poll-tax.

Wraw's authority seems to have extended all over western and northern Suffolk : only the district about Ipswich appears to have been dominated by bands independent of him. But in other directions his name is heard even beyond the limits of his native county. Emissaries acting under his direction stirred up riot in the county of Cambridge, and were found in Norfolk also.[1] A curious passage in the *Chronicon Angliae*[2] states that his enthusiastic followers hailed him as 'King of the Commons', but that he refused the title, saying that he already possessed one crown, that of the ecclesiastical tonsure, and would not take another. He bade the mob, if they must choose a king, elect his lieutenant, Robert Westbroun. This must all be idle talk : the whole story sounds most improbable.

To complete the picture of Suffolk during the third and fourth weeks of June, it is only necessary to give a few details about the eastern side of the county. Here the insurrection broke out two days later than in the district dominated by Wraw. It was not till June 14 that two small bands appeared in the district south of Ipswich. But on the following day the peasantry began to flock together under two local leaders, John Battisford, the parson of Bucklersham, and Thomas Sampson of Harkstead, a wealthy tenant farmer.[3] We know nothing about the grievances of these persons nor of the particular ends which they wished to attain. But on June 16 they entered Ipswich at the head of several thousand men, meeting no opposition from the burgesses. They sacked the houses of the Archdeacon of Suffolk, of John Cobat, collector of the Poll-tax, and several other wealthy residents. One murder was committed, that of a certain William Fraunces, but no more. Their bands then spread themselves over all the eastern hundreds of Suffolk as far as the sea, picking up two more leaders in the persons of two squires named

---

[1] See Réville, p. 80, and Powell, p. 49.   [2] *Chron. Angl.* p. 310.
[3] His stock and chattels were valued by the escheators at no less than £69. See Powell, pp. 143, 144.

James Bedingfield and Richard Talmache of Bentley. Their main work was the burning of manor rolls, and the plundering of the houses of justices of the peace, escheators, tax-collectors, and other officials. The victim who was most sought for was a certain Edmund Lakenheath, a justice and the owner of four or five manors. He was chased to the coast, and escaped in a boat, only, however, to fall into the hands of a French privateer, who held him to ransom for 500 marks, a sum which the unfortunate Lakenheath, whose landed property had all been devastated, had the greatest difficulty in collecting.[1]

On the whole, however, the rebels of eastern Suffolk were not so violent in their proceedings as were their neighbours in the west. But if they committed fewer murders, and were not so given to wholesale arson, they were no whit behind the western men in theft. The indictment rolls are full of cases of blackmail, extortion of money by threats, and carrying off of cattle and horses. One act of a local leader, the squire James Bedingfield, deserves special note, as showing a desire to organize the forces of rebellion which we find nowhere else in East Anglia. He went to William Rous, chief constable of the hundred of Hoxne, and forced him to levy ten archers from the hundred, who were to be kept permanently under arms. ' The said William gave him the archers, being under fear of death, and each of them was to receive 6d. a day, by the order of the said James.' [2]

When we cast our eyes north of the Waveney and the Brandon, and examine the history of the rising in the county of Norfolk, we find that we have to deal with a separate piece of history which has comparatively little to do with the tale of the Suffolk rising. Though Wraw's name is once or twice mentioned in the Norfolk documents, we have for the most part to deal with an entirely different set of leaders. It is quite clear, however, that the impulse to rise came from Suffolk; the first troubles broke out in villages on the southern border of the county, and only began on June 14, two days after Wraw had raised his standard at Liston, and one day

[1] See Réville, p. 83, and Powell, pp. 22, 130.   [2] Powell, pp. 130, 131.

after he had made his triumphal entry into Bury. On that morning we find a case of blackmailing at Watton near Thetford, which belonged to the Knights of St. John, who seem everywhere to have paid dearly for the unpopularity of the chief, Sir Robert Hales, the treasurer.[1] A certain Thomas Smyth extorted from the local representative of the order a quittance for the debts which he owed, and also went off with a promise of twenty marks. He had threatened to call in the Suffolk rebels unless he was satisfied. On the same day John Gentilhomme and Richard Filmond of Buxton were moving the countryside further to the east, ' riding from village to village, raising the hue and cry, and calling out the commons to rise against the crown and the laws of England '.[2]

It seems to have taken no more than thirty-six hours to set western Norfolk in a flame; evidently the news of what was going on in Essex and Suffolk spread round the county in a moment. On the 16th outrages are reported from half a dozen different districts, reaching as far as East Dereham and Wymondham; on the following day, Monday, June 17, anarchy had set in throughout the region between Norwich and the Wash, and bands, many hundreds strong, were passing from village to village working their wicked will on every one who was rich, defenceless, or unpopular.

The peculiar characteristics of the rebellion in western Norfolk were, that it was sporadic, non-political, and apparently destitute of all rational object. There was no single leader in command, to draw together the forces of the movement, as Tyler had done in Kent or Wraw in Suffolk. We find a score of bands, each cleaving close to its own district, and each led by two or three chiefs of the most approved insignificance. They seem, for the most part, to have guided their followers into acts of mere brigandage : it is curious to find that the manorial grievances, so prominent in other counties, are hardly heard of in this neighbourhood.[3] Records

---

[1] Réville, p. 84.   [2] Réville, document on p. 115.
[3] For this curious fact see the notes on Réville, pp. 94, 95. He says there was only *one* exception, having missed the case of Methwold, for which see Powell, pp. 27, 28.

exist of felonies committed in no less than 153 villages, but in only *two* cases are they connected with attacks on the landlord *qua* landlord.   These two exceptions took place at John of Gaunt's manor of Methwold (near Brandon) on June 16, and at the Abbot of Bury's manor of Southry (near Downham) on June 17.   In each case we are told that the local mob sought out and destroyed the court-rolls during the course of their pillage.   But it is worth while noting that both the duke and the rulers of the monastery were personally unpopular beyond the majority of landowners. It would seem that western Norfolk must have been exceptionally free from the usual sources of rural friction, apparently dues and fines and corvées must have been commuted ere now in most villages.

The amount of mischief done by the rebels in a countryside where neither political nor manorial grievances took a prominent place among the causes of trouble, is therefore all the more astonishing.   From the bulky rolls of indictments which compose the epitaph of the rising we draw a picture of half a county given over for ten days to mere objectless pillage.   Looking through the individual cases, we see that only in a small minority of them were the persons injured either squires, knights, or landlords of any sort.   In many instances we find that the rebels had been carrying off the oxen and sheep of a farmer, or the meagre chattels of a parish priest, or the stock-in-trade of a village tradesman.   In still more they were merely in search of hard cash, and did not disdain the most modest contributions—by dreadful threats of injury to limb or life wretched sums of a few shillings[1] were wrung from men who can have been hardly richer than their plunderers.   It was only on rare occasions that the money carried off by the rebels attained a respectable figure.   Evi-

---

[1] See the cases cited in Réville, pp. 89-91, e. g., John Lothale of Wymondham extorts 13s. 4d. from Richard Palmer, by threatening 'to break both his arms and his legs'.   John Carlton constrains Richard, vicar of Mattishall, to pay him 6s. 8d.   Robert Tuwe and others of Southry wish to blackmail Robert Gravel; when he demurs they place his head upon the block, and under the axe the poor man discloses his little hoard of eight marks, which (along with twenty-eight cattle) the band carries off in triumph.

dently we are dealing with an outburst of village ruffianism, not with a definite social or political propaganda. The King's law had ceased to run for the moment, and things had relapsed into the state ' when they may take who have the power, and they may keep who can '. The rebels in western Norfolk did not pretend to be levying subscriptions to maintain the common cause, or to be fining persons who had offended against public opinion. They merely took money where they could steal it, and divided it among themselves.

The only spot where we find anything more than mere brigandage is the town of Lynn, Bishop's Lynn as it was called in those days, when it depended on the see of Norwich, and had not yet become King's Lynn by passing into royal demesne. Here we read that the cry against ' traitors ', so well known in Kent, was raised, and several persons were arrested and imprisoned, but were released in consequence of the intercession of divers burgesses of repute, who were anxious to restrain the mob of artisans and shipmen.[1] Only two men perished at the hands of the rioters of Lynn : one was a Fleming whose nationality seems to have been his whole crime ; of the other we know not even the name.

A few miles north of Lynn there was an exciting man-hunt on June 17–18. The two most unpopular individuals of this north-western corner of Norfolk were John Holkham, a justice, and Edmund Gurney, the steward of the estates of John of Gaunt within the county. The hue and cry was raised against them by a certain Walter Tyler, a namesake of the Kentish captain, and they were chased for twenty-four hours, till, tracked down to the coast, they procured a small boat at Holme-by-the-Sea and launched out into the deep. This being reported to their pursuers, a dozen of them seized a larger boat and put out to run them down. The chase lasted for twenty miles, and was just about to terminate in the capture of the exhausted fugitives when night came down and hid them from their enemies. So, ' though they had completely despaired of saving their life or members ',[2]

---

[1] ' Magno prece bonorum hominum evaserunt illaesi.' See Réville, p. 96.

[2] See Document in Powell, pp. 135–6.

Holkham and Gurney slipped away, landed at Burnham, and escaped.

Turning from western to eastern Norfolk, we find ourselves confronted with a very different picture. Here, as in Suffolk and Kent, the rebellion had found a leader, and was worked from a single centre and with a definite purpose. The protagonist in the local drama was a certain Geoffrey Litster, a man who emerged from obscurity much after the fashion of Tyler; just like the Kentishman we find him suddenly exalted to command by his fellows at the outset of the rising, without being able to guess at the reason of his promotion. He was a dyer of Felmingham (near North Walsham), and not a rich man in his own class, for his stock-in-trade was valued at no more than 33s. after his death.[1] Yet he clearly possessed the capacity to compel obedience, and for the short week of his rule enjoyed an undisputed authority in the whole eastern half of Norfolk, from Holt and Cromer down to Yarmouth and Diss. He seems to have been a busy, enterprising man, with a programme of his own, which ran to something more than Wraw's gospel of pillage. We seem to trace in his actions an attempt to conform to the propaganda that had been set forth in Kent and London. He was the enemy both of the 'traitors' who conducted the King's government, of the oppressive landlords who enforced manorial customs, of the foreign merchants and artisans who were hated as trade rivals, and of the burgess-oligarchs of the great towns. Against every one of these classes we shall find him taking very stringent and drastic measures of repression. His right-hand man and chief executive officer was that unscrupulous and unquiet knight Sir Roger Bacon of Baconsthorpe. How it came to pass that the dyer commanded and the gentleman obeyed we cannot guess, but all the evidence shows that Bacon, in spite of his superior status, was no more than the lieutenant of Litster.

On June 17 the whole of the bands of East-Central Norfolk concentrated on Mousehold Heath, the regular mustering-place of the county from the earliest times down to the last

---

[1] Escheator's Inquisition Norfolk and Suffolk, 5–6 Ric. II, m. 12.

great East Anglian rising of Kett in 1549. Litster was already their chosen chief : how and why they had elected him to the post we are not told. But it was part of his plan to exhibit at the head of his bands men of higher social status than himself : Sir Roger Bacon was already at his side, of his own free will; but the dyer sought for a still more dignified colleague. He sent a party to seek for William Ufford, the Earl of Suffolk, who was known to be residing at one of his Norfolk manors. But on their approach the Earl fled, leaving his dinner half eaten on the table, and, disguised in the cloak of a varlet, rode off across country 'per deserta, per loca ultra citraque posita ',[1] till he finally reached St. Albans and comparative safety. In default of him Litster's followers collected five knights and brought them to their chief. These were Sir William Morley, uncle of the young Lord Morley, Sir John Brewes, Sir Stephen Hales, Sir Roger Scales, and Sir Robert Salle. The first four found favour in Litster's sight : they were evidently scared into obsequious obedience, and he made them members of his staff, if we may use the term. Sir Robert Salle, an old soldier of fortune, who had risen from the ranks in the wars of Edward III, was of less malleable stuff. He withstood the rebel leader to the face, and used such plain language about him and his followers that the mob rushed in upon him, threw him down, and beheaded him there and then, before the chapel of the Magdalen on Mousehold Heath.[2]

The great city of Norwich was but a mile or so distant from

---

[1] *Chron. Angl.* p. 305.

[2] Sir Robert, though born the son of a mason, had won great fame in the wars, and had been knighted by the sword of Edward III himself. He was, says the Chronicle in *Hist. Rev.* (p. 522), 'grand larron et combatour ', and had amassed a considerable fortune abroad. In his house at Norwich were £200 worth of valuable chattels. Froissart says that he was constable of Norwich, and rode out to endeavour to appease the rebels, who offered him the command of their host, and on his refusal fell upon him. He adds that the knight got his sword out and slew twelve men before he was knocked down and killed. All this must be incorrect ; he does not seem to have held the post of constable, and *Chron. Angl.* and the *Hist. Rev.* Chronicle both say that he was captured, that he spoke his mind too freely, and was then beheaded, not slain in affray. 'Non diu permansit vivus inter eos, qui dissimulare nescivit, ut ceteri, sed coepit eorum facta condemnare publice . . . sic expiravit miles qui

the mustering-place of the rebels, and it was with the object of taking possession of the county capital that they had assembled. It seemed at first as if they might meet with resistance. The citizens shut their gates, and raised their drawbridges : if they had possessed a vigorous leader they might perhaps have held their own : but the Earl of Suffolk, who ought to have put himself at the head of the forces of order, had fled away, and Sir Robert Salle was dead. The Mayor and aldermen dreaded the insurgents : they had probably heard already of what had happened four days before in London, when Tyler entered the city. But their resolve to resist the insurgents was sapped by the sinister temper displayed by the lower class, who were evidently desirous of admitting Litster and his crew. After some hours of painful indecision, the municipal authorities sent out a deputation to confer with the rebels, and finally agreed to open their gates and pay down a large fine, on condition that the ' true commons' should pledge themselves to abstain from slaughter, pillage, and arson. Litster accepted the terms, took the money, and entered Norwich in triumph ; his forces marched in with Sir Roger Bacon riding at their head in armour ' with pennons flying and in warlike array '.

Then followed the scenes of riot that might have been expected : instead of keeping their agreement Litster and his men at once betook themselves to plunder, and were eagerly aided by the rabble of the city. Their first act was to arrest, maltreat, and finally behead Reginald Eccles, a justice of the peace, one of a class which everywhere bore the brunt of the wrath of the multitude. They then sacked the houses of all whom they chose to consider traitors, the dead Sir Robert Salle, the Archdeacon of Norwich, Henry Lomynour late member of Parliament for the city, and many others. There was, however, no general massacre, nor were the mass of the burgesses assaulted or plundered : so far the rebel chief seems to have kept up a sort of discipline.

Litster then established himself in the castle, and ban-

mille ex iis solus terruisset, si contigisset ei aperto Marte puguasse contra eos.'
Chron. Angl. p. 305.

queted there in state, the four knights who were his captives
being compelled to serve as the great officers of his table :
Sir Stephen Hales carved for him, and the others acted as
butler, chamberlain, and so forth.   Struck with joy at the
magnificent spectacle the insurgents saluted their leader as
' King of the Commons ', a title in which (as we are told) he
gloried during the short week that he had yet to live.

King Geoffrey, however, was no mere spectacular monarch.
Next morning his forces were moving in all directions : one
party was sent to the priory of Carrow, to seize its deeds and
court-rolls, which were brought into Norwich and burnt before
Litster's face.   A more important detachment, under Sir
Roger Bacon, set out for Yarmouth and reached it that same
evening [June 18].   The men of this great port were odious to
their neighbours precisely because of the excellent charters
which they possessed.   Their most cherished privilege was a
market monopoly, which provided that no one for seven miles
around should buy or sell save in Yarmouth market.   This
was most inconvenient to villagers who would have preferred
to go to Lowestoft, Beccles, and other local centres.   Another
grant, which gave the borough control of the roadstead of
Kirkley and its harbour dues, was equally hateful to the
seafaring folk of Lowestoft, who wished to have their share
in its conveniences.[1]   Many Suffolk men therefore came to
join in Bacon's assault on Yarmouth.   The burgesses, as
terror-stricken as their fellows at Norwich, made no resistance, and allowed the rebels to enter the town with banners
flying.   Bacon immediately demanded the town charter,
and tore it into two halves : one he kept for Litster and
Norfolk, the other he sent to John Wraw, as the representative of Suffolk.   He then broke open the gaol, and setting
free one of the four prisoners whom he found there, an
Englishman from Coventry, beheaded the three others,
apparently because they had the misfortune to be Flemings.[2]

This was not all : after maltreating and threatening many

[1] See Rolls of Parliament, iii. 94–5.
[2] Or rather Dutchmen, their names being John of Roosendaal, Copyn de
Sele of ' Cerice ' (i. e. Zierickzee), and Copyn Isang.

of the burgesses, the intruding horde sacked a considerable number of houses, including those of Hugh Fastolf, a collector of the Poll-tax, and William Ellis, member for Yarmouth in the Parliament of 1377. They also found and tried three more unfortunate Flemings, 'quorum nomina ignorantur'[1]; all three were beheaded. Moreover, they established new custom-house officers of their own at Kirkley Road, to levy the harbour dues which had hitherto been the perquisite of the men of Yarmouth.

It is curious to find that while on one side of the mouth of the Yare Flemings were being murdered merely because they were foreigners, on the other a stranger of the same race was acting as a prominent chief among the insurgents. For at Lowestoft, only ten miles from Yarmouth, a Hollander named Richard Resch is recorded to have placed himself at the head of the mob, and to have killed with his own hand a certain John Race.[2] There is no parallel instance of a foreigner among the rebels to be found throughout the whole length and breadth of the counties affected by the rebellion.

On June 19, 20, and 21, we find Litster's host, the 'Great Company' as it was called (*magna societas*), busy at various points between Norwich and the sea. The 'King of the Commons' himself visited many villages, superintended the burning of an infinite number of deeds and court-rolls, dispossessed many persons from lands and tenements to which others laid claim, and presided at several trials both of 'traitors' and of persons accused of ordinary felonies. One or two of these unfortunates were put to death. It would seem that Litster tried to keep up a certain amount of discipline among his followers; at least ordinary theft, as opposed to charter-burning or the destruction of the houses of traitors, was far less common in Eastern than in Western Norfolk.[2] Rich abbeys like St. Bennet-at-Holme, Binham, Bromholm, where mere robbers would have found much attractive plunder, suffered nothing save the destruction of their court-rolls and documents. There are comparatively few indictments, after the suppression of the rebellion, for theft and

[1] See Réville, p. 111.   [2] See Powell, p. 24, and Réville, p. 108.

robbery. The worst offender indeed in this respect, seems to have been no peasant but Sir Roger Bacon, who used the authority delegated to him by Litster to enrich himself by blackmailing, and even by forcing his neighbours to transfer their manors to him for a nominal price.[1]

When he had got all eastern Norfolk in his hand, Litster took a step which shows that he was not thinking merely of his royalty of the moment, but wished to establish a *modus vivendi* for the future. No doubt he had already heard the news that Tyler was dead, and that the King was collecting an army at London. At any rate, about June 20 or 21 he resolved to send an embassy to the capital, to request the grant of a charter of manumission for all Norfolk, such as had been given at Mile End to the men of Essex and Hertfordshire, as also of a general pardon to himself and his followers for all their irregularities committed during the last week. He selected as his ambassadors two of the knights whom he was holding as hostages, Sir William Morley and Sir John Brewes, and joined with them three of his trusted lieutenants who bore the uneuphonious names of Trunch, Skeet, and Kybytt : all of them are found as 'capitanei malefactorum' in the narratives of the doings at Norwich and Yarmouth. They were to seek from the King 'a charter more special than all the charters granted to other counties ',[2] and in order to propitiate the royal clemency bore with them a considerable sum of money, the whole of the large fine which had been levied on the city of Norwich on June 17. Evidently then the captain of the 'Great Company' had established a public treasury, and had not allowed his followers to seize and divide all that they had extorted.

[1] We have already alluded to the case of Bacon's dealings with William Clere on p. 103.

[2] 'Cumque iam fatigari communes coepissent, et multi dies pertransissent, consilium inierunt ut mitterent duos milites, cum tribus in quibus confidebant, ad regem, Lundonias vel ubicunque possent eum invenire, pro carta manumissionis et remissionis obtinenda. Quae ut specialior esset caeteris cartis, aliis comitatibus concessis, magnam summam pecuniae quam coeperant a civibus Norwichensibus, praefatis nunciis tradiderunt, ut videlicet pacem et libertatem (quam non meruerant) pecunia impetrarent.' *See Chron. Angliae,* p. 300.

The ambassadors started from Norwich or its neighbourhood; Litster was touring round the hundreds of northeastern Norfolk when he sent them forth. For some unknown reason they took not the direct road to London, via Ipswich and Colchester, but a more circuitous road by Cambridge: but they had got no further than Icklingham near Newmarket when they encountered an adversary who made a prompt end of their mission. This was Henry Despenser, the warlike Bishop of Norwich, who now [June 22] becomes the most prominent figure in the history of the Rebellion in the Eastern Counties. But before dealing with his achievements, we must trace out the course of the insurrection in Cambridgeshire—the last of the three East Anglian counties with which we are now concerned.

CHAPTER VIII

THE REBELLION IN CAMBRIDGESHIRE AND HUNTINGDONSHIRE

IN the fourteenth century the shire of Cambridge was sharply divided into the Fen and the Upland. The northern half of the shire was a great stretch of marsh, hardly peopled save for the settlements that had grown up around the great abbey of Ely and the smaller foundation of Thorney. The southern half was a thickly settled region, full of agricultural villages, and similar in general character to West Suffolk, its nearest neighbour. The smaller county of Huntingdon, enclosed in the concave front which Cambridgeshire shows on its inner side, was divided in an exactly similar fashion to its greater neighbour. Its north-eastern third was a fen running into the marshes of Ely and Whittlesey, in whose midst lay the great abbey of Ramsey ; the rest was a well-peopled agricultural region.[1] The chief towns of the two shires, Cambridge and Huntingdon, were flourishing little boroughs, the one with some 3,500 the other with about 2,000 inhabitants. They differed only in the fact that the latter was purely a market town, while the former had, growing in its midst, the University, a corporation for which it had exactly the same lively detestation that Oxford felt for its gownsmen. The privileges which royal favour had secured to the two Universities were in each case a grave cause of offence to the municipality, and in every time of national disturbance the strife between town and gown was prone to break out. The University was hated by the burgesses of Oxford and Cambridge almost as much as the abbot was hated by those of Bury or St. Albans.

---

[1] The total population of the shire of Cambridge was in 1377 27,000, that of Hunts. 14,000. In each case the Fen was hardly inhabited and the population was concentrated in the Upland.

Oxford was not included in the boundaries of the area of the revolt of 1381, but Cambridge lay within them, with results disastrous to the gownsmen for the moment, but to the townsmen in the long run.

The rebellion in Cambridgeshire broke out only on June 14, the day preceding Tyler's death. Before that moment we can hardly trace any sign of the approach of the trouble : an isolated act of violence on June 9 at Cottenham may have had no connexion with the great rising.[1] But an assault on a manor belonging to the knights of St. John on June 14 was certainly the first token of the coming storm. For the Hospitallers in all parts of England were a favourite prey of the rebels, owing to the unpopularity of their prior, the unfortunate Robert Hales. Moreover, the locality of this first outbreak was the village of Chippenham, on the very edge of Cambridgeshire, and in close touch with Wraw's sphere of activity about Bury and Mildenhall in Suffolk.

On the next day, Saturday, June 15, the date of the great scene at Smithfield, rebellion flared up simultaneously in at least a dozen separate points in Cambridgeshire. We are fortunately so well provided with local documents, that we can trace two distinct origins for the revolt. The first was the arrival of emissaries from London, full of the news of Tyler's early successes. The second was the trespassing of a detachment from Wraw's Suffolk bands over the borders of Cambridgeshire.

That the news from the capital travelled down into the Fenland with all possible celerity is shown from the fact that two incendiaries from London, who had been present on June 13 at Tyler's triumphal entry into the city, and at the subsequent riot and arson, were already active in Cambridgeshire thirty-six hours later, on the morning of the fifteenth. These were John Stanford, who was a saddler in London, but owned property at his native place of Barrington near Cambridge, and John Greyston of Bottisham, who had chanced to be staying in the capital when the rebels entered

---

[1] See Powell, p. 43, and Réville, indictment-documents in the Appendix, p. 241.

it, and had hurried home as soon as he was sure of their victory.[1]

On June 15, Greyston was riding about the villages in the neighbourhood of his own domicile, declaring that the King had given him a warrant to raise an armed force and to destroy ' traitors ' ; he summoned the peasants to join him under pain of death, and had the effrontery to display to the unlettered mob an old Chancery document, which he happened to possess, as being the royal mandate addressed to him. In a similar vein John Stanford went about Abington and other places, declaring that he had the King's sign-manual in a box, which he exhibited, and that it authorized him to arrest and punish traitors. It is a sufficient commentary on the character of these two worthies to state that, though they destroyed no traitors, they started operations, the one by blackmailing the wealthier inhabitants of his own village, and the other by stealing a horse, value two marks, from a local farmer.

Meanwhile, other firebrands of revolt had entered the county from its eastern side. John Wraw had now been acting as dictator in West Suffolk for some three days, and was sending his emissaries abroad to spread the insurrection on every side. His chief agents on this side were Robert Tavell, who had taken a prominent part in the Bury riots, and a chaplain named John Michel, an Ely man, who had gone off to join the Suffolk rioters a few days before, and returned furnished with Wraw's mandate to raise the people in the Fens.[2]

But though Stanford and Greyston, Tavell and Michel, each became the centre of a small focus of disorder on June 15, they were by no means the chief leaders of the Cambridgeshire insurrection. The place of honour must be claimed for two wealthy local landowners, John Hanchach of Shudy Camps, and Geoffrey Cobbe, of Gazeley, who put themselves at the head of the rising for reasons to us unknown. Their conduct is as great an enigma as that of Sir Roger Bacon or Sir Thomas Cornerd in East Anglia. Hanchach owned pro-

[1] See Powell, pp. 42-3, and Réville, p. c.   [2] See Powell, pp. 42-4.

perty in five townships ; [1] Cobbe's yearly income is assessed at £22, a sum which must have placed him high among the landed gentry of the shire. Were they men with a grievance, or merely turbulent fellows who could not resist the opportunity of leading a mob to riot and pillage ? Whether they acted from principle or interest they conducted matters with a reckless violence which can only be paralleled from the most mob-ridden corners of Norfolk.

A glance at the details of the havoc committed by the Cambridgeshire bands shows that the programme in this county was exactly the same as that which was carried out in East Anglia. We find the usual outbreak against manorial dues : emissaries rode up and down the county proclaiming that the King had freed all serfs and that no one for the future owed suit or service to his lord.[2] In a score of villages there were bonfires of charters and documents belonging to unpopular landowners. Some of these burnings were accompanied by the sack or destruction of the manor house, some were not. The classes of people against whom the main anger of the rebels was directed were, as in East Anglia, justices of the peace, commissioners of the Poll-tax, royal officials in general, and clerical landlords such as the Abbots and Priors of Ely, Ramsey, Thorney, and Barnwell, the Prioress of Icklington and the Knights Hospitallers at Duxford and Chippenham. We naturally find the sheriff of the county, Henry English of Ditton Valence, among the sufferers, as also the justices Roger Harleston and Edmund Walsingham, and the Poll-tax collectors Thomas Torell and John Blanchpayne. A special animosity was displayed against Thomas Haselden, the steward of the household of the Duke of Lancaster. We do not know whether it was because of his own sins, or merely because of his master's unpopularity in the realm, that the two chief rebels of the shire, Hanchach and Cobbe, united their forces for the thorough devastation of his manors of Steeple Morden and

---

[1] He owned lands in Linton, Babraham, Abington Parva, Hadenham, and Cambridge town. See Powell, p. 44.

[2] See the case of Adam Clymme in Réville, p. c, and in Powell, p. 49.

Gilden Morden.   Haselden himself was absent in Scotland in the train of John of Gaunt, or he would assuredly have come to an evil end.[1]

The only person of note who actually met his death in the Cambridgeshire riots was the wealthy justice Edmund Walsingham, who was seized by local rioters at Ely, whither he had fled from his manor of Eversden, and there decapitated after a mock trial.   His head was placed on the town pillory [June 17].   A lawyer of the name of Galon seems also to have been put to death in the same place, where, says Capgrave, 'their entent was to kille all the men that lerned ony lawe'.[2]   Murder, however, seems to have been the exception in the shire, though every other form of violence abounded.

A special interest attaches to the doings of the burghers of Cambridge town during the four short days when the insurrection was at its height.   To them the rebellion of 1381 was mainly an opportunity for revenging themselves on their two enemies, the University and the suburban monastery of Barnwell.   It was at dusk on Saturday, June 15, that the town rose; the people were already aware that tumults had broken out in all the rural villages around, and John Hanchach with some of his followers from Shudy Camps had already come into the town to proffer his assistance. The signal for insurrection was given by the tolling of the bells of Great St. Mary's church, and a mob assembled in front of the Guildhall and elected two brothers, James and Thomas of Grantchester, as their chiefs.   After a short debate they resolved to start operations by an attack on the gownsmen, and, with the two Grantchesters and Hanchach at their head, went in a body to visit William Wigmore, the bedel of the University.   He had already fled, but his goods were plundered and the town-crier proclaimed that 'any one who met him might slay him at sight'.

It may be asked why the mob visited their first wrath on the bedel, and not on the Chancellor, the official head of the University.   The explanation is simple; the Chancellor was

[1] See Powell, p. 44.   [2] Capgrave, *Chron. Angl.* p. 237.

no less a person than that John de Cavendish, the Chief Justice of England, who on the previous day [June 14] had been murdered by the Suffolk rebels at Lakenheath. This was unknown to the Cambridge townsfolk, who went to his house, 'threatened him with fire and sword', and finding him not on the premises had to content themselves with wrecking his furniture.[1]

Then, at something past ten o'clock at night, the rioters moved on to Corpus Christi College, a corporation specially obnoxious to them because it owned much house-property in the town : it is said that a sixth of the borough paid rent to it.[2] Hearing of the coming storm, the masters and students fled, and the mob was able to sack the College without resistance. They gutted the buildings from cellar to roof, stole £80 worth of plate, burnt the charter-box, and finally carried off doors and glass windows, and any other parts of the fittings which they could detach and turn to account. The adjacent hospital of Corpus Christi was also wrecked.

This plunder seems to have ended this lively Saturday night : but on Sunday morning the townsfolk resumed their plan of operations against the University. They began by entering St. Mary's church during mass-time, and seizing the great chests in which the University archives, as also its common-plate and 'jewels', were kept. Next they moved on to the house of the Carmelites (now represented by Queens' College), broke into the chapel, and there carried off other chests and boxes, containing the books which formed the University Library ; its value was afterwards estimated at the modest sum of £20.

Having got possession of this property, the townsmen proceeded to burn it all in the Market Square. A certain old woman named Margery Starre is recorded to have flung parchment after parchment into the flames, to the cry of 'Away with the learning of clerks! Away with it!' Hence comes the fact that the early history of Cambridge University

---

[1] See Fuller's *History of the University of Cambridge*, pp. 115-16.

[2] This came from many deceased townsfolk having left houses in 'candle rents' to the College, i. e. for the sustentation of lights and the saying of masses for their souls. See Fuller, ibid.

is very difficult to substantiate. The archives, from which it might have been written, perished, along with the Library, in the smoke of this unholy bonfire.[1]

The evidence of the royal charters and the private gifts on which the wealth of the University rested being thus annihilated, the townsfolk thought that the way was clear for the drawing up of a new *modus vivendi* between town and gown. They prepared a document by which the University was made to surrender all the privileges which it enjoyed under royal donations, and to engage that its members should for the future plead in the borough courts only. For further security the gownsmen were compelled to bind themselves in a bond of £3,000 not to bring any actions against the town, for damages suffered during the last two days. Some sort of congregation of terrified Masters of Arts was got together and forced to assent to and seal this unsatisfactory compact [June 16].[2]

The University having thus been humbled, the men of Cambridge turned to deal with their other local enemy, the Prior of Barnwell. With him they had an old-standing quarrel, concerning the right of free pasturage over certain meadows called Estenhall. The earlier riots had been led by Hanchach, the two Grantchesters, and other unofficial persons; but for the attack on Barnwell, the townsfolk resolved to put themselves under the conduct of their Mayor, Edmund Redmeadow (or Lister), who had hitherto stayed in the background. He was evidently a feeble and cautious personage, who wished to keep out of trouble, but on being beset by an angry mob who (according to his own statement) threatened to behead him unless he went forth as their captain, he consented to lead the crusade against the Prior. They marched out over 1,000 strong by Barnwell Causeway, and fell upon the priory, pulling down walls and felling trees to the value of £400, draining the fish-ponds, and carrying off the store of turfs for the winter. The enclosures round the Estenhall meadows were, of course, obliterated to the last stake. To buy off personal violence and the destruction of

---

[1] See Powell, p. 52, and Fuller, p. 116.   [2] See Fuller, p. 116.

his chapel and other buildings, the Prior was compelled to sign a document binding himself in the sum of £2,000 not to prosecute the town or any individual townsman for the damage that had been done to the monastery.[1]   There is no need to speak of other disorders in Cambridge town—the sack of the tenement of Blanchpayne, the collector of Poll-tax, and such like details.   In these respects, the borough behaved only after the fashion of its rural neighbours.

From Cambridgeshire the tumults, as we have already shown, spread into the neighbouring shire of Huntingdon. Here, however, the rebellion was not nearly so acute : the town of Huntingdon held aloof from the movement, closed its gates against rioters, and even repelled by force the attempt of an armed band to enter—an instance of loyalty to the powers of order almost unparalleled during the whole of the rebellion in Eastern England.[2]   In the rural districts there was a moderate amount of disturbance—the tenants of the Abbot of Ramsey, for example, refused to pay him their dues—but nothing that could be compared to the troubles of Cambridgeshire.   An attempt of a small raiding band from Ely to plunder the Abbey itself met (as we shall see) with no success [June 18].[3]

But a little further to the north the rebellion flamed out much more fiercely in the estates of the wealthy Abbey of Peterborough, in the corner of Northampton that runs up to meet the shire-boundaries of Cambridge and Huntingdon in the heart of the fenland.   Here the peasantry found the Abbot a hard master, and were resolved to free themselves from their manorial grievances, while the townsfolk apparently were not disinclined to join them in an assault on the Abbey of the ' Golden Borough '.   There was a general rising on Monday, June 17, a date which shows that the trouble was the result of the successful outburst of Cambridgeshire during the two preceding days.   How it was nipped in the bud we must next proceed to show.

---

[1] Réville, Appendix, document no. 128.
[2] See the Charter granted them by the King on Dec. 12 for their faithful services, in Réville, p. 250.   [3] See p. 85, *supra*.

CHAPTER IX

THE SUPPRESSION OF THE REVOLT IN THE EASTERN COUNTIES

OF all the magnates of England, Bishop Henry of Norwich was the only one who showed real presence of mind and active energy in dealing with the insurrection. While veterans of the old French Wars like Warwick and Salisbury seemed to have lost their heads, and made no resolute effort to crush the rising at its commencement, this resolute and narrow-minded churchman showed how much could be accomplished by mere daring and single-hearted perseverance. Despenser was the grandson of the well-known favourite of Edward II, and the brother of a famous soldier of fortune, who had served Pope Urban V in Italy, and had used his favour with the pontiff to get his kinsmen put in the way of clerical promotion. It is said that Henry himself had seen service abroad in his brother's band, and felt the helmet sit more naturally on his head them the mitre. This much is certain, that when the nobles of England were tried by the test of sudden insurrection he showed himself the best fighting-man in the whole house of peers.[1]

He was, as it chanced, absent from his diocese when the rebellion broke out, being far from its limits, in the county of Rutland, at 'Burleigh House by Stamford Town', when the crisis came. For a few days such rumours of the rising as reached him pointed to nothing more than local tumults in Kent and Essex. But presently came the news, not only that the rebels of the south were marching on London, but that his own East Anglians had begun to stir. The tale of Wraw's doings near Sudbury on June 12 must have reached him two days later, and almost at the same time he must have heard

---

[1] See his Biography in Capgrave's *De Illustribus Henricis*, pp. 170-5.

that not only Suffolk but the nearer shire of Cambridge was on the move, for the first troubles in that region commenced as early as the fifteenth of June, so that the Bishop found that, in order to return to his diocese he would have to cut his way through a countryside that was up in arms.

Despenser had been travelling with no more than the ordinary retinue of a great prelate, eight lances, as we are told, and a few archers.[1]   But he saw that it was his duty to make his way to his own centre of influence, and set forth without hesitation at the head of this small band.

He was nearing Peterborough, the first stage of his homeward journey, when he received the news that the tenants of the abbey had just risen in arms, and were about to fall upon the monks, demanding the usual grant of charters and abolition of serfdom.[2]   The Bishop halted a few hours to gather in some recruits from the local gentry and the friends of the monastery, and then dashed into the town. He had taken the enemy by surprise, and, small as was the number of his followers, they beat the rebels out of the abbey just at the moment that they were commencing the sack. ' Some fell by lance or sword without the minster, some within, some even close to the altar.   So those who had come to destroy the church and its ministers perished by the hand of a churchman.   For the bishop's sword gave them their absolution.'[3]   Despenser tarried in Peterborough long enough to restore order ; he saw certain leaders hanged offhand, imprisoned others, and then moved on into the county of Huntingdon.

It was at Ramsey that he first met the insurgents of the Fens ; a band from Ely, headed by Robert Tavell, a lieutenant of Wraw, had entered the place, and was blackmailing the monastery.   Despenser fell upon them, and took them all prisoners [June 18].   Handing them over to the Abbot of Ramsey[4], the energetic Bishop pushed on next day

---

[1] *Hist. Angl.* p. 306.
[2] Knighton's Continuator, ii. p. 140.   [3] Ibid. p. 141.
[4] The Abbot had to account to the Escheators of Cambridgeshire for seventeen horses, nineteen saddles, and certain weapons belonging to Tavell's band (see Powell, p. 46).

to Cambridge, which (as we have seen) was a great local
centre of disorder.   Here, according to his eulogist Capgrave,
he ' slew some of that wicked mob, imprisoned others, and
the rest he sent to their homes, after taking from them
an oath that they would never again take part in such
assemblies '.[1]   We know from the Rolls of Parliament that
he made an example of John Hanchach, the wealthy local
landowner who had both led the attack on the estates of
John of Gaunt's steward[2], and also participated in the
assault on the University.   He was beheaded in Cambridge
market-place, and apparently others suffered with him.   But
the majority of the rebel leaders of the shire were more
fortunate : Geoffrey Cobbe, the other squire who had taken
a leading part in the troubles, Stanford, who had first come
down from London and stirred up the insurrection, Redmeadow, the Mayor of Cambridge, who had (willingly or
unwillingly) conducted the attack on the Priory of Barnwell,
all escaped with prison or reprimand.

As to Cambridge town, the Government, when the pacification of the land was complete, saw that the Mayor had been
but the tool of his townsfolk.   He was merely removed from
office as ' notoriously insufficient '[3], and suffered no further
penalty.   It was the borough itself that was chastised, and
the chastisement took the form that was most certain to
humble its pride.   Not merely were the old privileges of
the University restored, but many new ones were granted, to
the detriment of the town's autonomy.   For the future the
gownsmen could not only claim to plead in their own
Chancellor's court, but they were entrusted with the charge
of many functions that would naturally have fallen to the
municipality.   They secured the oversight of all victuals in
the market, the right to license all lodgings, the privilege of
punishing forestallers and regraters, the control of ' focalia ',
i.e. all firestuffs, turf, timber, and coal, and (most offensive
of all to the townsfolk) the management of Stourbridge Fair,
the great temporary mart in which the most important com-

[1] See Capgrave, *De Illustribus Henricis*, p. 172.
[2] See *supra*, p. 124.   [3] See Réville, Appendix, document no. 126.

mercial transactions of the fenland counties were conducted. The riots of June 15–16, 1381, in short, were as fatal to their instigators in the one University town, as those of St. Scholastica's day, 1354, had been in the other. Oxford and Cambridge were now on a level in respect of the abnormal immunities and privileges granted to the gownsmen in dealing with the town—rights that in many cases were destined to last down to our own day.

It may be worth noting that Cambridge wellnigh suffered the fate of Bury St. Edmunds in being put out of the law of the land for a space. But, like Canterbury and St. Albans, it was ultimately pardoned, and not enrolled as an 'excepted borough' by the Parliament that sat in the ensuing autumn.

Having, as it would seem, made Cambridge his head quarters on June 19 and June 20, the Bishop moved on via Newmarket into his own diocese. It was probably on the morning of the 22nd that he met, at Temple-Bridge, near Icklingham, on the Suffolk border, the troop of ambassadors whom Litster had sent forth on their mission to London. They ran straight into his band of men-at-arms, and were arrested. Despenser, seeing the knights Morley and Brewes, began to question them as to their purpose. They explained the situation to him, whereupon the Bishop, with small delay, had their colleagues, Skeet, Trunch, and Kybett, beheaded by the wayside. He sent their heads to be fixed on the pillory at Newmarket,[1] and pressed forward on his way into Norfolk.

The moment that his approach was noised abroad, the oppressed loyalists of Western Suffolk and Norfolk came flocking in to his banner. 'All the knights and men of gentle blood who had hid themselves for fear of the commons, when they saw their bishop in helm and cuirass, girt with his two-edged sword, joined themselves to his company.'[2] It was accordingly at the head of a considerable force that on June 24 he presented himself at the gates of Norwich. The main body of the rebels, and Litster their chief, had left the city, and the burghers gladly received Despenser. He 'saw and bewailed the destruction of houses and places that had been made by

---

[1] *Chron. Angl.* 306.   [2] Ibid. 307.

the furious people ', and as a token of his pity gave back to
the city the sum of money which he had seized in charge of
Litster's ambassadors at Temple-Bridge ; it had been originally (as will be remembered) a forced contribution extorted
from Norwich by the rebels.[1]   The corporation returned it to
him as a free gift, begging him to use it as a fund for the pay
of his troops.

Why the ' King of the Commons ' had evacuated Norwich
we cannot tell : perhaps he had feared to offer battle there
because of the notorious ill-will of the citizens, who might
have betrayed him to the enemy.   He had fallen back on
North Walsham, and had sent urgent messages to all his
partisans [2], to bid them mobilize at that place and 'strive to
tame the malice of the bishop'.   It would seem that the
muster was less numerous than Litster had hoped, for the
news from London had now had ten days to circulate, and
every one knew that Tyler was dead and that the Kentishmen
had dispersed.   Moreover, the easy success which Despenser
had won at Cambridge and Peterborough must have caused
the rebels to doubt their own strength.

Nevertheless, the ' King of the Commons ' had gathered
a numerous following, and had done his best to give them
a chance of victory.   He had fortified a position at North
Walsham with a ditch and palisades, and had covered his
flanks and rear with wagons chained wheel to wheel, and piles
of furniture—not merely (as the chronicler suggests) in
order to prevent his lines from being turned, but also in order
to keep his bands from slinking off to the rear when the
fighting began.   When the Bishop arrived in front of the
enemy, he took a rapid survey of the defences, and came to
the conclusion that they could be carried by a resolute
charge.   Hardly allowing time for the archers to open the
fight, he delivered a direct frontal attack with his cavalry.

[1] See *supra*, p. 116.

[2] Among the indictments of the Norfolk Juries is one against a certain John
Gyldyng who had been carrying Litster's message to Causton, Corpusty, and
Dalling on June 25, ' dicendo diversis hominibus quod bonum esset, et
proficuum communibus, arrestare episcopum, et illum obstupare de malicia sua '.
See Réville, p. 138.

He himself was the first to leap the ditch and burst through the palisades, his knights followed, and all together came hurtling in upon the rebels.[1]   Litster's men stood for a short time, but presently broke and strove to flee.   Many escaped, but their own rear defences hindered their retreat, and some were slain and more captured.   Among the prisoners was Litster himself, whom the Bishop promptly adjudged to be hanged, and afterwards beheaded and quartered.   Then with a sudden relapse into a clerical point of view, he remarked that the man must not be denied the last offices of religion. He confessed and absolved the rebel himself, and walked beside him to the gallows as he was drawn along on his hurdle, sustaining his head lest it might be dashed against the stones of the road.[2]

Thus died Geoffrey Litster, the least unworthy of the leaders of the insurrection of 1381 ; he was not such a ruffian as Tyler or Wraw, and had evidently both a turn for organization, a plan of operations, and a steadfast courage.   With his fall the Norfolk rising came to a sudden end : in no corner of the county did the rebels again offer battle to the Bishop.   Where-ever Despenser came he conquered : he had nothing to do but to hunt down the surviving chiefs and deal with them as he pleased.   Some were hung offhand : the majority, however, were consigned to Norwich gaol, and remanded till the normal processes of law could be resumed.   By the first week of July the juries of the hundreds were drawing up the regular lists of indictments, and the time of martial law was over.   We learn from the surviving documents of this month that most of Litster's lieutenants had been captured. Some were duly tried and hanged, but many were spared ; among those who got off with their lives were Sir Roger Bacon, Thomas Gissing, and several others who deserved the gallows as much as any of those who perished.   In Norfolk, as in the home counties and London, the rolls of 1382 and

---

[1] I follow the detailed account in *Chron. Angl.* 307-8, rather than that of Capgrave, as the latter lived further from the date of the rebellion, and gives many false details—e. g. that the Bishop had started from *London* instead of Burleigh—a very odd blunder.

[2] *Chron. Angl.* 308.

1383 are full of records of pardons ; that of Bacon is said to have been granted in response to the solicitation of the young Queen Anne, whom Richard II had wedded in the winter that followed the rebellion.[1]

In Suffolk the repression of the insurgents was even more prompt and easy than in Norfolk. The Earl of the shire, William Ufford, arrived at Bury on June 23 with 500 lances detached from the royal army at London. Before this formidable force, the rebel bands melted away, without making the least show of resistance. Their leader, the greedy and unscrupulous Wraw, showed himself an arrant coward. Instead of offering battle to the forces of order, as Litster had done, he fled and hid himself. When captured he wished to turn King's evidence, and drew up a long indictment against all his lieutenants, seeking to implicate them in the responsibility for each of his own actions.[2] It is satisfactory to know that he did not thus obtain his pardon ; the Bury murders had to be punished, and Wraw went to the gallows. Thomas Sampson, the leader of the Ipswich rebels, was more fortunate ; though condemned to death, he was kept eighteen months in prison and finally pardoned on January 14, 1383. So also was Robert Westbroun, the rival of Litster for the title of ' King of the Commons '.

It is possible to collect a list of twenty-eight rebels who were formally tried and executed in Norfolk, and of sixteen who suffered in a similar way in Suffolk.[3] This does not include the names of those who, like Skeet, Trunch, and Kybett, suffered under the Bishop's martial law in the first days of repression. The indictment-rolls too are incomplete, so that it is probable that a good many unrecorded cases should be added to those of which we have knowledge. If we take into consideration also the number of those who fell in battle at North Walsham, we are driven to conclude that East Anglia was more hardly hit by the reaction than any

---

[1] See Powell, p. 39.

[2] It will be found at length in pp. 175-82 of Réville's Appendices. This detestable priest did his best to get all his followers hanged.

[3] See Réville, p. 157.

other of the districts which had taken part in the rebellion, with the exception of Essex.

Few of the trials present any points of importance ; the interminable delations to which Wraw gave vent, while he was trying to save his neck, are only useful as showing in detail the way in which his lieutenants had harried the countryside in their day of power.   More interesting were the cases of John Wright, and of George Dunsby, a Lincolnshire man who had carried incendiary messages from the ' Great Company ' all over Norfolk.   Both these leaders gloried in their doings,[1] and went to death maintaining that they had served the commons faithfully.   It is unfortunate that the details of their defences have not been preserved ; they might have given us useful hints as to the way in which the rebellion was regarded by its more conscientious and manly supporters, the men who had not joined the rising for mere plunder, but in order to win their freedom, or to serve some even more ideal end.

The only trial in East Anglia which presented points of constitutional importance was that of the burgesses of Bury. Their town, as we already have had occasion to note, was the only one in all England which was excluded from the general amnesty which was proclaimed at midwinter.   ' The King ', as the Rolls of Parliament tell us, ' excludes the burgesses of Bury from his grace, because of their outrageous and horrible misdeeds, long continued, and will not have them share in the general pardon, nor take part in it.'[2]   It was not till the following year that they were finally allowed to buy the reversal of their outlawry by a payment of 2,000 marks. Half of this was raised at once, but the second moiety proved hard to levy, all the more because 500 marks of it was assigned to the abbey as compensation for the atrocities that had been committed within it by the rebels.   The men of Bury put off as long as they could the payment of this debt due to the hated corporation.   It was not till January 1386, nearly five years after the rebellion, that the last fractions of this

---

[1] See Dunsby's trial in Powell, p. 127.
[2] Rolls of Parliament, iii. 118 a.

heavy fine were paid off. Meanwhile the burgesses had been compelled in 1384 to go bail for themselves, in the enormous sum of £10,000, that they would never again engage in sedition. On the slightest movement reported to the King, the bail money, representing more than the total value of the town, was to be escheated to the crown. Seven hundred and twenty-two persons were inserted by name as responsible each for their share in this guarantee. This number probably represents the total number of householders in the place, as the sum of adults there resident had been reported in 1377 at 2,445 persons.[1] This device seems to have been effectual in restraining the energies of the turbulent town, which made no further attempt to resume its old quarrel with the abbey for many a long year.[2] Considering the massacres of June 15 it cannot be said that the fine of 2,000 marks was an unduly heavy punishment, from the point of view of a Government set upon restoring law and order. The provocation received by the town, during many generations of autocratic government by the abbots, could hardly have been taken into account by the ministry, who had only to deal with the actual facts of the revolt.

[1] See Tables in Appendix II.
[2] For a detailed account of the case of the burgesses of Bury see Réville, pp. 165-71.

CHAPTER X

Troubles in the Outlying Counties of the North and West

No county west of Cambridge, Hertfordshire, and Essex can be said to have formed part of the main area of insurrection in June 1381. Nevertheless, sporadic disturbances broke out in regions so far from the main *foci* of rebellion as Yorkshire and Somersetshire. They deserve a few words of notice, if only as illustrating the extraordinary divergency of the causes which led various English communities into the paths of treason. If none of these isolated outbreaks in the North and West grew to any serious height, it was largely because the wave of revolt, travelling slowly from the south-east onward, reached the outlying counties so late that the reaction was already in progress at London before the outbreak began at York or Scarborough or Bridgewater. The Government hastily dispatched the intelligence of Tyler's death to every corner of the realm, and bade the local magnates arm. Just at the psychological moment when the North or West might have flared up into general insurrection, came the chilling news that the main force of the rebels had been dispersed and their leader slain. The signs of approaching trouble at once died down, and no rising took place, save in a very few places, where special circumstances had precipitated a local outburst.

Going west from London we have noted that in all Hampshire only Winchester seems to have been disturbed, and that here a municipal quarrel between the town oligarchy and the lower classes was the cause of trouble. In Wiltshire the escheators write [1] that having been directed to render an account for the goods of any rebels in the county, they have to report that no such persons were to be found there. The only trace

[1] See Réville, Appendix, document 200.

of trouble in this region is a complaint that lead, stone, and tiles have been stolen from the royal castle of Mere ; if anything very serious had occurred we should assuredly know of it. Oddly enough there had been serious riots in Salisbury town nine months before, in September 1380, evidently arising from a strife between the local oligarchy and the commons. We have only the vaguest hint that the troubles may have broken out again in 1381.[1] In Somersetshire there was a curious local outbreak on June 19–20, about Bridgewater, headed by a priest named Nicholas Frompton and a yeoman named Thomas Engilby. It seems to have been the result of an old quarrel about an advowson. Frompton claimed a vicarage belonging to the Knights of St. John, to which he said that he had been legally presented. He was in London at the time of the murder of Sudbury and Hales, and, having seen the manner in which the Hospitallers were treated in the capital, thought that he could take his own private revenge on them. Hurrying back to Bridgewater, he raised a mob, whose captain was Engilby, and entering the house of the Knights forced the master to transfer to him the living which he claimed. Other men of Bridgewater seized and tore up bonds representing debts which they owed to the Hospitallers : they even forced the master to sign an acknowledgement binding him to pay the town £200. After this Engilby led his band out into the neighbouring villages of East Chilton and Sydenham, killed two men named Baron and Lavenham, and burnt the manor-rolls of Sir James Audley and John Cole. He also sacked several houses in the town, and broke open its gaol.

On June 21 the tumult subsided as fast as it had risen, probably on the receipt of news from London of the complete dispersion of the Kentish rebels. Engilby fled, leaving his forty-shilling freehold a prey to the escheators. Yet we are astonished to find that, though he was condemned to death in default upon July 16, he received a free pardon so early as March 18, 1382. Of Frompton's fate we know nothing.[2]

[1] See Réville, documents, pp. 280-1.
[2] See Réville, Appendix, document 203.

We hear nothing of troubles in the rest of Somersetshire, so that the Bridgewater rising would appear to have been a perfectly isolated affair. Nor are any special misdoings reported from Dorset, Devon, or Cornwall, though a writ of February 1382 complains that 'homicides, highway robbery, burglary, and riotous gatherings have been more common than usual in these shires ',[1] and charges the justices of the peace to see to their repression. But this represents not insurrection, but the ordinary increase of crimes against property in a period when the King's law had not been running smoothly.

In Berkshire, Buckinghamshire, and Oxfordshire there is a similar lack of evidence of any political or agrarian disturbance. Even the town of Oxford failed to take advantage of the general anarchy for an assault on the University, such as had been common in earlier decades of the century. One manor in Buckinghamshire[2] was raided by Hertfordshire rioters from across the county border, but no more. A few individuals from each of these three counties seem to have straggled up to London to take part in the riots in the capital, and so fell into the hands of the Mayor and his court-martial during the day of retaliation. One of them, an Oxfordshire man from Barford St. John, tried to save his neck by inventing a preposterous tale that two of his fellows had received a bribe of £100 from John de Vienne, the admiral of France, to stir up rebellion in England as a diversion for a projected French invasion of the south coast.[3] He met the credit that he deserved.

Bedford, Northampton, and Leicester, were decidedly more affected by the revolt than their south-midland neighbours. Not only are Bedfordshire men noted among the prisoners arrested in London, but a considerable number of townsfolk of Luton are found on the escheators' rolls as 'fugitivi pro insurrectione '.[4] Yet there was no general rising in the shire. So was it also in Northamptonshire; we hear of

---

[1] See Réville, document on p. 285.   [2] Langley Marish.

[3] It is clear that this was all wild invention, and it is curious that M. Petit-Dutaillis seems inclined to treat it seriously—see his preface to Réville, p. 58, where he severely blames the intrigues of the French admiral.

[4] See Réville, document on p. 276.

leagues of tenants refusing to pay manorial dues, and of a
vain attempt of a demagogue, named William Napton, to stir
up the lower orders of the county town against their Mayor.
But at Peterborough only was actual insurrection and violence found, and there it reigned for no more than one single
day. We have a vivid picture in the chronicle of the Continuator of Knighton, showing how the town of Leicester
was affected on Monday and Tuesday, June 17–18, by a false
rumour that the main army of rebels from London was
marching upon their town, because its castle was a
stronghold of the hated John of Gaunt. More courageous
than most of his fellows, the Mayor of Leicester called out the
full levy of his burgesses, some 1,200 strong, and prepared
to defend his charge. For two days they stood in order of
battle on Galtre hill, outside the gates, expecting an enemy
who never appeared, ' quia iidem profani essent Londoniis '.[1]
The greatest anxiety prevailed in the town, and the
guardian of the Duke of Lancaster's chattels in the castle
packed them all up in carts, and brought them to the abbey
for shelter and sanctuary. But the abbot refused to take
them in, saying that it would ruin him and his monks if such
wares were found under his roof when the rebels arrived.
They had ultimately to be stacked in the church of St. Mary
by the Castle. While the Duke's goods were thus bandied to
and fro, his wife was undergoing a very similar experience.
The Duchess Constance, who had apparently been lying at
one of her husband's midland castles when the rebellion broke
out, had fled North to his great fortress of Pontefract. The
castellan was disloyal and cowardly enough to refuse her
entrance, lest her presence should draw the insurgents in his
direction. It was only after long nocturnal wanderings that
she found refuge in Knaresborough.[2]

Meanwhile, all this panic had little or no solid foundation ;
no riots broke out in rural Leicestershire, the worst that
happened being that the tenants of two manors belonging
to the Knights of St. John (here, as always, prominent objects

---

[1] See Knighton's Continuator, pp. 142-3. [2] Ibid. p. 144.

of public dislike) were egged on by a local priest to refuse their dues, and to burn the tithe-corn which had been collected in the Knights' barns.[1]

The same phenomena were seen in the larger shire of Lincoln.   There was enough discontent in the county to induce the Government to bid the Earl of Nottingham and the other great landowners to arm and prepare to march if troubles should begin.   But they never had occasion to move, the sole overt act being a strike against manorial dues on the part of the villeins of Dunsby and other estates belonging to the Hospitallers.   It may be remembered that a Dunsby man, a messenger from his village to the East Anglian insurgents, was one of those who was executed at Bury by the Earl of Suffolk.[2]   No open rebellion or armed gathering seems to have occurred in the whole of the wide expanse of the Lincolnshire Fen and Wold.

The whole of the West Midlands, from Gloucestershire to Derby and Nottingham, seem to have been practically undisturbed by the insurrection.   If there were any signs of local disturbance they were no more than those which were common in all counties of mediaeval England, even during years of complete political apathy.   Village ruffianism was a normal feature of the life of the fourteenth century.   An obscure disturbance in the Cheshire peninsula of Wirral, between Dee and Mersey, merits notice only because of its isolation.

North of the Humber, however, there were three isolated outbreaks, all in large towns, which deserve some investigation. Two of them are clear instances of attacks on the local burgess oligarchy by the local democracy ; the third witnesses to a state of something not far from endemic civil war in the greatest city of Northern England.

Scarborough was a busy little port of about 2,500 souls, much given to privateering against the Scots and not averse to occasional piracy.   It was evidently divided by bitter feuds, for on June 23, after the receipt of the news of the

---

[1] The promoter of mischief was William Swepston, parson of Askettleby, and the manors were the neighbouring villages of Rothley and Wartnaby, near Loughborough.   Réville, Appendix, p. 252.

[2] See *supra*, p. 136.

capture of London by Wat Tyler,[1] certain townsmen, to the number of at least 500 men, assembled under the leadership of Robert Galoun,[2] William Marche, a draper, and Robert Hunter, and proceeded to make a systematic attack on 'all against whom they had old quarrels, or wished to pick new ones'. They had adopted a common uniform of a white hood with a red tail,[3] and had sworn a great oath to maintain each other in all their doings. They began by seizing on Robert Acklom, bailiff of the town, and consigning him to prison, and then declared that he and all other municipal officers were deposed from office. Having thus cleared the ground and given themselves a free hand, they went round blackmailing and maltreating all the richer burgesses. Some of them were besieged in their own houses for many hours, others taken out and lodged in the town gaol along with the bailiff. From one three pounds was extorted, from another ten marks, from a third as much as twenty, but this was only after the poor man, a certain William Manby, had been led to the gallows and threatened with instant death unless he gave up his little store. In every case the sole object of the rioters seems to have been the settling of old scores and the gathering in of money.

It was natural, therefore, that, on the restoration of order, after the news of the collapse of the insurrection in the south, the Government should punish the Scarborough men in the same fashion of fines. The town had to pay 400 marks, and forty-two excepted persons, leaders and prominent offenders during the riot, had to buy pardons for themselves by contributions over and above this general penalty. Robert Galoun, Hunter, and the others escaped the death penalty, which they richly deserved, but did not obtain their pardons

---

[1] 'Percipientes et scientes levaciones et congregationes in partibus australibus perpetratas, per rebelles et inimicos domini regis', says the indictment. Réville, Appendix, document 152.

[2] Robert Galoun must have been a man of wealth, as the King disallowed and confiscated a pious foundation which he had started. See Réville, p. ciii.

[3] The dress was 'unica secta capuciorum alborum cum liripipis rubeis'. The liripipe was the long 'weeper' or tail, often wound round the neck. See ibid. document 153.

till May 1, 1386. It is probable that they had spent a good deal of the intervening time as prisoners in Scarborough Castle, before being released on bail.[1]

The case of Beverley was rather worse than that of Scarborough. The long and tedious documents which set forth the progress of the troubles in this little town of 4,000 souls, the commercial centre of the East Riding, show that there had been for many years a venomous quarrel between the local oligarchs, the ' probiores et magis sufficientes burgenses ' and the commonalty. The magnates were accused of having levied taxes unfairly, of selling public property for their private profit, of using municipal justice as a means to crush their enemies with heavy fines.[2] In especial we are informed that they had taken advantage of the secret murder of a certain William Haldane by fathering it upon the leaders of their political opponents, who were in no way guilty, and getting them cast into the King's prison. The beginning of these accusations runs back as far as 1368, far into the reign of Edward III. If half what is related by John Erghom, the leading spirit among these strangely-named ' probiores viri ', is true, he must have been a sort of Critias in little.

It must not be supposed, however, that the ' viri mediocres ', who formed the party of opposition in Beverley, were passive victims of the oligarchs. Long before the great rebellion began they had bound themselves in a league to resist their oppressors. On May 7, three weeks before the first outbreak in Essex, a mob had broken into the Guildhall of the town, stolen and divided £20 in hard cash, and made off with the town seal and a quantity of its charters.

This outrage had been condoned, and the leaders had received the King's pardon, apparently because of the pro-

---

[1] Réville, Appendix, p. 256, last lines.

[2] Great play is made in the indictment of the fact that the oligarchs had raised for the building of a certain barge for the town more money than the vessel really cost. Also they had illegally levied rates called *bustsilver* and *pundale* from a number of small artisans &c. whose names are annexed at length. But the great accusation is that whereas John Wellynges had really murdered William Haldane, Erghom and his friends maintained and abetted him, and accused of the crime John Whyte and others of their enemies. See Réville, document no. 161, pp. 263-7.

vocation that they had received, when in the end of June
the news of Tyler's doings reached Beverley. The 'mediocres
viri' saw their opportunity, and rose in force, adopting like
their fellows at Scarborough a common uniform of white
hoods. Headed by one Thomas Preston, a skinner, and by
two tilers named John and Thomas Whyte, they beset all
their adversaries, and forced them 'by rough threats, by the
imprisoning of their bodies, and by other irrational and un-
heard of methods, to acknowledge themselves debtors, and
to sign bonds for large sums'. Apparently these were the
sums which the oligarchs were supposed to have been illegally
exacting from the town during the last ten or fifteen years.
Both parties appealed to the King when order was restored,
and each set forth the misdeeds of the other. After mature
consideration, Richard and his council resolved to side with
the 'probiores viri', as was perhaps natural under the circumstances. They were pardoned for their illegal doings on
paying a small fine,[1] but the community of Beverley was
saddled with a contribution of no less than 1,100 marks, by
a royal ordinance issued in the year following the revolt.[2]

At Scarborough and Beverley the revolt took the definite
form of a rising of the smaller citizens against the greater.
But at York the tumults of the summer of 1381 were a much
more confused and unintelligible business. Long before the
troubles began in the south, there had apparently been civil
strife raging in this city between two parties headed respectively by John Gisburn, the late Mayor, and Simon Quixley,
the present occupier of the municipal chair. As early as
January twenty persons had been arrested and sent to prison
for breaking the King's peace.[3] In May the council wrote
from London to direct the Archbishop and the Earl of Northumberland to intervene and terminate the quarrel between
Gisburn and his party and the 'communitas' of York, i.e.
the faction at present in power.[4]

The mediation of these magnates was clearly of no effect,

---

[1] Erghom, the chief criminal, paid a sum of ten marks in the hanaper on
receiving pardon. See Réville, p. 266.   [2] Réville, Appendix, document 172.
[3] Ibid. document no. 174.   [4] Ibid. document no. 176.

if ever it was put into use.   For the next group of documents show that on July 1 there was a great riot at the gate called Bootham Bar.   We have documents emanating from each side.   On the one hand, the jurors of the city of York, acting under the inspiration of Mayor Quixley, lay an indictment to the effect that Gisburn and certain of his partisans had come to the gates on horseback armed with iron bars and other weapons, had assaulted a party of citizens who strove to keep them out, and had then ridden round the streets distributing a badge, and binding all their friends with a great oath to maintain them in their quarrel.   The jurors add that Gisburn was an issuer of false money [1] and a notorious patron of robbers, and that two of his chief followers had committed murders some years back, one in 1372, and the other in 1373.

On the other hand, we have an indictment evidently drawn up by Gisburn's friends, stating that Quixley and his allies, the bailiffs of York, have seized and imprisoned five innocent persons, and, by threatening them with death, have induced them to sign bonds for large sums of money, claimed as due to certain friends of the Mayor, and also to promise not to pursue the magistrates in the royal courts for their illegal violence. [2]

The King cites both parties to appear before the Chancellor to answer for their misdeeds, and with a fine impartiality terminates the proceedings by fining the whole city of York 1,000 marks, after which he pardons all the citizens alike, except a certain few excepted by Parliament from the amnesty. The names of these persons show that they were mainly of Gisburn's party.   As has been truly observed ' mediaeval justice was mainly finance, though mediaeval finance was not always justice '.

Thus ended this squalid and obscure municipal quarrel, which had obviously no relation to the general causes of the rebellion of 1381.   It merely broke out with violence at this

---

[1] Perhaps he had farmed the royal mint of York, and was accused of issuing light money.

[2] Réville, Appendix, document no. 179.

[3] Ibid. document no. 180.

moment because all parties, hearing heard the news of tumult
in the south, had concluded that the King's law no longer
ran, and that it was an admirable time to settle old grudges
by armed force. In short, the case was the same as at
Scarborough and Beverley, and indeed the same as at Bury,
Cambridge, or St. Albans. During the 'Anarchy' of 1381
every man and every faction strove to win what could be
won by the strong hand.

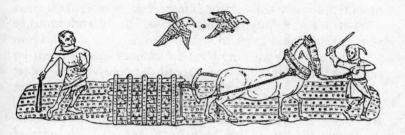

CHAPTER XI

HAVING dealt in detail with all the events of the summer
of 1381, in every shire from Somerset to Norfolk, and from
York to Kent, it only remains that we should endeavour to
sum up their general result.

All through the autumn the Government was harassed by
rumours that the rebellion was about to break out once more.
The fact that the insurgents had never tried their armed force
against that of the crown, save at the two small combats of
Billericay and North Walsham, had evidently made them
doubt whether they had been fairly beaten. We hear of
half a dozen cases of bands reassembling in East Anglia and
in Kent, and of leaders who tried to rekindle the embers of
sedition during August and September. None of these
attempts achieved any success; the great mass of the people
had tasted the results of anarchy, and were not anxious to
set it once more on foot. The desperate men who strove to
renew the insurrection met with little support. Only one of
these plots has any interest, and that merely because of the
curious revulsion in political feeling to which it bears evidence. At the first outbreak of the revolt in June, John of
Gaunt had been (with the possible exception of Archbishop
Sudbury) the most unpopular person in the realm. It was
the King who was to right all wrongs and terminate all
grievances. But after Richard's revocation of the Mile End
charters, and his drastic declaration to the rebels that 'villeins
they were and villeins they should remain', public opinion
swerved round. We find that a number of obscure persons
who were plotting to raise a new insurrection about Maidstone in September and October, proposed that the King
should be dethroned, and the Duke of Lancaster placed in his

seat. This, we are told, was merely because they had heard that John had been very liberal in granting exemption from servile dues to his tenants in the northern counties.[1] But the plot was betrayed at once to the sheriff, Sir William Septvans, its framers were arrested, and the movement (which must have been purely local) was suppressed before it had got into the stage of practical action.[2]

The autumn was occupied in the steady but not too merciless punishment of the rebel leaders. There were few hangings or beheadings when once the first flush of panic was over, and the Government was already beginning to turn clemency into a means of filling the exchequer, by allowing rebels of the minor sort to buy their pardons by payments into the Chancellor's hanaper. All serious danger was over when on November 3 the Parliament was summoned to sit at Westminster. It met on November 13, and sat for a month; then, after having been prorogued for the Christmas holidays, it reassembled and transacted business from January 27 to February 25, 1382.

The chief duty of the two Houses during this session was to take into consideration the state of affairs which the rebellion had created. As was natural, after the terrors which its various members had gone through during the summer, it showed itself very reactionary in its policy. One of its first acts was to pass an act of indemnity for all those who, like Mayor Walworth and Bishop Despenser, had put rebels to death without due form of law during the first days of repression.

The chief minister who faced the Parliament in the King's name was William Courtenay, who was Bishop of London when he took over the Great Seal and became Chancellor on August 10, but had received the Archbishopric of Canterbury on September 9. The new Treasurer, in place of the mur-

---

[1] This they had learnt, said Cote the informer against them, from pilgrims who came out of the North Country. See *Arch. Cant.* iv. p. 85.

[2] The original informer was one Borderfield, who told all to the sheriff before the band was ready for action. They had met on Sept. 30 at Broughton Heath, and were had up for trial on Oct. 8. Six or seven, including their leader, a mason named Hardyng, were hanged. See ibid. pp. 67–86.

dered Sir Robert Hales, was Sir Hugh Segrave. Courtenay, best known as a bitter enemy of John of Gaunt, and of the Lollards, opened the proceedings with a long English sermon, setting forth, no doubt, the evils of rebellion. But it was Segrave who took the main part in laying the problem of the day before the House of Commons. The King, as he said, had issued, under constraint of the mob at Mile End, many charters enfranchising villeins and abolishing manorial dues. Such charters were null and void, because the sovereign had no power to publish, without the consent of Parliament, any such decrees, which granted away the rights of many of his loyal subjects, before the consent of their representatives in Parliament had been obtained. Knowing this he had revoked all the charters by his proclamation of July 2. But he was informed that certain lords were willing to enfranchise and manumit their villeins of their own free will ; if this was so the King would have no objection to sanction such emancipations.

This last clause is curious ; the ministers must have known perfectly well that the two Houses were in no mood to deal tenderly with their serfs at this moment. Did they wish to set themselves right with the peasantry, so far as was possible, by throwing the responsibility for the retention of villeinage on the Parliament ? Or was there some obscure working of conscience in the young King's mind, causing him to make a feeble representation in favour of the serfs, because he had, after all, promised them much that he had never intended to perform ? Or again—for a third alternative is possible—did Richard and his Council sincerely believe that it would be for the advantage of the realm that manorial servitude should be abolished, and so think it their duty to lay this suggestion before Parliament ?

Whatever was their object, they received an answer of the most decided sort from the two Houses. ' Prelates, lords temporal, citizens, knights and burgesses responded with one voice that the repealing of the Charters had been wisely done. And they added that such a manumission of serfs could not have been made without the consent of those who had the main interest in the matter. And, for their own parts, they would never consent of their own free will, nor otherwise, nor ever would do it, even if they all had to live and die in one day.'[1] Immediately after this declaration, Courtenay resigned the Great Seal, being too busy with the duties of his newly obtained archbishopric to combine with them those of Chancellor ; the example of Sudbury's tenure of the two offices had not been encouraging. Courtenay was replaced [November 18] by Richard, Lord Scrope, the same man who had already held that office at the time of the Parliament of Gloucester. His assumption of office was only one of several changes made at this time, all intended, as it would seem, to conciliate the opinion of Parliament. Thus an old and trusted public servant, enjoying the full confidence of the two houses, received the chief ministerial post : but almost as much importance attached to the appointment of two permanent guardians for the young king. A petition having been made that his household should be reformed, Richard made no opposition, and in due course the Earl of Arundel and Michael, lord de la Pole, were given him as tutors, taking an oath to live with him always in the palace ' pour gouverner et conseiller sa personne '. It is curious to note that these two tutors whom the Parliament gave the King were to become, one his greatest enemy, the other his best friend. Both were to end disastrously, Arundel on the scaffold for crossing Richard's purpose, de la Pole in exile for serving him too loyally.

The next step of the Commons was to demand by petition that the King should grant a general amnesty to all those who had taken part in the late troubles, save certain important leaders and notable malefactors. This was readily conceded, the new Chancellor taking the opportunity of getting the House to renew the subsidy on wool as a token of gratitude for the royal clemency. The rather lengthy list of persons excluded comprised 287 names, of which a very large proportion were London criminals.[2] The Commons had at first proposed to leave outside of the law the towns of Canterbury, Cam-

---

[1] *Rot. Parl.* iii. 100.   [2] No less than 151 of the names belong to London.

bridge, Bridgewater, Bury St. Edmunds, Beverley and Scarborough. But at the King's suggestion they left Bury alone on the list, and the other five were allowed to buy their pardon by the heavy fines of which we have already spoken.

We have seen also, when dealing with the history of the repression of the revolt, that by far the larger number of the 287 persons left unpardoned by the general amnesty were ultimately allowed to go free, after a greater or less term of imprisonment, and a notable fine, when they were able to bear it. For the next three years the King was pardoning a few rebels almost every week, and chiefs so notorious as Sir Roger Bacon, Thomas Farringdon, Aldermen Tonge, Horne and Sibley, Sampson of Ipswich, and Westbroun the ' King of the Commons ', all returned to their homes sooner or later, in a sufficiently humbled frame of mind, as is to be supposed.[1] The last outstanding matter of importance from the rebellion was the case of the burgesses of Bury, and even they (as we have already seen) were pardoned in December 1382, though they did not pay off the last instalment of their heavy fine till January 1386. By that time the rebellion was only an old and evil memory in the minds of men. Later political events were gradually causing its terrors to be forgotten.

It remains to ask what was the general result of this great convulsion. The popular theory down to the few last years was that formulated by Thorold Rogers, that though the formal victory lay with the lords, the real gains had fallen to the peasants, that, to use his words ' the War of 1381 had as its effect the practical extinction of villeinage. Though the Parliament refused emancipation with a great show of indignation, the judges, as I am convinced, at the King's own instance, began to interpret servile tenures in a sense favourable to the serfs, and to protect them against arbitrary oppression. By the fifteenth century, villeinage was only a legal fiction '.[2] In a similar strain Bishop Stubbs writes that

[1] See pp. 82, 89, 98, 135.
[2] For a lengthy setting forth of this see *Six Centuries of Work and Wages*, pp. 264–71.

' although the villeins had failed to obtain their charters and had paid a heavy penalty for their temerity in revolting, yet they had struck a vital blow at villeinage. The landlords gave up the practice of demanding base services ; they let their land to leasehold tenants, and accepted money payment in lieu of labour : they ceased to recall the emancipated labourer into serfdom, or to oppose his assertion of right in the courts of the manor and the county '.[1]

Later researches, such as those of Professors Maitland and Cunningham, Mr. Powell and André Réville, have shown that this statement of the consequences of the Great Revolt in 1381 is too sweeping, and is not founded on a sufficient number of observed facts in manorial records. It is true that serfdom is on the decline during the last year of the fourteenth century, and still more so during the first half of the fifteenth. But the immediate result of the rebellion does not seem to have been any general abandonment by the lords of their disputed rights. Indeed the years 1382 and 1383 are full of instances which seem to prove that the first consequence of the suppression of the revolt was that many landlords endeavoured to tighten the bonds of serfdom, and to reassert rights which were slipping from their grasp. Now, in the moment of wrath and repression, was the time for them to reclaim all their old privileges. A case can be quoted in Suffolk [2] where a lord claimed and obtained 28 years' arrears of base services owed to him by a recalcitrant tenant [1382]. In another instance in the same county a number of villeins who had withheld their labour dues for the lesser term of three years are declared to be wholly in the wrong, and told in words that recall King Richard's speech at Waltham, that ' Serfs they are and serfs they must remain '.[3] In this manor, Littlehawe, near Bury St. Edmunds, the villeins had obtained exemplifications from Domesday Book,

---

[1] *Constitutional History*, ii. 503.
[2] The manor of Barton Parva, one of those belonging to Bury, where in spite of all the terrors of 1381, the monks start in 1382 to revindicate rights that had almost passed into oblivion. See Powell, p. 64.
[3] Powell, pp. 64-5.

to prove that there ought to be no serfdom in the manor, perhaps by the council of two priests, who are said to have acted as their advisers. They had refused their services in 1382–3–4, tendering instead a rent of 4*d*. an acre for their holdings. They were found guilty, fined £3, and told to resume their *corvées*. Professor Maitland quotes similar instances, in which every incident of villeinage is levied with the minutest care, in the years following the revolt : in one manor (Wilburton, Cambs.) it was not till the late date 1423, that the labour-rents of the tenants ceased to be exacted.[1]

We may well believe that many landlords were taught caution by the events of June 1381, and that they conducted the rural machine with comparative moderation for the future, lest another outburst of discontent should ensue. But there can be no doubt that the old system went on ; it had received a rude shock, but had not been completely put out of gear.

The best proof of this is that for the next ten years the archives of England are full of instances of conflict between landlord and tenant precisely similar to those which had been so rife in the years immediately preceding the rebellion. We have countless cases of oaths and conventicles entered into by peasants to resist their lords, of secret outrages and of open riots against unpopular lords and bailiffs. If we had not the chronicles of Tyler's rising, we should never have gathered from the court rolls of the manors that there had been an earth-shaking convulsion in 1381. The old quarrels go on in the same old weary way. Parliament still continued to harp on its ancient theme of violations of the Statute of Labourers. So far from being cowed or converted by the recent insurrection, it continued for some years to devise new remedies for the perversity of the working-classes. The session at Cambridge in September 1388 was singularly fruitful in futile devices of the usual sort. The peasantry proved as obstinate as ever, and continued the struggle, but it cannot be proved that their resistance was a whit

[1] See his 'History of a Cambridgeshire Manor' in the *English Historical Review* for 1894.

more effective after than before 1381. It is interesting, however, to find that the terms of the Charters which they had won in Tyler's time now served as the ideals which they hoped some day to achieve The much-tried tenants of St. Albans are accused by their abbot of having made many copies of the document which they had extorted from him, ' as evidence that they should have the said liberties and franchises in time to come '.[1] The theory that the fair rent of land should be 4d. an acre, popularized at the Mile End Conference, also reappears regularly in the subsequent demands of the villeins of manors where a strike or an agricultural union was on foot. Sometimes such folks dreamed of extending their local grievances once more into a general insurrection like that of 1381. In the very next year there was a widespread plot in Norfolk raised ' by certain men inspired by the Devil, whose minds had not been chastened by the perils of others, whom the deaths and torments of their fellows had not tamed ', to slay the bishop of Norwich as a sacrifice to the *manes* of Geoffrey Litster. They had also planned to fall upon the folks congregated at St. Faith's fair, and force them all to take an oath to rise in the name of the ' true commons ', and they intended to make the marsh-girt abbey of St. Benet's-at-Holme their central fortress. But they were put down before anything had got to the stage of action.[2] A similar conspiracy, also in Norfolk, was reported two years later, when certain riotous persons proposed ' to carry out all the designs of the traitors and malefactors who feloniously rose against their allegiance in the fourth year of King Richard '. They were delated and captured before they had time to do much harm.[3] There were agrarian troubles on a large scale in Sussex in 1383, when a mob stormed Lewes Castle, and burnt all the rolls, rentals, and charters of the Earl of Arundel, its proprietor. Still greater troubles, which almost attained to the dignity of a formal insurrection, broke out in 1392-3 : they affected Cheshire and West Yorkshire, districts

[1] *Rot. Parl.* iii. 129. [2] See details in *Chron. Angl.* p. 354.
[3] See document in Réville, p. cxxxiv.

which had (save for a trifling rising in Wirral) been untouched by the revolt of Tyler's year. In short, the great rebellion which we have been investigating does not mark the end any more than it marks the beginning of the struggle between the landholder and the peasant.

It is the same in the towns: the strife between the local oligarchs and the local democracy in some places, between factions divided by less obvious lines in others, went on for many years after 1381. In London the war of the 'victualling' and 'clothing' guilds was flaring up fiercely in the period that immediately followed Tyler's triumph and fall. Riots that often became regular street-battles were in progress during the turbulent mayoralty of John of Northampton (1382–3), who was the champion of the commons, and the advocate of cheap food. There was another outbreak in 1393, so violent that the King deposed Mayor Hynde, and appointed Sir Edward Dalingridge as a military governor for the city, suspending the civil administration for many months. This affair had started with an assault on a Lombard: but attacks on Flemings, so prominent during Tyler's rising, are still more frequent in after days. All London was roused against them by 'bills' posted everywhere in 1425, and it is said that there was a plot for their general massacre in 1468.[1] Provincial towns too continued to have their riots from time to time, all through the times of Richard II and his fifteenth-century successors. Norwich was up four times between 1433 and 1444. Those who list may find turbulence enough in the annals of Lincoln, or Bristol, or Exeter. In short, all the incidents of the great rebellion can be paralleled from the century that follows. The only difference is that the troubles are once more scattered and sporadic, instead of simultaneous.

Neither villeinage and all the manorial grievances in the countryside, nor the class-war within the towns, were in any sense brought to an end by the great popular outburst that we have been investigating. The problems were settled, so far as they were ever settled, by the slow working out of

[1] See Gregory's *Chronicle*, pp. 158 and 237.

economic changes. If in 1481 we find copyholders and rent-paying yeomen where villeins had most abounded in 1381, it was due to the working of causes which had already begun to be visible long before the year of the rebellion, and which did not attain their full operative force till more than a generation after it was over. In the first chapter of this book it was shown that the letting of the lord's demesne land to farmers, small and great, was growing common even in the time of Edward III. As the lords abandoned more and more the attempt to work their home-farms by forced labour, they had less and less use for the *operationes* of their villeins. When all demesne land had been let on lease, or turned into pasturage, there was little gain to be got from enforcing the servile status of the old *nativi*. Gradually they were allowed to commute all their liabilities for money, and for the most part became copyholders. Villeinage died out from natural causes and by slow degrees : it could still be spoken of as a tiresome anachronistic survival by Fitz-herbert in 1529,[1] and Queen Elizabeth found some stray villeins on royal demesne to emancipate in 1574. But by the time of the sixth Henry it had for all intents and purposes ceased to play any great part in the rural economy of England. It had vanished away imperceptibly, because it had ceased to serve any practical purpose ; it certainly had not been destroyed, once and for all, by the armed force of rebellion in Wat Tyler's ' Hurling time '.

---

[1] ' Howe be it, in some places the boundmen continue as yet, the which, me seemeth, is the gretest inconvenience that is now suffered by the lawe, that is to have any Christen man bounden to another, and to have the rule of his body lands and goods. . . . For as me seemeth there shoulde be no man bounde but to God, and to his kynge and prince over him : . . . and it woulde be a charitable dede to manumyse all that be bond, and make them free of body and blode.' *Boke of Surveyenge*, p. 50.

APPENDIX I

THE POLL-TAX ROLLS IN THE RECORD OFFICE

THE documents relating to the Poll-tax of 1381, which are to be found in the Record, consist of (1) A complete summary of the results for all England save the Palatine counties of Durham and Chester, to be found in ' Lord Treasurer's Remembrancer's Enrolled Accounts, No. 8 ', in which are also to be found two summaries of the results of the Poll-tax of 1377 (51 Edw. III), when a groat per head was levied all round the realm on persons over fourteen years of age. (2) Of ' views of account', giving the summary of shires and towns : of these some thirty only survive. (3) Of the detailed rolls of the townships, arranged in their hundreds, and of the cities and towns. This series is most imperfect, and the surviving rolls are often mutilated, dirty, and illegible. There is nothing from the outlying shires of Cornwall, Devon, Northumberland, Westmoreland, Cumberland. No single shire is complete ; those of which the largest percentage of rolls survive are Berks., Essex, Suffolk, Surrey, and the East Riding of Yorkshire. I append a list of them, so far as they can be identified, for it is possible that some more small fragments may exist, misplaced among the rolls of the Poll-tax of 1377. When the headings and dates have been lost (as is often the case) it is easy to confuse the two sets of returns —a broken list of fourpenny contributors from the end of a mutilated scroll may belong to either. Of course in any large fragment the identity is settled by the prevailing shilling-assessment of 1381, which cannot belong to a document of 51 Edw. III.

The manner in which the returns of the townships have been prepared varies indefinitely according to the idiosyncrasies of the constables who drew them up. In some regions, e.g. Suffolk and Essex, the lists have full details of the trade and status of each contributary, and often add notes as to the relationship of individuals. In other districts there is nothing given but a bare list of names, not even the relationship of husband and wife, father and son being indicated, and the occupation of no single person being given. For example, if John Attewell, tailor, with

Margery his wife, and his children John and Isabel, had lived in Hinckford hundred in Essex, we should find them returned thus—

Scissor. Johannes Attewell et Margeria, uxor ejus,
Johannes Attewell, filius ejus,
Isabella Attewell, filia ejus ;

but if the family had lived in some parts of Berkshire, we should simply get—

Johannes Attewell, senior,
Margeria Attewell,
Johannes Attewell, junior,
Isabella Attewell.

In some regions we find *vidua* after widows' names, so can distinguish between the younger and the older women who are without husbands ; but this is rather exceptional ; the region where I found it most prevalent was Staffordshire.

I looked through many dozens of townships from Essex, Gloucestershire, Suffolk, Staffordshire, Berks., Surrey, and Bedfordshire, in order to see whether the preponderance of males over females which I have noted in Chapter II was universal. It seemed to be so, but in some districts it was decidedly more marked than in others. Essex and Suffolk are worst in their preposterous suppression of the females. In a *very* few cases did I find the preponderance of females over males which must really have been common or even normal. Pebmarsh, in Essex, and Horningsheath Parva, in Suffolk, were examples. Families, where the family relationship is indicated, seem to have been much smaller than we should have expected. The largest family-group that I found was in Surrey, where one John Fraunceys had three sons and three daughters, all unmarried and living with him. No doubt the prevailing system of early marriages led to the sons establishing themselves outside the paternal domicile at an early age. But still the numbers of homonymous families in a village are generally less than we should expect, though in some places a good many of them are to be found. I am driven to conclude that families were not usually large. Of course we have no indication of the number of children under fifteen, since they did not pay the tax. But the families belonging to men of forty or fifty must have been grown up, and settled near them—the indications are against their being very numerous.

The surviving rolls, arranged under shires, are the following :—

BEDFORD.   One long mutilated and very illegible roll, apparently containing a considerable portion of the shire.   But the amounts paid seem to suggest the Poll-tax of 1379 rather than that of 1381.   Also the 'view of account' for the shire for 1381.

BERKSHIRE.   Detailed rolls of the inhabitants of the hundreds of Faringdon, Ganfield, Lambourne, Ock, Kintbury Eagle, and Sutton.

BUCKS.   Nothing but 'view of account' for the shire.

CAMBRIDGESHIRE.   Details of Cambridge town only.

CORNWALL.   Nil.

CUMBERLAND.   Nil.

DERBYSHIRE.   Detailed roll of the hundred of High Peak, and 'view of account' for the shire.

DEVON.   Nil.

DORSET.   Imperfect roll of Dorchester town only.

ESSEX.   Detailed rolls of the hundreds of Chelmsford, Thurstable, Chafford, Beacontree, Ongar, Wytham, Waltham, and Hinckford : also of towns of Colchester and Walthamstow.

GLOUCESTER.   Fourteen scraps, containing great parts of the hundreds of Bradley, Berkeley, and Rapsgate.

HEREFORD.   Short 'view of account' for the whole shire only.

HERTFORD.   Ditto.

HUNTINGDON.   Ditto.

KENT.   A very mutilated detailed roll of Canterbury city, and short 'view of account' of the shire.

LANCASHIRE.   Detailed rolls of Blackburn Wapentake, and part of Sulford.

LINCOLNSHIRE.   Detailed rolls of Calceworth and Skinbeck Wapentakes, and short 'views of account' for Lindsey, Kesteven, Holland, and Lincoln city.

MIDDLESEX.   Nil.

NORFOLK.   Detailed rolls of the hundreds of Shropham, Freebridge, Tunstead, and Lynn town, also 'view of account' of the shire.

NORTHANTS.   Fragmentary detailed rolls of Wileybrook hundred and Northampton town, and 'view of account' of the shire.

NOTTS.   'View of account' of Nottingham town only.

NORTHUMBERLAND.   Nil.

OXFORD. Detailed rolls of Oxford town and the villages of Adderbury and Bloxham, and short ' view of account ' of the shire.

RUTLAND. ' View of account ' of the shire only.

SHROPSHIRE. Detailed rolls of the hundreds of Sottesdon and Bradford, and the town of Shrewsbury.

SOMERSET. Detailed rolls of Bath and Wells, and ' view of account ' of the shire.

SOUTHAMPTON. ' View of account ' only.

STAFFORD. Detailed roll of Cuttleston hundred only.

SUFFOLK. Detailed rolls of the hundreds of Corsford, Mutford, Blithing, Plymsgate, Thingoe, Finberg Magna, Stowlangtoft, Wirdswell, Euston, Buxhall, Flempton, Westcretyng, Stow-market, Wetherden, Stow, Thweyt, Fakenham, Barwe, and short ' view of account ' of the shire.

SURREY. Detailed rolls of the hundreds of Godalming, Chadyn-field, Haslemere, and the town of Southwark.

SUSSEX. Mutilated rolls of the Tithing of East Lavant and of Chichester town, and ' view of account ' of Chichester.

WARWICK. Mutilated roll of Tamworth, and ' view of account ' of the shire and of the town of Coventry.

WESTMORELAND. Nil.

WILTSHIRE. ' View of account ' of the city of New Sarum only.

WORCESTER. ' Views of account ' of the shire and city.

YORKSHIRE. East Riding. Detailed rolls of the Wapentakes of Ouse, Derwent, Harthill, and Buckrose, and ' view of account ' of Hull.

West Riding. Nil [though the Poll-tax of 1379 is well represented].

North Riding. ' View of account ' of Scarborough, and a mutilated fragment of the wards.

Ainsty of York, ' view of account ' only.

APPENDIX II

THE POPULATION OF ENGLAND IN 1381

THE following are the figures returned by the collectors of the
Poll-tax of 1381, as summarized in Lord Treasurer's Remembrancer's Enrolled Accounts : Tax Accounts, No. 8, in the
Record Office. Set over against them are the similar returns of
the Poll-tax of 1377—the fifty-first year of Edward III, when
a groat, not a shilling, was extracted per head. It is clear that
we must not press the returns for the outlying counties too far :
although the whole sum due was supposed to have been collected
before April 21, and although many shires professed that they
had paid up every exigible shilling, yet figures like

	Anno 1377	Anno 1381
Cornwall	34,274	12,056
Cumberland	11,841	4,748
Devon	45,635	20,656
North Riding	33,185	15,690
West Riding	48,149	23,029

do not seem to represent a complete census, ' cooked ' by the
constables and sub-collectors, but rather to be incomplete. There
are, unfortunately, no surviving detailed rolls for any of these
regions, save for a scrap of the North Riding, so that we cannot
verify what proportion of the townships had paid up when the
returns were compiled.

But the really monstrous part of the statistics was not the
returns of these outlying shires, but those of the inlying regions
of the East and South, where every village purported to have
furnished a full account of its inhabitants, as is shown by the rolls
surviving in such considerable numbers for Suffolk, Essex,
Surrey, Berks., &c. Far more noteworthy than the Northumbrian or Cornish totals are figures like

	Anno 1377	Anno 1381
Berks	22,723	15,696
Essex	47,962	30,748
Hants	33,241	22,018
Kent	56,557	43,838
Norfolk	88,797	66,719
Wilts	42,599	30,627

Here it is mere trickery and corruption that is displayed, not an imperfect return.

In comparing the detailed figures of 1377 and 1381 we find that the local authorities seem to have taken a perverse pleasure in reckoning into, or out of, the shire-total, certain small towns. In 1377, Grimsby, Southwark, Scarborough are not differentiated from the shires in which they lie. In 1381, Carlisle, Derby, Dartmouth, Hereford, Rochester, Stamford, Boston, Yarmouth. Newark, Ludlow, Lichfield, Beverley, all of which gave separate returns in 1377, are thrown back into the shire total.

The reader will note that the relative size of the great English towns runs as follows :—London, York, Bristol, Coventry, Norwich, Lincoln, Salisbury, Lynn, Boston, Newcastle-on-Tyne, Beverley.

L. T. R. Enrolled Accounts.   Tax Accounts, No. 8.

	51 Edw. III [1377]	4 Rich. II [1381]
Comitatus Bedford	20,339	14,895
Comitatus Berks............	22,723	15,696
Comitatus Bucks.	24,672	17,997
Comitatus Cantabrigiae	27,350	24,324
villa de Cantebr.'..........	1,902	1,739
Comitatus Cornubiae	34,274	12,056
Comitatus Cumbriae	11,841	4,748
civitas Karliol	678	no separate return
Comitatus Derby............	23,243	15,637
villa de Derby	1,046	no separate return
Comitatus Devon	45,635	20,656
civitas Exon...............	1,560	1,420
villa de Dertemuth	506	no separate return
Comitatus Dorset	34,241	19,507
Comitatus Essex	47,962	30,748
villa de Colchestr'	2,955	1,609
Comitatus Gloucestriae	36,730	27,857
villa Gloucestriae..........	2,239	1,446
villa de Bristoll	6,345	5,652
Comitatus Hereford	15,318	12,659
civitas Hereford	1,403	no separate return
Comitatus Hertford..........	19,975	13,296
Comitatus Hunts	14,169	11,299
Comitatus Kent	56,307	43,838
civitas Cantuar.	2,574	2,123
civitas Roffen.	570	no separate return
Comitatus Lancastriae	23,880	8,371
Comitatus Leycestriae	31,730	21,914
villa de Leycester	2,101	1,708

	51 Edw. III [1377]	4 Rich. II [1381]
Comitatus Lincoln.		
Lindesey	47,303	30,235
Kesteven	21,566	15,734
Holand	18,592	13,795
civitas Lincoln	3,412	2,196
clausum de Lincoln	157	no separate return
villa de Stamford	1,218	no separate return
villa de Boston	2,871	no separate return
villa de Grymesby	no separate return	562
Comitatus Middesex	11,243	9,937
civitas London	23,314	20,397
Comitatus Norffolk	88,797	66,719
civitas Norwyci	3,952	3,833
villa de Lenne	3,127	1,824
villa de Jernemuth	1,941	no separate return
Comitatus Northamptoniae	40,225	27,997
villa Northamp.'	1,477	1,518
Comitatus Northumbriae	14,162	return missing
villa Novi Castri super Tynam	2,647	1,819
Comitatus Nottingham	26,260	17,442
villa de Nottingham	1,447	1,266
villa de Newark	1,178	no separate return
Comitatus Oxon	24,981	20,588
villa Oxon	2,357	2,005
Comitatus Roteland	5,994	5,593
Comitatus Salopiae	23,574	13,041
villa Salopiae	2,082	1,618
villa de Lodelowe	1,172	no separate return
Comitatus Somerset	54,603	30,384
civitas Bathon	570	297
civitas Welles	901	487
Comitatus Stafford	21,465	15,993
civitas Lychfeld	1,024	no separate return
Comitatus Suffolk	58,610	44,635
villa Gippewici	1,507	963
villa Sti Edmundi	2,445	1,334
Comitatus Surrey	18,039	12,684
villa de Southwerk	no separate return	1,059
Comitatus Sussex	35,326	26,616
civitas Cicestriae	869	787
Comitatus Suthampton	33,241	22,018
Insula Vecta	4,733	3,625
villa de Suthhampton	1,152	1,051
Comitatus Warrewici	25,447	20,481
villa de Coventre	4,817	3,947
Comitatus Westmoreland	7,389	3,859

	51 Edw. III [1377]	4 Rich. II [1381]
Comitatus Wigorniae	14,542	12,043
civitas Wigorn	1,557	932
Comitatus Wyltes	42,599	30,627
civitas Novi Sarum	3,226	2,708
Comitatus Eboraci		
Estrithing................	38,238	25,184
Westrithing	48,149	23,029
Northrithing	33,185	15,690
civitas Eboraci............	7,248	4,015
villa de Beverley	2,663	no separate return
villa de Scardeburg	no separate return	1,480
villa de Kyngeston super Hull	1,557	1,124
Totals	1,355,201	896,481

The clerical population of England, arranged under dioceses, appears as follows in the Clerical Poll-tax of 1381. [L. T. R. Enrolled Accounts Subsidies, No. 4.] The figures include not only all the clergy in full orders, regular and secular, but also nuns, and persons in minor orders, acolytes, subdeacons, &c. The return of the diocese of Carlisle is missing. Unlike the lay statistics for the year, the clerical ones show a shrinkage of numbers, but no very great one, since the Poll-tax of 1377. The difference is 1,415, but the comparison cannot be made exact, as the diocese of Durham is missing in the earlier, and the diocese of Carlisle in the later, roll.

Bath and Wells.
    Archdeaconries of Bath and Wells 714
    Archdeaconry of Taunton 324
Canterbury.
    Archdeaconry of Canterbury 787
    Deanery of South Malling 27
    Deaneries of Shoreham and Croydon................. 96
    Deanery of Bocking 27
Chichester.
    Archdeaconry of Chichester and Cathedral of Chichester . 355
    Archdeaconry of Lewes 363
Coventry and Lichfield.
    Archdeaconry of Coventry 491
    Archdeaconry of Chester 308
    Archdeaconry of Salop............................. 177
    Archdeaconry of Derby 392
    Archdeaconry of Stafford 376

Durham.

  Archdeaconry of Durham 335
  Archdeaconry of Northumberland 268
Ely.   Diocese of Ely 759
Exeter.   Archdeaconry of Cornwall 450
  Archdeaconry of Exeter 283
  Archdeaconry of Totnes 419
  Archdeaconry of Barnstaple 208
Hereford.
  Archdeaconry of Hereford 454
  Archdeaconry of Salop. 226
Lincoln.
  Archdeaconries of Lincoln and Stow 2,506
  Archdeaconries of Hunts. and Beds. 1,137
  Archdeaconries of Bucks. and Oxon. 1,124
  Archdeaconries of Northampton and Leicester 1,827
  St. Albans 148
London.
  Archdeaconry of London 895
  Archdeaconry of Essex 404
  Archdeaconry of Middlesex 433
  Archdeaconry of Colchester 444
Norwich.
  Archdeaconries of Norfolk and Norwich 1,913
  Archdeaconries of Suffolk and Sudbury 1,298
Rochester.   Diocese of Rochester 275
Salisbury.
  Archdeaconries of Dorset and Sarum 1,225
  Archdeaconries of Berks. and Wilts. 839
Winchester.
  Archdeaconry of Winton........................... 950
  Archdeaconry of Surrey 337
Worcester.
  Archdeaconry of Worcester 600
  Archdeaconry of Gloucester 783
York.
  Archdeaconries of York, Richmond, East Riding, Cleve-
    land 2,389
  Archdeaconry of Nottingham 469

                                           Total   20,676

APPENDIX III

DETAILED POLL-TAX
RETURNS OF A TYPICAL HUNDRED

As a sample of a Poll-tax account of 1381, I here annex the rolls of thirteen townships of an Essex hundred—Hinckford, on the border of Suffolk. I selected this hundred on account of the elaborate definition of the status of each person, and the careful indication of relationships between individuals of the same family. Few rolls are so full and satisfactory in this respect. In this hundred, it will be noted, lay Liston, the place at which the rebel chief Wraw assembled the band with which he invaded Suffolk, and started the East Anglian rebellion.

Note the absurd disproportion of the sexes in most of the townships. Felsted shows—

	Men.	Women.
Married pairs	54	54
Other men	47	—
Other women	—	10
	—	—
Total	101	64

This must have been one of the most shamelessly 'cooked' returns in the whole realm. But Bumstead is almost as bad with—

	Men.	Women.
Married pairs	45	45
Other men	36	—
Other women	—	17
	—	—
Total	81	62

Stebbing falsifies on the same scale as Bumstead with—

	Men.	Women.
Married pairs	62	62
Other men	24	—
Other women	—	8
	—	—
	86	70

There is one village in the hundred, 'Pebymersh' (now Pebmarsh), which unlike all the rest seems to show a clear majority of women—46 to 33 as far as can be made out. The lists of the remaining few places are terribly mutilated by large holes, which make all calculation impossible. But they do not seem, as far as they can be collated, to show any preponderance of the female sex—rather the reverse.

The total of the fully legible townships works out as follows—

	Men.	Women.
Alhamston et Buris .	49	33
Bewchamp Oton....	39	37
Bumstede	81	62
Felstede	101	64
Fynchyngfelde	92	85
Gelham	16	14
Gosfeld	49	45
Hythingham Sibill ..	111	103
Ovyton............	5	2
Pebymersh....... ..	33	46
Pentelowe	30	21
Salyng Magna	16	17
Stebbing	86	70
Sturmer	61	52
Total	769	651

Or very nearly five men to four women. In Thingoe Hundred, Suffolk, which Mr. Powell worked out, the proportion was 487 to 383.

Lay Subsidy Roll, Essex, Hinckford Hundred, No. $\frac{107}{68}$ (4 Rich. II).

VILL' DE ALHAMSTON ET DE BURIS.

Liberi tenentes	ß	d
... Quilter et uxor eius .	ij	vj
Radulfus Clerk et uxor eius	iij	
Henricus Whych et uxor eius	ij	vj
Johannes Turk . . .		xij
Matilda fitz Geffrey . .		xij
Roger Pach'		xij
Matilda uxor eius . . .		xij
Willelmus Schanke et uxor eius	ij	
Maget [? Margaret] Aleyn		xij
Johannes Catere . . .		xij
Philippus Weypyld et uxor eius	ij	
Willelmus Sparwehauk .		xij
Adam Bechhey et uxor eius	ij	vj

Adam Bernard et uxor	ß	d
eius	ij	
Johannes Cobbe . . .		xij
Alicia Aunger		xij
Johannes famulus eius .		xij
Robertus Aunger et uxor eius	ij	vj
Johannes Sparlyng et uxor eius	ij	
Robertus Wegayn . . .		xij
Johannes Clerk . . .		xij
Laborarii		
Ricardus atte Broke et uxor eius	ij	
Katerina atte Staple . .		xij
Alicia Sparhauk . . .		xij
Robertus Bisschop et uxor eius	ij	

	s	d
Rogerus Southfen . . .		viij
Walterus Taylor . . .		xij
Johannes Brok et uxor eius . . .	ij	vj
Johannes Ruddok . . .		vj
Johannes Reynold . . .		xij
Nicholas Newer et uxor eius . . .	ij	
Ricardus atte Pit . . .		xij
Johannes Newyr . . .		viij
Ricardus Bust . . .		viij
Ricardus Mody . . .		iiij
Johannes Balddewene et uxor eius . . .	ij	
Thomas Mody . . .		xij
Johannes Schachelok et uxor eius . . .	ij	
Johannes Mody . . .		xij
Johannes Simeon et uxor eius . . .	ij	vj
Johannes Kyl et uxor eius . . .	ij	
Johannes White et uxor eius . . .		xviij
Margeria Payn . . .		viij
Hugo Frankeleyn . . .		vj
Aluredus Payn et uxor eius	ij	

	s	d
Thomas Scubbard et uxor eius . . .	ij	
Johannes Resshey et uxor eius . . .		iiij

Fabri

	s	d
Ricardus Donyng . . .		xviij
Alicia Mot . . .		iiij
Johannes Squepyr . . .		viij
Willelmus Dunnyng et uxor eius . . .	iij	
Walterus Wley et uxor eius . . .	ij	
Johannes Hyrde . . .		xij
Thomas Basse . . .		vj

Piscatores

	s	d
Thomas Kyl . . .		xviij
Johannes Wetherisfeld .		xij
Agnes Gode . . .		xij

Textor

	s	d
Willelmus Geddyng et uxor eius . . .	ij	vj

Summa personarum iiij ij proxima Summa iiijli ijs.

VILLA DE BEWCHAMP OTON.

Liberi tenentes

	s	d
Ricardus de Eston et uxor eius . . .	iij	
Ricardus Jernays et uxor eius . . .	iij	
Johannes Albon et uxor eius . . .	iij	
Willelmus atte Frede et uxor eius . . .	ij	vj
Robertus filius eius . .	xij	
Isabella filia eius . . .	viij	
Johannes Myldeman et uxor eius . . .	ij	
Robertus atte Fen . .	xl	
Willelmus famulus eius .	xij	
Avicia ancilla eius . . .	viij	
Matilda Ode . . .	xij	
Johannes Albon junior et uxor eius . . .	ij	
Johannes Gerold et uxor eius . . .	ij	
Alicia filia eius . . .	viij	
Simon Thresscher et uxor eius . . .	xxx	
Christina filia eius . .	vj	
Christiana * . . . . . . ylle	xij	
Johannes Thomas et uxor eius . . .	ij	

Johannes Swan . . .	xij
Isabella filia eius . . .	xij
Johannes Turnour et uxor eius . . .	xxx
Johannes May . . .	vj
Johannes Hyrde et uxor eius . . .	xxx
Thomas Hopelyr et uxor eius . . .	ij

Laborarii

Johannes Baylyfh et uxor eius . . .	xviij
Johannes Hyrde et uxor eius . . .	ij
Johannes filius eius . .	xij
Johannes Bertelot . .	xij
Sewalus Snelhauk et uxor eius . . .	ij
Rogerus Thresscher' et uxor eius . . .	ij
Johannes Adam et uxor eius . . .	ij
Johannes Adam junior .	xij
Willelmus Huberd et uxor eius . . .	ij
Isabella Webbe . . .	xij

* Hole in MS.

	s	d
Christo[pherus]*...Warde		vij
Willelmus Reve et uxor eius		ij
Willelmus Reve junior .		x
Simon Obyte et uxor eius		ij
Johannes Katelote et uxor eius		ij
Ricardus Robert . . .		iiij
Stephanus Folcher et uxor eius		xij
Alicia Ethe		xij
Hawkyn Lech et uxor eius		ij
Ricardus Catelote et uxor eius		xviij
Johannes famulus eius . .		x
Simon Thurston et uxor eius		ij
Mabilla uxor Johannis Folchyr		vj
Johannes Scoccel et uxor eius		ij

Scissores

	s	d
Thomas . . l . . . ones et uxor eius . .		ij

Proxima Summa Personarum lxxvj Proxima Summa iij li xvj s.

VILLA DE BŨMSTEDE AD TRIM.

Liberi tenentes

	s	d
Ricardus Messyng et uxor eius		iij
Robertus Rewe et uxor eius		iij
Robertus Roylyngh et uxor eius		ij
Johannes Frere et uxor eius		ij
Willelmus Belyngton . .		ij
Edmundus Bendych et uxor eius		iij
Willelmus Robcot et uxor eius		ij
Johannes Trumpe . . .		ij
Johanna Bley		xij
Thomas Hicche et uxor eius		ij
Johannes Heldeborow et uxor eius	ij	viij
Johannes Holmsted . .		xij
Willelmus Fayr et uxor eius		ij
Agnes Cote		vj
Thomas Punge		xij
Walterus Smyth et uxor eius	ij	vj
Walterus famulus eius .		vj
Johannes Cote		xij
Johannes Ballard et uxor eius		ij
Willelmus Colham . .		xij
Johannes Godard et uxor eius		xx

Laborarii

	s	d
Johannes filius Thome Hicche		xij
Isabella filia Thome Hicche		xij

	s	d
Johannes le Eyr et uxor .		ij
Robertus Chaumberleyn et uxor eius	ij	vj
Ricardus Chapman . .		xij
Willelmus Man et uxor eius		ij
Johannes Everard et uxor eius	ij	viij
Willelmus Bakhouse et uxor eius		ij
Robertus Stevene et uxor eius		ij
Margareta Herstede . .		xij
Rogerus Coo		xij
Katerina Tussy . . .		xij
Johanna Talbot . . .		xij
Johannes famulus eius .		xij
Ricardus Plowwrithe et uxor eius	ij	vj
Johannes Cook et uxor eius	ij	vj
Johannes Wyte		xij
Johannes Whichele et uxor eius		ij
Henricus Cherchehall .		xij
Johannes Tresscher . .		xij
Johannes famulus Vicarii de Bumstede		xij
Galfridus Clek		xij
Walterus Wendene . .		vj
Margareta Spycer . . .		xij
Margareta Aleyn . . .		xij
Alicia Aleyn		viij
Johannes Powney . . .		xij
Ricardus Spyrman et uxor eius		ij
Johannes Chippeman .		xij
Johannes Lowt		xij
Johannes Sturmer . . .		xij
Thomas Joie		xij

* Hole in MS.

	£	d
Willelmus Serjaunt et uxor eius		ij
Johannes Halton et uxor eius		ij
Johannes Derkyn et uxor eius		ij
Agnes Westmenster . .		xij
Amicia' Hunte . . .		vj
Johannes Webbe . . .		xij
Ricardus Webbe et uxor eius		ij
Johannes Asschindon et uxor eius		ij
Johannes Trois junior et uxor eius		ij
Johannes Yonges et uxor eius		ij
Rogerus Holdeborough et uxor eius		ij
Johannes Holdeborwgh' et uxor eius . . .		xij
Simon Godefray et uxor eius		ij
Ricardus Huthe et uxor eius		ij
Ricardus Cote		xij
Johannes Whyte et uxor eius		xij
Alicia filia eius . . .		vj
Johannes Fynch . . .		iiij
Johannes Modwe . . .		xij
Katerina uxor eius . .		xij
Thomas filius eius . . .		xij
Johannes Troys senior et uxor eius		ij
Johannes Snelhauk et uxor eius		xx
Robertus Somenor . .		viij
Thomas Martyn et uxor eius		xij

	£	d
Robertus Martyn . . .		viij
Willelmus Broon . . .		xij
Agnes Walkelyn . . .		xij
Henricus Waryn et uxor eius	ij	vj
Rogerus Molesfeld' et uxor eius	ij	vj
Katerina Dowce . . .		xij
Radulphus Coo et uxor eius		ij
Ricardus Derekyn . .		vj
Johannes Bayle . . .		vj
Margareta Cokkow . .		vj
Walterus Hende et uxor eius		ij
Thomas Asschindone . .		xij
Cristiana uxor Thome Yonge		vj
Johannes filius Johannis Hynde		viij
Gonnora uxor Roberti Somonor		vj

Scissores

	£	d
Thomas Yunge . . .		xij
Willelmus Penne . . .		xij
Willelmus Rede et uxor eius		ij
Johannes Mahew . . .		xij

Fabri

	£	d
Willelmus Leweneth et uxor eius	ij	vj
Nicholas Eyr et uxor eius	ij	

Proxima Summa personarum cxlv Summa vij li x s.[1]

VILLA DE FELSTEDE.

Frankelyn

Edmundus Helpistone .}		
Christina uxor eius . . } iij		

Liberi tenentes

Walterus Horstede .}		
Alicia uxor eius . . . } ij	*	
Johannes Stevene .}		
Matilda uxor eius . . }	*	*
Robertus Stase .}		
Matilda uxor eius . . } ij	*	
Rogerus Prat . . . .}		
Katerina uxor eius . . } ij	vj	

Stephanus Clement . . }		
Alicia uxor eius . . . } ij	vj	
Johannes Chabbac . . }		
Margereta uxor eius . . } ij		
Walterus Edwyne . . . }		
Cecilia uxor eius . . . } ij		
Nicholas Hedwene et uxor eius . . .	*	
Willelmus Blacston et uxor eius		xviij
Ricardus Herny . . .		xij
Johannes Drane senior et uxor eius		ij

* Hole in MS.
1 The total stated is 145 persons; but only 143 are named—presumably a married pair has dropped out.

	s	d
Galfridus Teffryn et uxor eius		ij
Thomas Coke et uxor eius		ij
Johannes Coke et uxor eius		ij
Johannes Sponer et uxor eius		ij
Walterus Oxenby . . .		xij
Thomas Steph'de et uxor eius		ij

Nativus tenens

	s	d
Walterus Reman et uxor eius		*

Laborarii

	s	d
Ricardus Prat . . . } Alicia uxor eius . . }		ij
Willelmus atte Mille . .		
Ricardus de Lenne et uxor eius		ij
Alicia serviens eius . .		xij
Johannes Wode et uxor eius		ij
Stephanus Serjaunt et uxor eius		ij
Thomas Herny . . .		xij
Ricardus Lymong . . .		xij
Phillipus Skeyt et uxor eius		ij
Willelmus Drane . . .		xij
Johannes Drane junior .		xij
Galfridus Drane et uxor eius		ij
Galfridus Ker et uxor eius		ij
Johannes Ker junior . .		xij
Robertus Ker et uxor eius		ij
Willelmus Schache . .		xij
Johannes Hyde . . .		xij
Johannes Swethey . . .		xij
Johannes Steph'de junior		xij
Elias Holles		xij
Walterus Oxenby et uxor eius		ij
Jacobus Lymuges et uxor eius		ij
Johannes Lymuges . .		xij
Thomas Stevene . . .		xij
Johannes Jacop . . .		viij
Ricardus Frenssch et uxor eius		ij
Ricardus Wryhte et uxor eius		ij
Rogerus Clement et uxor eius		ij
Johannes Carter . . .		xij

	s	d
Robertus Attebregge et uxor eius		ij
Johannes Attenoke . .		xij
Johannes Bret junior et uxor eius		ij
Johannes Bret senior et uxor eius		ij
Thomas Crek . . .		xij
Johannes Garlonde . .		xij
Willelmus Bygge et uxor eius		ij
Robertus Carder . . .		xij
Johannes Oxenhey . .		xij
Johannes Wode . . .		xij
Johanna serviens Stephani Serjaunt . .		vj
Robertus Harwerd . .		*
Nicholas Prat . . .		iiij
Nicholas Edwyne . . .		xij
Ricardus Edwyne . . .		xij

Carpentarii

	s	d
Johannes Bel . . . } Christina uxor eius . . }		ij
Thomas Seward . . .		xij
Margareta Seward . . .		xij
Willelmus Hedwyne et uxor eius		ij
Johannes Smyth et uxor eius		ij
Johannes Wryhte et uxor eius		ij
Stephanus Herlowe . .		xij
Johannes Herlowe et uxor eius		ij
Matilda Bollis . . .		xij
Katerina Bynso . . .		xij
Johannes Peche . . .		xij

Scissores

	s	d
Johannes Beneyt et uxor eius		xvii
Johannes Beuchamp . .		xij
Johannes Routh et uxor eius		ij
Simon Smyth et uxor eius		ij
Willelmus Chalke et uxor eius		ij
Willelmus Reman . .		xij
Henricus Reynold et uxor eius		ij
Margareta Sutor . . .		xij
Henricus Dale senior . .		xij
Henricus Dale junior . .		viij
Alicia Swetyng		xij

Fabri

	s	d
Willelmus Frensch et uxor eius		ij
Egidius Smyth		xij

* Holes in MS.

	s	d			s	d
Johannes Skynner . . .		xij	Johannes Arch			xij
Johannes Goodsoule et uxor eius		ij	Johannes Tyler			xij
Thomas Reynyr . . .		xij	Robertus Aleyn			xij
Thomas Sacoward et uxor eius		ij	Robertus Attewode . .			xij
Thomas Brounyng et uxor eius		xvj	Emma Attegoter . . .			vj
Willelmus Fuller et uxor eius		ij	Lora Brounyng			xij

Fuller

Johannes Canyl et uxor eius . . . . . . ij

Pandoxatores

		s	d
Johannes Swetyng. . .			xij
Johannes Rowth . . .			xij
Radulphus Peche senior et uxor eius		ij	

Draperes

Johannes Kent et uxor eius . . . . . . ij
Johannes Bernard . . . xij

Sutores

Johannes Wystok et uxor eius . . . . . . ij
Agnes Arnold . . . . xij

Sellarius

Alexander Steph'de senior xij

Textores

Johannes Lynlyf . . . xij
Johannes Swet . . . xij

Carnifices

Johannes Bocher et uxor eius . . . . . . ij

Proxima Summa Personarum clxv Summa viij li v š.

VILLA DE FYNCHYNGFELDE.

Liberi tenentes

Willelmus Coleman . . ⎫
Margareta uxor eius . . ⎬ ij vj
Galfridus Spryngold . . ⎭
Alicia uxor eius . . . ⎱ ij vj
Johannes Hulde . . . ⎰
Margareta uxor eius . . ⎰ ij vj
Thomas Revel et uxor eius . . . . iij
Nicholas Conspol et uxor eius . . . . . . ij vj
Willelmus Colbayn et uxor eius . . . . . ij
Willelmus Shaldeforde et uxor eius . . . . . ij vj
Ricardus Bulmar et uxor eius . . . . . . ij vj
Walterus Carter et uxor eius . . . . ij
Robertus Roys et uxor eius . . . . ij vj
Robertus Huril et uxor eius . . . . ij
Willelmus Hundyswode et uxor eius . . . . ij
Walterus Revel et uxor eius . . . . ij vj
Willelmus Parkyr et uxor eius . . . . . . ij vj
Robertus Webbe . . . ij
Johannes Stonham . . xij

Johannes Kent et uxor eius . . . . ij
Johannes Houte et uxor eius . . . . ij
Margareta Houte . . . xij
Robertus Reys junior et uxor eius . . . . . xij
Johannes Goodrych . . xij
Johannes Fostyr et uxor eius . . . . xviij
Agnes Brokhole . . . xij
Johannes Wetyn et uxor eius . . . . ij
Johannes Caketone et uxor eius . . . . . ij
Johannes Huberd et uxor eius . . . . ij
Johannes Botoner . . . xij
Johannes Ilfot et uxor eius . . . . xvj
Ricardus Stebbyng et uxor eius . . . . . xviij
Albanus Mortymyr et uxor eius . . . . . ij

Laborarii

Johannes Caterel et uxor eius . . . . xviij
Thomas Recok et uxor eius . . . . . . ij vj
Ricardus Holde . . . vj

	s	d
Johannes Chouk . . .		vj
Johannes Smyth et uxor ejus	ij	
Sabina Revel		xij
Johannes Meller . . .		viij
Johannes Aloys et uxor ejus		xviij
Thomas Cuntone et uxor eius	ij	
Willelmus Meller et uxor eius	ij	
Willelmus Hundene et uxor eius	ij	
Johannes Blakes et uxor eius	ij	
Petronilla Fostyr . . .		xij
Johannes Page et uxor eius		xij
Ricardus Tetford et uxor eius	ij	
Johannes Spelman et uxor eius	ij	vj
Alicia Carter		xij
Gilbertus Hed et uxor eius	ij	
Galfridus Webbe et uxor eius	ij	
Willelmus Olyve et uxor eius	ij	vj
Willelmus Oborne et uxor eius	ij	
Johannes Sweyth et uxor eius	ij	
Gilbertus Cnevet et uxor eius	ij	
Robertus Coke et uxor eius		xij
Gilbertus Gelham et uxor eius	ij	vj
Johannes Horde et uxor eius		xij
Willelmus famulus Willelmi Colbayn et uxor eius	ij	
Johannes Clerk et uxor eius		xviij
Thomas Hendewode et uxor eius	ij	
Agnes Kempe		xij
* . . . ? ? . . . fermarius apud Cokefield . . .		xij
* . . . Beloge		xij
Lucia Speleman		xij
Robertus Bernerewe . .		xij
Sabina Piccat		iiij
Agnes Kent		xij
Thomas Brewer et uxor eius		xij

	s	d
Galfridus Oborne . . .	*	*
Johannes Carter et uxor eius		vj
Robertus Driver et uxor eius	*	xviij
Johannes Derkyn . . .		vij
* . . . ? ? . . . K et uxor eius		ij

Sutores

	s	d
Radulfus Herny et uxor eius	ij	
Willelmus Bermerowe et uxor eius	ij	vj
Willelmus Colyn et uxor eius	ij	
Johannes Jeman et uxor eius	ij	
Johannes Jeman junior .		xij
Petrus Conspol et uxor eius	ij	
Robertus Cox		xij

Scissores

	s	d
Johannes Blake . . .		xij
Thomas Brond et uxor eius	ij	
Ricardus Stedeman et uxor eius	ij	
Johannes Hulde . . .		vj
Hugo Lyng' et uxor eius		xviij
Ricardus Bromleye . .		xij
Walterus Cokat et uxor eius	ij	
Ricardus Bacon et uxor eius	ij	

Carpentarius

	s	d
Robertus Stonhard et uxor eius	ij	

Pistor

	s	d
Gilbertus Coleman et uxor eius	ij	vj

Pastores

	s	d
Thomas Blake et uxor eius	ij	
Johannes Peselond et uxor eius	ij	

Fabri

	s	d
Johannes Kyng et uxor eius	ij	
Johannes Prentys . . .		
Agnes Lowe	ij	vj
Johannes Cok et uxor eius	ij	
Simon atte Grove et uxor eius	ij	

* Hole in MS.

	ß	đ
Johannes Doreward et uxor eius	ij	
Johannes Kent et uxor eius	ij	vj
Johannes Walle et uxor eius	ij	vj
Walterus Coo et uxor eius	ij	vj
Ricardus Tyele et uxor eius	ij	vj
Johannes Pete et uxor eius	ij	
Johannes Cranschauke et uxor eius	ij	

Proxima summa personarum clxxvii Summa viiili xviiß

VILL' DE GELHAM PARVA [now YELDHAM].

Liberi tenentes

Johannes Sybyle et uxor eius	ij
Robertus Pecoc et uxor eius	ij
Thomas Cok et uxor eius	ij
Johannes Haale et uxor eius	ij
Johannes Godyng et uxor eius	iij
Johannes Godfrey	xij
Johannes Robet et uxor eius	ij

Laborarii

Thomas Sybile et uxor eius	ij
Ricardus de Potton' et uxor eius	ij
Johannes famulus eius	xij
Willelmus Haale et uxor eius	ij

Famuli

Margeria Rekedon'	xij
Johannes Haale et uxor eius	ij
Robertus Robet	xij
Ricardus Raffrex et uxor eius	ij
Rogerus Roger et uxor eius	ij
Robertus Godfrey et uxor eius	xij

Proxima Summa personarum xxx Summa xxxß.

VILL' DE GOSFELD.

Armiger

Ricardus de Lyon	x
Antiocha(?) uxor Willelmi de Coggyshal	iij iiij
Johanna de Shordelowe	xx

Frankeleyn

Johannes Haukwode et Margareta uxor eius.	x

Liberi tenentes

Alicia Chiltere	ij(?) vj
Willelmus atte Bigynge	ij(?) vj
Emma Longewode	xij
Johannes Flechyr et uxor eius	ij
Johannes Geray et uxor eius	ij vj
Robertus Attestrete et uxor eius	ij
Thomas Heyward et uxor eius	ij
Johannes * . . . na	xij
Johannes * . . . leyr	xij

Johannes Birde et uxor eius	ij
Johannes Belcham et uxor eius	xvj
Johannes William et uxor eius	xij
Robertus Periton et uxor eius	ij
Willelmus Bayly	vj
Willelmus Bernerowe	xij
Ricardus Cotte et uxor eius	xij
Johannes Hanekoc et uxor eius	ij

Laborarii

M *	xij
Jankyn Holder	iiij
Johannes Sprenger	iiij
Margareta serviens domine de Coggishale	xij
Alicia Bloy	xij
Johannes Simond	xij
Johannes Tussent et uxor eius	ij

* Holes in MS.

	s	d
Galfridus Smyth et uxor eius		ij
Laurentius Capper et uxor eius		ij
Johannes Attestrete et uxor eius		xij
Alicia filia Willelmi Bygynge		vj
Johannes Spensyr et uxor eius		ij
Walterus Taylor et uxor eius		ij
Willelmus Abot et uxor eius		xvj

Famuli

	s	d
Johannes Peyton et uxor eius		ij
Johannes Benteleye et uxor eius		ij
Willelmus Tempernoyse et uxor eius		ij
Alicia serviens Johannis Haukwode		xij
Johannes Bygynge		ij
Johannes Carter		xij
Johannes Wriyte et uxor eius		ij
Agnes Beste		iiij
Ricardus Chylterne		vj
Stephanus Geray		viij

	s	d
Walterus Nithelane et uxor eius		viij
Johannes Palmer et uxor eius		ij
Johannes Randulf et uxor eius		ij
Ricardus Boton' et uxor eius		ij
Editha filia eius		xij
Alicia filia eius		xij
Johannes Aylewyn et uxor eius		ij

Famuli et Laborarii

	s	d
Johannes Brokat et uxor eius		ij
Willelmus Calch et uxor eius		ij
Johannes Henkyn et uxor eius		ij
Johannes Chambre et uxor eius		ij
Johannes Pakeman et uxor eius		ij
Willelmus Hunte		xij
Margareta Chilterne		xij
Johannes Chambyrleyn		xij
Johannes Cok		xij

Proxima Summa personarum iiij^{xx} xiiij Summa iiijli xiiij s.

VILL' DE HYTHINGHAM SIBILL.

Liberi tenentes

	s	d
Johannes Dier et uxor eius		xx
Gilbertus Cole et uxor eius		xx
Johannes Onwyn et uxor eius		xx
Johannes Herny et uxor eius		xx
Nicholas Dauenant et uxor eius		iiij
Gilbertus Streyk et uxor eius		ij
Johannes Medwe et uxor eius	ij	vj
Juliana Combwell		xviij
Willelmus Kempe et uxor eius	ij	vj
Thomas Kentissch et uxor eius		iiij

Laborarii

	s	d
Johannes Carter et uxor eius	ij	vj
Johannes Tyler et uxor eius	ij	vj

	s	d
Willelmus in ye Aldris et uxor eius		ij
Johannes filius eius		xij
Willelmus famulus eius		xij
Agnes Peuer'		xij
Johannes Portyr et uxor eius		xij
Robertus Boket		xij
Johannes Waryn junior et uxor eius		xvj
Willelmus Boton' et uxor eius		ij

Famuli et laborarii

	s	d
Ricardus Rich et uxor eius		ij
Willelmus Seward et uxor eius		ij
Nigellus Red et uxor eius		ij
Emma filia eius		xij
Willelmus Combwell		xij
Johannes Combwell		xij
Margareta Combwell		xij
Johannes Lyr' et uxor eius		ij
Johannes Tyler et uxor eius		xx

	s	d		s	d
Johannes Tyler Crekys (?) et uxor eius	ij		Ricardus Clap et uxor eius	ij	
Henricus Tyler		xij	Johannes Scubbard et uxor eius	ij	
Johannes Mayhew et uxor eius		xij	Thomas filius eius . . .		xij
Henricus filius eius . .		xij	Johannes Bornard . .		xij
Johannes famulus eius .		xij	Ricardus Bornard et uxor eius	ij	
Agnes Morise		xij	Johannes Moun et uxor eius	ij	
Johannes Hankyn et uxor eius	ij		Willelmus Cokkot et uxor eius	ij	
Johanna Meller		xij	Andreas Wyeyn et uxor eius	ij	
Johannes Sparchance et uxor eius	ij		Juliana filia eius . . .		xij
Walterus Wriyte et uxor eius	ij		Willelmus Northfolk et uxor eius	ij	
Thomas Badekyn . . .		xij	Johannes Parkyr et uxor eius	ij	
Johannes Lord et uxor eius		xviij	Ricardus Fippe et uxor eius	ij	
Johannes Tofte et uxor eius	ij		Adam Bloy et uxor eius .	ij	
Johannes Hille et uxor eius	ij		Johannes Speyney et uxor eius	ij	
Willelmus Polsted et uxor eius	ij		Petrus Alselot et uxor eius	ij	
Johannes Walton . . .		xij	Gilbertus Orgon et uxor eius	ij	
Ricardus Upholder et uxor eius	ij		Willelmus Storeys et uxor eius	ij	
Johannes Peyton' et uxor eius	ij		Ricardus atte Hol et uxor eius	ij	
Ricardus Honewyk et uxor eius	ij		Willelmus Botyld et uxor eius	ij	
Johannes Webbe et uxor eius	ij		Johannes With yᵉ co(?)et uxor eius	ij	
Katerina Grey		xij	Johannes Clopton et uxor eius	ij	
Walterus Brokat et uxor eius		xvj	Willelmus Aleyn et uxor eius	ij	
Margareta Jemes . . .		xij	Willelmus Wyeyn et uxor eius	ij	
Johannes Godiskot et uxor eius	ij		Walterus With yᵉ co(?)et uxor eius	ij	
Emma Hunte		xij	Willelmus Cole et uxor eius		xvj
Alicia Crowe		xij	Johannes Batayle senior et uxor eius . . .	ij	
Willelmus Lizefot et uxor eius	ij		Johannes Cok et uxor eius	ij	
Willelmus Smyth et uxor eius	ij		Johannes Batayle junior et uxor eius . . .	ij	
Johannes Peyton et uxor eius	ij		Willelmus Combwell et uxor eius	ij	
Willelmus Dikyrt et uxor eius	ij vj		Johannes Clap et uxor eius	ij	
Walterus filius eius . .		xij	Thomas Sowter et uxor eius		xvj
Willelmus Baker et uxor eius	ij		Henricus Fowtrer et uxor eius	ij	iiij
Johannes Undal et uxor eius	ij				
Willelmus Herny et uxor eius	ij				
Walterus Brag' et uxor eius	ij				
Ricardus Heyward et uxor eius	ij				

	s	d
Johannes Symor et uxor eius	ij	iiij
Simon Wytene et uxor eius	ij	
Willelmus Larke et uxor eius	ij	
Johannes Wyeyn		xij
Johannes Heyward		xij

Fuller

	s	d
Johannes Rich et uxor eius		xij

Tegulator

	s	d
Johannes Tyler senior et uxor eius		ij

Pastores

	s	d
Johannes Pikot		xij
Robertus Pikot		xij
Johannes Helder		xij
Johannes Gemes		xij

Scissores

	s	d
Walterus Dereman et uxor eius		ij
Johannes Smyth junior et uxor eius		ij
Matilda atte Brok		xij
Willelmus Spelyng		xviij

	s	d
Willelmus Clerk et uxor eius	ij	
Johannes Smyth senior et uxor eius	ij	
Johannes Bassch et uxor eius	ij	
Johannes Honewyk et uxor eius		xvj
Johannes Bidon et uxor eius	ij	iiij
Johannes Fot famulus eius		xij
Radulphus Mot et uxor eius		xvj

Draperes

	s	d
Johannes Cook et uxor eius	ij	
Margareta Reve		xij

Carpentarii

	s	d
Johannes Medwe et uxor eius	ij	
Johannes filius eius		xij

Fabri

	s	d
Johannes Ferour et uxor eius	ij	

Proxima Summa personarum ccxiiij Summa xᵭi xiiij š.

VILL' DE OVYTON.

	s	d
Ricardus Gylot et uxor eius	ij	
Johannes Bery		xij
Johannes Sebyle		xij
Svenus Lyon		xij

	s	d
Johannes Lowelond et uxor eius	ij	

Proxima Summa personarum vij Summa vij š.

VILLA DE PENTELOWE.

Liberi tenentes

	s	d
Nicholas Clerk et uxor eius	ij	vj
Ricardus Clerk et uxor eius	ij	vj
Johannes Buntyng		xviij
Thomas Gerneys et uxor eius	ij	vj
Willelmus Gerneys et uxor eius	iij	iiij
Willelmus Reve et uxor eius	ij	vj
Stephanus Gerneys et uxor eius	ij	
Simon Dereby et uxor eius	ij	
Johannes Olyver		xviij
Johannes Dawnce junior		xij
Johannes Crysale senior et uxor eius	ij	vj

	s	d
Reginaldus Promet' et uxor eius	ij	vj

Laborarii

	s	d
Johannes Dawnce senior et uxor eius		xij
Thomas Reve et uxor eius		xx

Famuli et Laborarii

	s	d
Johannes Bret et uxor eius	ij	
Johannes Whypp		xij
Willelmus Kylat		xij
Robertus Auton		vj
Johannes O(l)eval		vj
Johanna Rokeber'		vj
Johannes Stokton		iiij
Margareta Reve		xij
Johannes Thomas et uxor eius	ij	

	s	d
Johannes Grey et uxor eius		ij
Johannes Clerk et uxor eius		ij
Walterus Plante et uxor eius		xij
Johannes Propechant' .		xij
Johannes Robac et uxor eius		xviij
Margareta Bontyng . .		xij
Thomas Crisal et uxor eius		xxij

	s	d
Johannes famulus Willelmi Gerneys		xj
Johannes Galor . . .		xj

Textores

Johannes Crisale . . .		xij

Proxima Summa Personarum li proxima Summa li s.

VILLA DE SALYNG MAGNA.

Frankelyn

Willelmus Attepark et uxor eius		ij
Galfridus Golde et uxor eius		ij
Johannes Aukier et uxor eius		ij
Johannes Brok et uxor eius		ij

Laborarii

Stephanus Pigott et uxor eius		ij
Christina Priour . .		xij
Galfridus Brok et uxor eius		ij
Willelmus Wolpot et uxor eius		ij
Johannes Wodeman et uxor eius		ij
Willelmus Rowhey et uxor eius		ij

Emma Standes		xij
Johannes Hilke et uxor eius		ij
Johannes atte Medwe et uxor eius		ij

Carpentarii

Johannes Wrihte et uxor eius		ij
Ricardus Peete et uxor eius		ij
Johannes Rowe et uxor eius		ij

Scissores

Johannes Stameris . .		xij
Johannes Gunnyl et uxor eius		ij

Proxima Summa Personarum xxxiij Summa xxxiij s.

VILL' DE STEBBYNG.

Domina de Wanton' . .		iiij

Famuli

Elisabeth serviens eius .		xij
Thomas famulus eius . .		xij

Liberi tenentes

Robertus Skene et uxor eius		iij
Johannes Holtes et uxor eius		iij
Andreas Nase et uxor eius	ij	vj
Willelmus Pyrye et uxor eius	ij	*
Robertus Ylger et uxor eius		ij

Stephanus Frankeleyn et uxor eius		ij
Ricardus Cuppere et uxor eius		ij
Ricardus Broun' et uxor eius		ij
Andreas Gy et uxor eius .	ij	vj
Robertus Putyng et uxor eius		xx
Simond Swetyng et uxor eius	ij	vj
Roger Fyssch et uxor eius	ij	*

Nativi tenentes

Willelmus Pyrie et uxor eius		iij

* MS. torn.

	s	d
Johannes Fulburn' et uxor eius		iij
Johannes Wyot et uxor eius		ij
Johannes Potter et uxor eius		ij
Henricus Brenstede et uxor eius		ij
Johannes Pleyhelle et uxor eius		ij *
Willelmus Ewat' et uxor eius		ij *
Johannes Clerk et uxor eius		ij
Willelmus Keng' et uxor eius		ij
Ricardus Clerk et uxor eius		ij vj
Ricardus Ram et uxor eius		ij vj
Robertus Lyttle et uxor eius		ij *
Willelmus Kempe et uxor eius		x*
Ricardus Ricun' et uxor eius		xvj
Johannes Reve et uxor eius		xij
Robertus Ynde		xij
Johannes Martyn		xij

Laborarii

	s	d
Johannes Theccher et uxor eius		iiij
Johannes Bumstede et uxor eius		xvj
Willelmus Punfred et uxor eius		vj
Ricardus Reng' et uxor eius		iiij
Thomas Lyttle et uxor eius		viij
Willelmus Sorel		x
Henricus Drane et uxor eius		ij
Johannes Menteney		xij
Willelmus Leyr'		xij
Willelmus Thorgod		xij
Willelmus Blake		xij
Johannes Polco et uxor eius		ij
Agnes Alard		xij
Johannes Lyttle		xij
Matilda Ram		xij
Johannes Bruer et uxor eius		ij
Johannes Koc'		xij
Johannes Col		xij

Bercarii

	s	d
Willelmus Kocston et uxor eius		iij
Johannes Tanner et uxor eius		ij

Scissores

	s	d
Clemens Wynd et uxor eius		ij
Johannes Pole et uxor eius	ij	vj
Willelmus Ewant junior et uxor eius		ij
Thomas Taylor et uxor eius		ij
Johannes Foukes		xij
Willelmus Londe' et uxor eius		ij

Textores

	s	d
Johannes Flemyng et uxor eius		ij
Johannes Hastiler et uxor eius		ij
Willelmus Webbe et uxor eius		ij
Johannes Moyn et uxor eius		ij
Johannes London et uxor eius		ij
Johannes Blakdene et uxor eius		ij
Ricardus Wyseden et uxor eius		ij

Carpentarii

	s	d
Nicholas Pape et uxor eius	ij	*
Johannes Britteman et uxor eius	ij	vj
Johannes Kocston et uxor eius	ij	iiij

Draperes

	s	d
Johannes Wryth et uxor eius		iiij
Johannes Dier et uxor eius		xij
Ricardus Taylor		iiij
Agnes Culond		ij

Molendinarius

	s	d
Johannes Miller et uxor eius		xvj

Carnifices

	s	d
Edmundus Koc' et uxor eius	ij	*
Walterus Goding et uxor eius		iiij

* MS. torn.

Fulleres	ß	ᵭ
Willelmus Crakebon et uxor eius		viij

Sutores		
Willelmus Wylle et uxor eius		ij
Johannes Ponu'*		xij

Fabri		
Stephanus Smyth et uxor eius		xij
Henricus Alard et uxor eius		ij

Pelliparii		
Johannes Skynner . .		iiij
Roger Trape		iiij

Famuli	ß	ᵭ
serviens Willelmi Wille .		xij
Serviens Walteri Godyng		xij
Serviens Vicarii Ecclesiae de Stebbing		iiij
Johannes famulus Johannis Felburn		xij
Henricus Pyrye . . .		xij
Eleanor Souch		xij
Galfridus Brighteman .		xij
uxor Willelmi Pekenot' .		xij
uxor Johannis Partrik .		xij

Tegulatores		
Hugo Tyler et uxor eius .	ij	
Roger Tye		xij

Proxima Summa personarum clv Summa vijᶩi xvß.

Lay Subs. Roll. Essex. No. $\frac{107}{68}$.

VILL' DE STURMER'.

Liberi tenentes	ß	ᵭ
Willelmus Bern et uxor eius	ij	vj
Thomas Bret et uxor eius	ij	vj
Willelmus Toller et uxor eius	iij	
Johannes Longe et uxor eius	iij	
Agnes filia eius . . .		xij
Robertus atte Welle . .		xij
Johannes Mayster et uxor eius	iij	
Johannes atte Hel et uxor eius	iij	
Willelmus Bret et uxor eius	ij	
Margareta filia eius . .		xij
Thomas Blomast . .		xvj
Willelmus atte Thorn et uxor eius	ij	vj

Laborarii	ß	ᵭ
Johannes Bret junior . .		vj
Alicia filia Thome Bret .		iiij
Agnes filia Willelmi Bern'		iiij
Johannes Deynys et uxor eius		ij
Willelmus filius Thome Hondr' et uxor eius .		ij
Walterus Mustard . . .		xij
Willelmus Turpayn . .		xviij
Johannes Fole et uxor eius		ij
Willelmus Chapman . .		xij
Edmundus Casse et uxor eius		xviij

	ß	ᵭ
Hugo Shepherd et uxor eius		ij
Gilbertus Drugge et uxor eius		xij
Johannes Sturdi et uxor eius		ij
Johannes Soow . . .		xij
Henricus Rande et uxor eius		ij
Thomas Morse		xij
Alicia Grey		x
Johannes atte Welle et uxor eius		vj
Amicia soror eius . . .		vj
Thomas Caunt		xij
Margareta Barwe . . .		xij
Johannes Hogoun et uxor eius		xij
Johannes Coppayl et uxor eius		xvj
Henricus Mayster . . .		vj
Robertus Bok et uxor eius		ij
Robertus Morse et uxor eius		xij
Willelmus Chapman et uxor eius . .		xij
Johannes Poterryle et uxor eius . .		ij
Edmundus Buk et uxor eius		ij
Agnes Casse		xij
Johannes Scheldrake et uxor eius . .		ij
Willelmus Hyrde et uxor eius	ij	vj

* MS. torn.

	s	d
Johannes Caunt et uxor eius		vj
Johannes Rande . . .		xij

Fabri

	s	d
Roger Smyth	ij	
Thomas famulus eius . .		xij
Alicia serviens eius . .		xij
Johannes Smyth et uxor eius	ij	vj
Johannes Bemuud et uxor eius	ij	vj
Robertus Hunter et uxor eius	ij	vj

Fulleres

	s	d
Galfridus Fuller et uxor eius		iij
Johannes Chon' et uxor eius		iij
Johannes Fullor et uxor eius		ij
Johannes Mustard et uxor eius		ij
Johannes suus socius . .		xij

Carpentarii

	s	d
Radulphus Wrihte . . .		xij

	s	d
Johannes Wrihte et uxor eius		ij
Johannes Hog et uxor eius		ij
Robertus Heyward . .		xviij
Johannes Beneyth et uxor eius		ij
Roger Folke et uxor eius .		ij

Sutores

	s	d
Johannes Wagge et uxor eius	ij	vj
Robertus filius eius . .		xij
Simon Kot et uxor eius .	ij	vj
Ricardus Bog et uxor eius		ij

Carucarii

	s	d
Johannes Haligod . . .		xij
Thomas Paty et uxor eius		xvj

Scissor

	s	d
Robertus Mayster et uxor eius		xij
Summa personarum cxiij		
Summa v℔ xiij s.		

N.B.—The reader should note the enormous proportion of artisans in some of the villages. The smiths in Alhamston, Felstede, Fynchyngfelde, and Sturmer, the weavers in Stebbyng, the tailors in Felstede, Fynchyngfelde, and Hythingham Sibill, the carpenters in Felstede and Sturmer seem out of proportion to all local needs. The figures suggest that these places were small industrial centres in these trades.

Note also that only Felstede and Stebbyng return *nativi tenentes*. Presumably land-holding villeins in the other villages must be mixed with the *laborarii*.

Felstede, Gosfeld, and Salyng Magna alone show resident 'frankeleyns', distinguished from *liberi tenentes*. Felstede enrolls three innkeepers: no other village shows them, though large places like Hythingham Sibill and Bumstede must have owned some.

Observe that in the whole 1,300 persons enrolled, we find only thirteen cases of 'filia eius' and one of 'soror eius' resident with a householder.

APPENDIX IV. WRIT OF INQUIRY AS TO THE FRAUDULENT LEVYING OF THE POLL-TAX.

L. T. R. Originalia, 4 Rich. II, m. 12.   Norfolkia De inquirendo pro Rege.

Rex vicecomiti Norfolkiae, Stephano de Hales chivaler, Hugoni Fastolf, Nicholao de Massyngham, Willelmo Wenlok clerico, Johanni de Ellerton servienti suo ad arma salutem.   Satis patet per veras et notabiles evidencias quod taxatores et collectores subsidii trium grossarum, quod nobis in ultimo parliamento nostro apud Northampton per dominos magnates et communitates regni nostri, in salvacionem et defensionem ejusdem regni nostri de qualibet persona laica ejusdem regni levandum, concessum fuit, in comitatu predicto per commissiones nostras nuper assignati, parcentes pluribus personis dicti comitatus, quasdam voluntarie et quasdam negligenter vel favorabiliter omiserunt, sic quod magna pars ejusdem subsidii in comitatu predicto per negligentiam et defectum ipsorum Taxatorum et Collectorum a nobis est cancellata et detenta, quae ad opus nostrum levare deberent si bene et fideliter taxata et assessa fuisset, quod non solum in nostri et dicti regni nostri grave prejudicium verum eciam in ordinacionum per nos et consilium nostrum pro salutacione et honore ejusdem regni nostri et subditorum nostrorum factarum et tractarum retardacionem et finalem turbacionem, nisi cicius in hac parte emendetur, dinoscitur redundare, nos volentes cum toto effectu hujusmodi periculis obviare, et de subsidio predicto juxta concessionem ejusdem fideliter respondere, de avisamento consilii nostri ordinavimus et assignavimus vos, quatuor tres et duos vestrum, ad supervidendum et inspiciendum omnes et singulas indenturas inter dictos Collectores et Constabularios ac alias gentes quarumcumque villarum et burgorum dicti Comitatus de taxacione et collectione dicti subsidii confectas, vel veras copias earundem taxaciones ac numerum et nomina omnium personarum per ipsos Taxatores et subtaxatores suos ad dictum subsidium assessarum continentes, ac ad perscrutandum et examinandum numerum quarumcumque personarum laicarum tam hominum quam feminarum Comitatus predicti tam infra libertates quam extra, que etatem quindecim annorum excedunt, veris mendicantibus et de elemosina solomodo viventibus dumtaxat exceptis, et ad vos informandum tam per sacramentum Constabulariorum et Ballivorum singularum villarum et burgorum ac aliorum proborum et legalium hominum de quolibet loco Comitatus predicti tam infra libertates quam extra, ubi necesse fuerit, quam aliis viis et modis, prout vobis magis expediens videbitur, de omnibus et singulis personis laicis quarumcumque villarum dicti Comitatus per dictos Taxatores et Collectores omissis vel concelatis, que hujusmodi subsidium solvere debuerunt, et ad numerum et nomina earundem redigendum in scriptis, et ea prefatis Taxatoribus et Collectoribus liberandum per indenturam inde inter vos et ipsos Taxatores et Collectores debite conficiendam, pro collectione et levacione dicti subsidii juxta formam concessionis ejusdem per eos fideliter faciendum, ac eciam ad conficiendum inter vos et Constabularios et duos alios homines cujuslibet villae dicti Comitatus indenturam de toto numero omnium personarum que in qualibet villarum predictarum inveniri poterunt, et que dictum subsidium secundam formam concessionis ejusdem solvere debent vel tenentur. Ita quod aliqua persona laica ejusdem Comitatus contra formam dictae concessionis nullatenus pretermittatur, et ad Thesaurarium et Barones de scaccario nostro de numero et nominibus ac singulis personis que sic inveneritis in qualibet villa et parochia cum omni celeritate possibili certificandum, et ad partes indenturarum vestrarum predictarum ibidem deferendum, et ad omnes illos quos in premissis seu aliquo premissorum contrarios inveneritis seu rebelles arestandum et capiendum et eos prisonis nostris mancipandum, in eisdem moraturos quousque de eorum punicione aliter duxerimus ordinandum. Et ideo vobis super fide et ligeancia quibus nobis tenemini, et sub forisfactura omnium que nobis forisfacere poteritis, injungimus et mandamus quod omnibus aliis premissis, et exoneracione quacumque cessante, vos quatuor tres vel duo vestrum de villa ad villam et loco ad locum infra Comitatum predictum tam infra libertates quam extra personaliter divertentes, hujusmodi perscrutacionem et examinacionem faciatis, et informacionem predictam viis et modis quibus melius poteritis capiatis, et premissa et omnia alia et singula faciatis et expleatis in forma predicta. Mandavimus enim prefatis Collectoribus quod ipsi indenturas suas predictas vel veras copias earundem vobis, quatuor tribus vel duobus vestrum, liberent indilate, et subsidium predictum de suis personis hujusmodi, quas eis per indenturas vestras sic certificaveritis, cum omni celeritate levari et colligi faciant, et nobis inde respondent ad scaccarium supradictum. Damus autem universis et singulis Ducibus Comitibus Baronibus militibus Maioribus Ballivis Ministris, et quibuscumque aliis ligeis et fidelibus nostris Comitatus predicti tam infra libertates quam extra, tenore presencium firmiter in preceptis, quod ipsi et eorum quilibet super fide et ligeancia quibus nobis tenentur, vobis, quatuor tribus et duobus vestrum, in premissis et quolibet premissorum diligenter intendentes, sint consulentes obedientes et auxiliantes: et tu prefatus vicecomes omnes et singulos qui in solucione subsidii predicti seu in aliquo premissorum rebelles vel contrarii fuerint capias, et in prisona nostra salvo custodiri facias in forma predicta. Et venire facias coram vobis, quatuor tribus vel duobus vestrum, ad dies et loca quos ad hoc provideritis vel providerint, quatuor tres vel duo vestrum, tam Constabularios et Ballivos quam alios probos et legales homines de qualibet villa seu parochia Comitatus predicti tam infra libertates quam extra de locis, ubi indigerint per quos etc. et inquiri (sic). In cujus etc. Teste Rege apud Westmonasterium xvj die Marcii. Eodem modo assignantur subscripti in Comitatu subscripto in forma predicta sub eadem data videlicet.

N.B.—Similar writs, varying only in the names of the commissioners in the first paragraph, are directed to fourteen shires of the South and East, and to the West Riding of Yorkshire, see p. 30, *supra*.

APPENDIX V

THE 'ANONIMAL CHRONICLE OF ST. MARY'S, YORK'

By the kind permission of Mr. G. M. Trevelyan, who discovered and transcribed this invaluable chronicle, of Dr. Poole who caused it to be inserted in the *English Historical Review*, Part 51 (1898), and of Messrs. Longmans, the proprietors of that admirable magazine, I am allowed to reproduce the document here. I have ventured to translate it, because the extraordinary jargon of corrupt Anglo-French in which it is written makes it extremely hard to follow. The author possessed a very poor vocabulary, and a wretched cramped quasi-legal style. His sentences wander about in the most illogical fashion, with clauses loosely connected by 'pour ceo que' or 'par quel encheson' or 'en quel temps'. They are often ungrammatical, lacking an apodosis, or a principal verb. I have had to break up a very large number of his sentences into two or three, in order to be intelligible. In three or four places the phrases are clearly incomplete, by reason of words having dropped out in the copy made by Francis Thynne, in or about 1592, the sole surviving text. But if the literary merit of the piece is *nil*, its historical value is enormous. It contains far more detailed facts about the rising than any other single chronicle, and a large proportion of them are unrecorded elsewhere. It is clearly the work of a contemporary, and in some parts of an eyewitness. I have followed it so closely in certain sections of my narrative that I thought it well to append it here. The back-file of the *English Historical Review* is hard to obtain outside great public libraries, and the general reader, if he ever glances at the original, will appreciate my reasons for translating the chronicle, instead of merely reprinting Mr. Trevelyan's text.

'Because in the year 1380 the subsidies were over lightly granted[1] at the Parliament of Northampton and because it seemed to divers Lords and to the Commons that the said subsidies were not honestly levied, but commonly exacted from the

---

[1] I do not pretend to be sure of what exactly the chronicler means by 'legerment grantés'—presumably 'granted without due consideration of details or difficulties of levying'.

poor and not from the rich, to the great profit and advantage of the tax-collectors, and to the deception of the King and the Commons, the Council of the King ordained certain commissions to make inquiry in every township how the tax had been levied. Among these commissions, one for Essex was sent to one Thomas Bampton, senechal of a certain lord, who was regarded in that country as a king or great magnate for the state that he kept. And before Whitsuntide he held a court at Brentwood in Essex, to make inquisition, and showed the commission that had been sent him to raise the money which was in default, and to inquire how the collectors had levied the aforesaid subsidy. He had summoned before him the townships of a neighbouring hundred, and wished to have from them new contributions, commanding the people of those townships to make diligent inquiry, and give their answers, and pay their due. Among these townships was Fobbing, whose people made answer that they would not pay a penny more, because they already had a receipt from himself for the said subsidy. On which the said Thomas threatened them angrily, and he had with him two sergeants-at-arms of our Lord the King. And for fear of his malice the folks of Fobbing took counsel with the folks of Corringham, and the folks of these two places made levies and assemblies, and sent messages to the men of Stanford to bid them rise with them, for their common profit. Then the people of these three townships came together to the number of a hundred or more, and with one assent went to the said Thomas Bampton, and roundly gave him answer that they would have no traffic with him, nor give him a penny. On which the said Thomas commanded his sergeants-at-arms to arrest these folks, and put them in prison. But the commons made insurrection against him, and would not be arrested, and went about to kill the said Thomas and the said sergeants. On this Thomas fled towards London to the King's Council; but the commons took to the woods, for fear that they had of his malice, and they hid there some time, till they were almost famished, and afterwards they went from place to place to stir up other people to rise against the lords and great folk of the country. And because of these occurrences Sir Robert Belknap, Chief Justice of the King's Bench, was sent into the county, with a commission of Trailbaston, and indictments against divers persons were laid before him, and the folks of the countryside were in such fear that they were proposing to abandon their homes. Wherefore the commons rose against him, and came before him, and told him that he was a traitor to the King, and that it was of pure malice that he would put them in default, by means of false inquests made before him. And they took him, and made him swear on the Bible that never again would he hold such a session, nor act as a justice in such inquests. And they made him give them a list of the names of all the jurors, and they took all the jurors they could catch, and cut off their heads, and cast their houses to the ground. So the said Sir Robert took his way home without delay. And afterwards the said commons assembled together, before Whitsunday, to the number of some 50,000, and they went to the manors and townships of those who would not rise with them, and cast their houses to the ground or set fire to them. At this time they caught three clerks of Thomas Bampton, and cut off their heads, and carried the heads about with them for several days stuck on poles as an example to others. For it was their purpose to slay all lawyers, and all jurors, and all the servants of the King whom they could find. Meanwhile the great lords of that country and other people of substance fled towards London, or to other counties where they might be safe. Then the commons sent divers letters to Kent and Suffolk and Norfolk that they should rise with them, and when they were assembled they went about in many bands doing great mischief in all the countryside.

Now on Whit Monday a knight of the household of our Lord the King named Sir Simon Burley, having in his company two sergeants-at-arms, came to Gravesend, and challenged a man there of being his born serf: and the good folks of the town came to him to make a bargain for the man, because of their respect for the king: but Sir Simon would take nothing less than £300, which sum would have undone the said man. And the good folks prayed him to mitigate his demand, but could not come to terms nor induce him to take a smaller sum, though they said to Sir Simon that the man was a good Christian and of good disposition, and in short that he ought not to be so undone. But the said Sir Simon was of an irritable and angry temper, and greatly despised these good folk, and for haughtiness of heart he bade his sergeants bind the said man, and to take him to Rochester Castle, to be kept in custody there: from which there came later great evil and mischief. And after his departure the commons commenced to rise, gathering in to them the men of many townships of Kent. And at this moment a justice was assigned by the King and Council to go into Kent with a commission of Trailbaston, as had been done before in Essex, and with him went a sergeant-at-arms of our Lord the King, named Master John Legge, bearing with him a great number of indictments against folks of that district, to make the King rich. And they would have held session at Canterbury, but they were turned back by the commons.

And after this the commons of Kent gathered together in great numbers day after day, without a head or a chieftain, and the Friday after Whit Sunday came to Dartford. And there they took counsel, and made proclamation that none who dwelt near the sea in any place for the space of twelve leagues, should come out with them, but should remain to defend the coasts of the sea from public enemies, saying among themselves that they were more kings than one (?)[1], and they would not suffer or endure any other king but King Richard. At this same time the commons of Kent came to Maidstone, and cut off the head of one of the best men of the town, and cast to the ground divers houses and tenements of folks who would not rise with them, as had been done before in Essex. And, on the next Friday after, they came to Rochester and there met a great number of the commons of Essex. And because of the man of Gravesend they laid siege to Rochester Castle, to deliver their friend from Gravesend, whom the aforesaid Sir Simon had imprisoned. They laid strong siege to the Castle, and the constable defended himself vigorously for half a day, but at length for fear that he had of such tumult, and because of the multitude of folks without reason from Essex and Kent, he delivered up the Castle to them. And the commons entered, and took their companion, and all the other prisoners out of the prison. Then the men of Gravesend repaired home with their fellow in great joy, without doing more. But those who came from Maidstone took their way with the rest of the commons through the countryside. And there they made chief over them Wat Teghler of Maidstone, to maintain them and be their councillor. And on the Monday next after Trinity Sunday they came to

[1] The text is obscure here, ' dissant parentre eux que ils fuerent pluseurs roys que un, et il ne voyderont autre roy forsque roy Richart sufferer ne aver '.

Canterbury, before the hour of noon; and 4,000 of them entering into the Minster at the time of High Mass, there made a reverence and cried with one voice to the monks to prepare to choose a monk for Archbishop of Canterbury, ' for he who is Archbishop now is a traitor, and shall be decapitated for his iniquity'. And so he was within five days after ! And when they had done this, they went into the town to their fellows, and with one assent they summoned the Mayor, the bailiffs, and the commons of the said town, and examined them whether they would with good will swear to be faithful and loyal to King Richard and to the true Commons of England or no. Then the mayor answered that they would do so willingly, and they made their oath to that effect. Then they (the rebels) asked them if they had any traitors among them, and the townsfolk said that there were three, and named their names. These three the commons dragged out of their houses and cut off their heads. And afterwards they took 500 men of the town with them to London, but left the rest to guard the town.

At this time the commons had as their councillor a chaplain of evil disposition named Sir John Ball, which Sir John advised them to get rid of all the lords, and of the archbishop and bishops, and abbots, and priors, and most of the monks and canons, saying that there should be no bishop in England save one arch-bishop only, and that he himself would be that prelate, and they would have no monks or canons in religious houses save two, and that their possessions should be distributed among the laity. For which sayings he was esteemed among the commons as a prophet, and laboured with them day by day to strengthen them in their malice—and a fit reward he got, when he was hung, drawn, and quartered, and beheaded as a traitor. After this the said commons went to many places, and raised all the folk, some willingly and some unwillingly, till they were gathered together full 60,000. And in going towards London they met divers men of law, and twelve knights of that country, and made them swear to support them, or otherwise they should have been beheaded. They wrought much damage in Kent, and notably to Thomas Haselden, a servant of the Duke of Lancaster, because of the hate that they bore to the said duke. They cast his manors to the ground and all his houses, and sold his beasts—his horses, his good cows, his sheep, and his pigs—and all his store of corn, at

a cheap price. And they desired every day to have his head, and
the head of Sir Thomas Orgrave, Clerk of Receipt and sub-
Treasurer of England.

When the King heard of their doings he sent his messengers to
them, on Tuesday after Trinity Sunday, asking why they were
behaving in this fashion, and for what cause they were making
insurrection in his land. And they sent back by his messengers
the answer that they had risen to deliver him, and to destroy
traitors to him and his kingdom. The King sent again to them
bidding them cease their doings, in reverence for him, till he could
speak with them, and he would make, according to their will,
reasonable amendment of all that was ill-done in the realm. And
the commons, out of good feeling to him, sent back word by his
messengers that they wished to see him and speak with him at
Blackheath.[1] And the King sent again the third time to say that
he would come willingly the next day, at the hour of Prime, to hear
their purpose. At this time the King was at Windsor, but he
removed with all the haste he could to London : and the Mayor
and the good folks of London came to meet him, and conducted
him in safety to the Tower of London. There all the Council
assembled and all the lords of the land round about, that is to
say, the Archbishop of Canterbury, Chancellor of England, the
Bishop of London, and the Master of the Hospital of St. John's,
Clerkenwell, who was then Treasurer of England, and the Earls
of Buckingham[2] and Kent, Arundel, Warwick, Suffolk, Oxford,
and Salisbury, and others to the number of 600.

And on the vigil of Corpus Christi Day the commons of Kent
came to Blackheath, three leagues from London, to the number
of 50,000, to wait for the King, and they displayed two banners
of St. George and forty pennons. And the commons of Essex
came on the other side of the water to the number of 60,000 to
aid them, and to have their answer from the King. And on the
Wednesday, the King being in the Tower of London, thinking to
settle the business, had his barge got ready, and took with him
in his barge the Archbishop, and the Treasurer, and certain others

---

[1] The text seems corrupt, ' Et les dist comons pur amites a luy, par ses mes-
sageurs que il se vodroit veer et parler ovesque eux al Blackeheathe '. A verb
is missing, and presumably the text should run, ' respondirent que ils vodroient
veer et parler ovesque luy '.

[2] An error. Buckingham was in Wales at the moment.

of his Council, and four other barges for his train, and got him to
Greenwich, which is three leagues from London. But there the
Chancellor and the Treasurer said to the King that it would be
too great folly to trust himself among the commons, for they
were men without reason and had not the sense to behave properly.
But the commons of Kent, since the King would not come to them
because he was dissuaded by his Chancellor and Treasurer, sent
him a petition, requiring that he should grant them the head of
the Duke of Lancaster, and the heads of fifteen other lords, of
whom fourteen (three?) were bishops,[1] who were present with
him in the Tower of London. And these were their names : Sir
Simon Sudbury, Archbishop of Canterbury, Chancellor of England,
Sir Robert Hales, Prior of the Hospital of St. John's, Treasurer
of England, the Bishop of London, Sir John Fordham, Bishop-
elect of Durham and Clerk of the Privy Seal, Sir Robert Belknap,
Chief Justice of the King's Bench, Sir Ralph Ferrers, Sir Robert
Plessington, Chief Baron of the Exchequer, John Legge, Sergeant-
at-arms of the King, and Thomas Bampton aforesaid. This the
King would not grant them, wherefore they sent to him again
a yeoman, praying that he would come and speak with them : and
he said that he would gladly do so, but the said Chancellor and
Treasurer gave him contrary counsel, bidding him tell them that
if they would come to Windsor on the next Monday they should
there have a suitable answer.

And the said commons had among themselves a watchword in
English, " With whome haldes you ? " ; and the answer was, " With
kinge Richarde and the true comons " ; and those who could not
or would not so answer were beheaded and put to death.

And at this time there came a knight with all the haste that
he could, crying to the King to wait ; and the King, startled at
this, awaited his approach to hear what he would say. And the
said knight came to the King telling him that he had heard from
his servant, who had been in the hands of the rebels on that day,[2]
that if he came to them all the land should be lost, for they would
never let him loose, but would take him with them all round
England, and that they would make him grant them all their
demands, and that their purpose was to slay all the lords and

---

[1] The figure fourteen is unintelligible—only three bishops are cited in the list
—the Primate, Courtenay of London, and Fordham elect of Durham.

[2] Text is possibly corrupt here.

ladies of great renown, and all the archbishops, bishops, abbots and priors, monks and canons, parsons and vicars, by the advice and counsel of the aforesaid Sir John Wraw (Ball).[1]

Therefore the King returned towards London as fast as he could, and came to the Tower at the hour of Tierce.   And at this time the yeoman who has been mentioned above hastened to Black-heath, crying to his fellows that the King was departed, and that it would be good for them to go on to London and carry out their purpose that same Wednesday.   And before the hour of Vespers the commons of Kent came, to the number of 60,000, to South-wark, where was the Marshalsea.   And they broke and threw down all the houses in the Marshalsea, and took out of prison all the prisoners who were imprisoned for debt or for felony.   And they levelled to the ground a fine house belonging to John Imworth, then Marshal of the Marshalsea of the King's Bench, and warden of the prisoners of the said place, and all the dwellings of the jurors and questmongers [2] belonging to the Marshalsea during that night.   But at the same time, the commons of Essex came to Lambeth near London, a manor of the Archbishop of Canterbury, and entered into the buildings and destroyed many of the goods of the said Archbishop, and burnt all the books of register, and rules of remembrances belonging to the Chancellor, which they found there.

And the next day, Thursday, which was the feast of Corpus Christi, the 13th day of June, with the Dominical Letter F, the said commons of Essex went in the morning [3] to Highbury, two leagues north of London, a very fine manor belonging to the Master of the Hospitallers.   They set it on fire, to the great damage and loss of the Knights Hospitallers of St. John.   Then some of them returned to London, but others remained in the open fields all that night.   And this same day of Corpus Christi, in the morning, the commons of Kent cast down a certain house

[1] Ball must be meant.   Wraw is not yet ' avandit ', being only named on the last page of the Chronicle.   The story agrees with the advice ascribed to Ball on the preceding page.

[2] Questmongers.   Dr. Murray comments thus on these people : 'they are generally mentioned along with jurors or *false* jurors, and seem to have been persons who made it their business and profit to give information, and cause judicial enquiries to be made against others, so as to get a share of the fines.'

[3] Date certainly wrong.   There is ample proof that Highbury was burnt on Friday.   See page 70.

of ill-fame near London Bridge, which was in the hands of Flemish women, and they had the said house to rent from the Mayor of London.   And then they went on to the Bridge to pass into the City, but the Mayor was ready before them, and had the chains drawn up, and the drawbridge lifted, to prevent their passage. And the commons of Southwark rose with them and cried to the custodians of the bridge to lower the drawbridge and let them in, or otherwise they should be undone.   And for fear that they had of their lives, the custodians let them enter, much against their will.   At this time all the religious and the parsons and vicars of London were going devoutly in procession to pray God for peace.   At this same time the commons took their way through the middle of London, and did no harm or damage till they came to Fleet Street. [And at this time, as it was said, the mob of London set fire to and burnt the fine manor of the Savoy, before the arrival of the country folk.]   And in Fleet Street the men of Kent broke open the prison of the Fleet, and turned out all the prisoners, and let them go whither they would.   Then they stopped, and cast down to the ground and burnt the shop of a certain chandler, and another shop belonging to a blacksmith, in the middle of the said street.   And, as is supposed, there shall never be houses there again, defacing the beauty of that street.   And then they went to the Temple, to destroy the tenants of the said Temple, and they cast the houses to the ground and threw off all the tiles, and left the roofing in a bad way (?)[1].   They went into the Temple church and took all the books and rolls and remembrances, that lay in their cupboards in the Temple, which belonged to the law-yers, and they carried them into the highway and burnt them there.   And on their way to the Savoy they destroyed all the houses which belonged to the Master of the Hospital of St. John. And then they went to the house of the Bishop of Chester, near the Church of St. Mary-le-Strand, where was dwelling John Fordham, Bishop-elect of Durham and clerk of the Privy Seal. And they rolled barrels of wine out of his cellar, and drunk their fill, and departed without doing further damage.   And then they went toward the Savoy, and set fire to divers houses of divers unpopular persons on the Western side[2]: and at last they

---

[1] 'E avaiglerent toutz les tughles, issint que il fueront converture en male araye.'   I do not quite understand this phrase.

[2] Gentz a que est maugrés del parte le West.

came to the Savoy, and broke open the gates, and entered into the place and came to the wardrobe. And they took all the torches they could find, and lighted them, and burnt all the sheets and coverlets and beds and head-boards of great worth, for their whole value was estimated at 1,000 marks. And all the napery and other things that they could discover they carried to the hall and set on fire with their torches. And they burnt the hall, and the chambers, and all the buildings within the gates of the said palace or manor, which the commons of London had left unburnt. And, as is said, they found three barrels of gunpowder, and thought it was gold or silver, and cast it into the fire, and the powder exploded, and set the hall in a greater blaze than before, to the great loss and damage of the Duke of Lancaster. And the commons of Kent got the credit of the arson, but some say that the Londoners were really the guilty parties, for their hatred to the said Duke.

Then one part of them went towards Westminster, and set on fire a house belonging to John Butterwick, Under-sheriff of Middlesex, and other houses of divers people, and broke open Westminster prison, and let loose all the prisoners condemned by the law. And afterwards they returned to London by way of Holborn, and in front of St. Sepulchre's Church they set on fire the house of Simon Hosteler, and several other houses, and broke open Newgate Prison, and let loose all the prisoners, for whatever cause they had been imprisoned. This same Thursday the commons came to St. Martin's-le-Grand, and tore away from the high altar a certain Roger Legett, a great 'assizer'[1], and took him into Cheapside and his head was cut off. On that same day eighteen more persons were decapitated in divers corners of the town.

At this same time a great body of the commons went to the Tower to speak with the King and could not get speech with him, wherefore they laid siege to the Tower from the side of St. Catherine's, towards the south. And another part of the commons, who were in the City, went to the Hospital of St. John's, Clerkenwell, and on the way they burnt the dwelling and houses of Roger Legett, the questmonger, who had been beheaded in Cheapside, and also all the rented houses and tenements of the

---

[1] 'Grand cisorer.' I can find no better explanation for *cisorer*. Professor Ker suggests that it is a corrupt form of sisour or cisour, an 'assizer'. Roger Legett is called a 'questmonger and sisor' by Stow, *Annals*, 286.

Hospital of St. John, and afterwards they came to the beautiful priory of the said Hospital, and set on fire several fine and delectable houses within the priory, a great and horrible piece of damage for all time to come. They then returned to London, to rest or to do more mischief.

At this time the King was in a turret of the great Tower of London, and could see the manor of the Savoy and the Hospital of Clerkenwell, and the house of Simon Hosteler near Newgate, and John Butterwick's place, all on fire at once. And he called all his lords about him to his chamber, and asked counsel what they should do in such necessity. And none of them could or would give him any counsel, wherefore the young King said that he would send to the Mayor of the City, to bid him order the sheriffs and aldermen to have it cried round their wards that every man between the age of fifteen and sixty, on pain of life and members, should go next morning (which was Friday) to Mile End, and meet him there at seven o'clock. He did this in order that all the commons who were encamped around the Tower might be induced to abandon the siege, and come to Mile End to see him and hear him, so that those who were in the Tower could get off safely whither they would, and save themselves. But it came to nought, for some of them did not get the good fortune to be preserved. And on that Thursday, the said feast of Corpus Christi, the King, being in the Tower very sad and sorry, mounted up into a little turret towards St. Catherine's, where were lying a great number of the commons, and had proclamation made to them that they all should go peaceably to their homes, and he would pardon them all manner of their trespasses. But all cried with one voice that they would not go before they had captured the traitors who lay in the Tower, nor until they had got charters to free them from all manner of serfdom, and had got certain other points which they wished to demand. And the King benevolently granted all, and made a clerk write a bill in their presence in these terms : " Richard, King of England and France, gives great thanks to his good commons, for that they have so great a desire to see and to keep their king, and grants them pardon for all manner of trespasses and misprisions and felonies done up to this hour, and wills and commands that every one should now return to his own home, and wills and commands that each should put his grievances in writing, and have them sent to him ; and he will provide, with the aid of his loyal lords and his good council, such remedy as shall be profitable both to him and to them, and to all the kingdom." On this document he sealed his signet in presence of them all, and sent out the said bill by the hands of two of his knights to the folks before St. Catherine's. And he caused it to be read to them, and the knight who read it stood up on an old chair[1] before the others so that all could hear. All this time the King was in the Tower in great distress of mind. And when the commons had heard the Bill, they said that this was nothing but trifles and mockery. Therefore they returned to London and had it cried around the City that all lawyers, and all the clerks of the Chancery and the Exchequer and every man who could write a brief or a letter should be beheaded, whenever they could be found. At this time they burnt several more houses in the City, and the King himself ascended to a high garret of the Tower and watched the fires. Then he came down again, and sent for the lords to have their counsel, but they knew not how they should counsel him, and all were wondrous abashed.

And next day, Friday, the commons of the countryside and the commons of London assembled in fearful strength, to the number of 100,000 or more, besides some four score who remained on Tower Hill to watch those who were in the Tower. And some went to Mile End, on the Brentwood Road, to wait for the coming of the King, because of the proclamation that he had made. But some came to Tower Hill, and when the King knew that they were there, he sent them orders by messenger to join their friends at Mile End, saying that he would come to them very soon. And at this hour of the morning he advised the Archbishop of Canterbury, and the others who were in the Tower, to go down to the Little Water-gate, and take a boat and save themselves. And the Archbishop did so, but a wicked woman raised a cry against him, and he had to turn back to the Tower, to his confusion.

And by seven o'clock the King came to Mile End, and with him his mother in a whirlecote[2], and also the Earls of Buckingham[3], Kent, Warwick, and Oxford, and Sir Thomas Percy, and Sir

---

[1] Or an old pulpit (chaire) (?).

[2] This is certainly a mistake. The Princess of Wales was left in the Tower according to the consensus of *Chron. Angl.*, Froissart, and the other chronicles. This is the only one which brings her to Mile End. A whirlecote is the fourteenth-century wheeled carriage.

[3] A mistake : Buckingham, as stated before, was in Wales.

Robert Knolles, and the Mayor of London, and many knights
and squires ; and Sir Aubrey de Vere carried the sword of state.
And when he was come the commons all knelt down to him, saying
"Welcome our Lord King Richard, if it pleases you, and we will
not have any other king but you ". And Wat Tighler, their leader
and chief, prayed in the name of the commons that he would suffer
them to take and deal with all the traitors against him and the
law, and the King granted that they should have at their disposition all who were traitors, and could be proved to be traitors by
process of law.   The said Walter and the commons were carrying
two banners, and many pennons and pennoncels, while they made
their petition to the King.   And they required that for the future
no man should be in serfdom, nor make any manner of homage
or suit to any lord, but should give a rent of 4d. an acre for his
land.   They asked also that no one should serve any man except
by his own good will, and on terms of regular covenant.

And at this time the King made the commons draw themselves
out in two lines, and proclaimed to them that he would confirm
and grant it that they should be free, and generally should have
their will, and that they might go through all the realm of England
and catch all traitors and bring them to him in safety, and then
he would deal with them as the law demanded.

Under colour of this grant Wat Tighler and [some of] the commons took their way to the Tower, to seize the Archbishop, while
the rest remained at Mile End.   During this time the Archbishop
sang his mass devoutly in the Tower, and shrived the Prior of the
Hospitallers and others, and then he heard two masses or three,
and chanted the *Commendacione*, and the *Placebo*, and the *Dirige*,
and the Seven Psalms, and a Litany, and when he was at the
words "Omnes sancti orate pro nobis ", the commons burst in,
and dragged him out of the chapel of the Tower, and struck and
hustled him rudely, as they did also the others who were with
him, and dragged them to Tower Hill.   There they cut off the
heads of Master Simon Sudbury, Archbishop of Canterbury, and
of Sir Robert Hales, Prior of the Hospital of St. John's, Treasurer
of England, and of Sir William Appleton, a great lawyer and
surgeon, and one who had much power (?) with [1] the king and the
Duke of Lancaster.   And some time after they beheaded John

---

[1] Grant maester ovesque le roy : but I suspect that this means ' chief physician
to the king, &c.'

Legge, the King's Sergeant-at-arms, and with him a certain juror. And at the same time the commons made proclamation that whoever could catch any Fleming or other alien of any nation, might cut off his head, and so they did after this. Then they took the heads of the Archbishop and of the others and put them on wooden poles, and carried them before them in procession, as far as the shrine of Westminster Abbey, in despite of them and of God and Holy Church : and vengeance descended on them no long time after. Then they returned to London Bridge and set the head of the Archbishop above the gate, with eight other heads of those they had murdered, so that all could see them who passed over the bridge. This done, they went to the Church of St. Martin's in the Vintry, and found therein thirty-five Flemings, whom they dragged out and beheaded in the street. On that day there were beheaded in all some 140 or 160 persons. Then they took their way to the houses of Lombards and other aliens, and broke into their dwellings, and robbed them of all their goods that they could lay hands on. This went on for all that day and the night following, with hideous cries and horrid tumult.

At this time, because the Chancellor had been beheaded, the King made the Earl of Arundel Chancellor for the day, and gave him the Great Seal ; and all that day he caused many clerks to write out charters, and patents, and petitions, granted to the commons touching the matters before mentioned, without taking any fines for sealing or description.

The next morning, Saturday, great numbers of the commons came into Westminster Abbey at the hour of Tierce, and there they found John Imworth, Marshal of the Marshalsea and warden of the prisoners, a tormentor without pity ; he was at the shrine of St. Edward, embracing a marble pillar, to crave aid and succour from the saint to preserve him from his enemies. But the commons wrenched his arms away from the pillar of the shrine, and dragged him away to Cheapside, and there beheaded him. And at the same time they took from Bread Street a valet named John Greenfield, merely because he had spoken well of Friar William Appleton, and of other murdered persons, and brought him to Cheapside and beheaded him. All this time the King was causing a proclamation to be made round the City, that every one should go peaceably to his own country and his own house, without doing more mischief ; but to this the commons gave no heed

And on this same day, at three in the afternoon, the King came to the Abbey of Westminster, and some 200 persons with him ; and the abbot and monks of the said Abbey, and the canons and vicars of St. Stephen's Chapel, came to meet him in procession clothed in their copes and their feet naked, half-way to Charing Cross. And they brought him to the Abbey, and then to the High Altar of the church, and the King made his prayer devoutly, and left an offering for the altar and the relics. And afterwards he spoke with the anchorite, and confessed to him, and remained with him some time. Then the King caused a proclamation to be made that all the commons of the country who were still in London should come to Smithfield, to meet him there ; and so they did.

And when the King and his train had arrived there they turned into the Eastern meadow in front of St. Bartholomew's, which is a house of canons : and the commons arrayed themselves on the west side in great battles. At this moment the Mayor of London, William Walworth, came up, and the King bade him go to the commons, and make their chieftain come to him. And when he was summoned by the Mayor, by the name of Wat Tighler of Maidstone, he came to the King with great confidence, mounted on a little horse, that the commons might see him. And he dismounted, holding in his hand a dagger which he had taken from another man, and when he had dismounted he half bent his knee, and then took the King by the hand, and shook his arm forcibly and roughly, saying to him, " Brother, be of good comfort and joyful, for you shall have, in the fortnight that is to come, praise from the commons even more than you have yet had, and we shall be good companions ". And the King said to Walter, " Why will you not go back to your own country ? " : But the other answered, with a great oath, that neither he nor his fellows would depart until they had got their charter such as they wished to have it, and had certain points rehearsed, and added to their charter which they wished to demand. And he said in a threatening fashion that the lords of the realm would rue it bitterly if these points were not settled to their pleasure. Then the King asked him what were the points which he wished to have revised, and he should have them freely, without contradiction, written out and sealed. Thereupon the said Walter rehearsed the points which were to be demanded ; and he asked that there should be no law within the realm save the law of Winchester, and that from henceforth there should be no outlawry in any process of law, and that no lord should have lordship save civilly,[1] and that there should be equality (?) among all people save only the King, and that the goods of Holy Church should not remain in the hands of the religious, nor of parsons and vicars, and other churchmen ; but that clergy already in possession should have a sufficient sustenance from the endowments, and the rest of the goods should be divided among the people of the parish. And he demanded that there should be only one bishop in England and only one prelate, and all the lands and tenements now held by them should be confiscated, and divided among the commons, only reserving for them a reasonable sustenance. And he demanded that there should be no more villeins in England, and no serfdom or villein-age, but that all men should be free and of one condition. To this the King gave an easy answer, and said that he should have all that he could fairly grant, reserving only for himself the regality of his crown. And then he bade him go back to his home, without making further delay.

During all this time that the King was speaking, no lord or counsellor dared or wished to give answer to the commons in any place save the King himself. Presently Wat Tighler, in the presence of the King, sent for a flagon of water to rinse his mouth, because of the great heat that he was in, and when it was brought he rinsed his mouth in a very rude and disgusting fashion before the King's face. And then he made them bring him a jug of beer, and drank a great draught, and then, in the presence of the King, climbed on his horse again. At this time a certain valet from Kent, who was among the King's retinue, asked that the said Walter, the chief of the commons, might be pointed out to him. And when he saw him, he said aloud that he knew him for the greatest thief and robber in all Kent. Watt heard these words, and bade him come out to him, wagging his head at him in sign of malice ; but the valet refused to approach, for fear that he had of the mob. But at last the lords made him go out to him, to see what he [Watt] would do before the King. And when Watt saw him he ordered one of his followers, who was riding behind him carrying his banner displayed, to dismount and behead

---

[1] 'Et que nul seigneur de ore en avant averoyt seigneurie, fors sivilement, ester proportione entre toutz gentz fors tant seulement le roy.' A word seems to have slipped out.

the said valet. But the valet answered that he had done nothing
worthy of death, for what he had said was true, and he would
not deny it, but he could not lawfully make debate in the presence of his liege lord, without leave, except in his own defence :
but that he could do without reproof; for if he was struck he
would strike back again. And for these words Watt tried to
strike him with his dagger, and would have slain him in the King's
presence ; but because he strove so to do, the Mayor of London,
William Walworth, reasoned with the said Watt for his violent
behaviour and despite, done in the King's presence, and arrested
him. And because he arrested him, the said Watt stabbed the
Mayor with his dagger in the stomach in great wrath. But, as
it pleased God, the Mayor was wearing armour and took no harm,
but like a hardy and vigorous man drew his cutlass, and struck
back at the said Watt, and gave him a deep cut on the neck,
and then a great cut on the head. And during this scuffle one
of the King's household drew his sword, and ran Watt two or three
times through the body, mortally wounding him. And he spurred
his horse, crying to the commons to avenge him, and the horse
carried him some four score paces, and then he fell to the ground
half dead. And when the commons saw him fall, and knew not
how for certain it was, they began to bend their bows and to shoot,
wherefore the King himself spurred his horse, and rode out to
them, commanding them that they should all come to him to
Clerkenwell Fields.

Meanwhile the Mayor of London rode as hastily as he could
back to the City, and commanded those who were in charge of
the twenty-four wards to make proclamation round their wards,
that every man should arm himself as quickly as he could, and
come to the King in St. John's Fields, where were the commons,
to aid the King, for he was in great trouble and necessity. But
at this time most of the knights and squires of the King's household, and many others, for fear that they had of this affray, left
their lord and went each one his way. And afterwards, when
the King had reached the open fields, he made the commons array
themselves on the west side of the fields. And presently the
aldermen came to him in a body, bringing with them their wardens,
and the wards arrayed in bands, a fine company of well-armed
folks in great strength. And they enveloped the commons like
sheep within a pen, and after that the Mayor had set the wardens

of the city on their way to the King, he returned with a company of lances to Smithfield, to make an end of the captain of the commons. And when he came to Smithfield he found not there the said captain Watt Tighler, at which he marvelled much, and asked what was become of the traitor. And it was told him that he had been carried by some of the commons to the hospital for poor folks by St. Bartholomew's, and was put to bed in the chamber of the master of the hospital. And the Mayor went thither and found him, and had him carried out to the middle of Smithfield, in presence of his fellows, and there beheaded. And thus ended his wretched life. But the Mayor had his head set on a pole and borne before him to the King, who still abode in the Fields. And when the King saw the head he had it brought near him to abash the commons, and thanked the Mayor greatly for what he had done. And when the commons saw that their chieftain, Watt Tyler, was dead in such a manner, they fell to the ground there among the wheat, like beaten men, imploring the King for mercy for their misdeeds. And the King benevolently granted them mercy, and most of them took to flight. But the King ordained two knights to conduct the rest of them, namely the Kentishmen, through London, and over London Bridge, without doing them harm, so that each of them could go to his own home. Then the King ordered the Mayor to put a helmet on his head because of what was to happen, and the Mayor asked for what reason he was to do so, and the King told him that he was much obliged to him, and that for this he was to receive the order of knighthood. And the Mayor answered that he was not worthy or able to have or to spend a knight's estate, for he was but a merchant and had to live by traffic: but finally the King made him put on the helmet, and took a sword in both his hands and dubbed him knight with great good will. The same day he made three other knights from among the citizens of London on that same spot, and these are their names—John Philpott, and Nicholas Bramber, and [blank in the MS.][1]: and the King gave Sir William Walworth £100 in land, and each of the others £40 in land, for them and their heirs. And after this the King took his way to London to the Wardrobe to ease him of his great toils.

Meanwhile a party of the commons took their way toward Huntingdon to pass towards the north, to ravage the land and

[1] The third person was John Standwyche. See page 79.

destroy the people : there they were turned back and could not pass the bridge of that town, by reason that William Wighman, Spigornel of Chancery, and Walter Rudham, and other good folk of the town of Huntingdon and the country round, met them at the said bridge and gave them battle, and slew two or three of them. The rest were glad to fly, and went to Ramsey to pass thereby, and took shelter in the town, and sent to the abbot for victuals to refresh them. And the abbot sent them out bread, wine, beer, and other victuals, in great abundance, for he dare not do otherwise. So they ate and drank to satiety, and afterwards slept deep into the morning, to their confusion. For meanwhile the men of Huntingdon rose, and gathered to them other folks of the country-side, and suddenly fell upon the commons at Ramsey and killed some twenty-four of them. The others took to headlong flight, and many of them were slain as they went through the countryside, and their heads set on high trees as an example to others.

At this same time the commons had risen in Suffolk in great numbers, and had as their chief Sir John Wraw, who brought with him more than 10,000 men. And they robbed many good folks, and cast their houses to the ground. And the said Sir John [to get] gold and silver [for his own profit?[1]], came to Cambridge.[2] There they did great damage by burning houses, and then they went to Bury, and found in that town a justice, Sir John Cavendish, Chief Justice of the King's Bench, and brought him to the pillory, and cut off his head and set it on the pillory. And afterwards they dragged to the pillory the Prior of that abbey, a good man and wise, and an accomplished singer, and a certain monk with him, and cut off their heads. And they set them on poles before the pillory, that all who passed down that street might see them. This Sir John Wraw their leader was afterwards taken as a traitor, and brought to London and condemned to death, and hanged, drawn, and quartered, and beheaded.

At the same time there were great levies in Norfolk, and the rebels did great harm throughout the countryside, for which reason the Bishop of Norwich, Sir Henry Despenser, sent letters to

---

[1] A son opes demesne. Professor Ker suggests that opes is an error for oyes, an inaccurate spelling of oes, 'need' or 'profit'.

[2] Almost certainly a mistake for Cavendish. The gold and silver was the spoil taken in the church there. See p. 105.

the said commons, to bid them cease their malice and go to their homes, without doing any more mischief. But they would not, and went through the land destroying and spoiling many townships, and houses of divers folk. During this time they met a hardy and vigorous knight named Sir Robert Hall [Salle], but he was a great wrangler and robber, and they cut off his head. Wherefore the said Bishop, gathering in to himself many men-at-arms and archers, assailed them at several places, wherever he could find them, and captured many of them. And the Bishop first confessed them and then beheaded them. So the said commons wandered all round the countryside, for default and mischief, and for the fear that they had of the King and the lords, and took to flight like beasts that run to their earths.[1]

Afterwards the King sent out his messengers into divers parts, to capture the malefactors and put them to death. And many were taken and hanged at London, and they set up many gallows around the City of London, and in other cities and boroughs of the south country. At last, as it pleased God, the King seeing that too many of his liege subjects would be undone, and too much blood spilt, took pity in his heart, and granted them all pardon, on condition that they should never rise again, under pain of losing life or members, and that each of them should get his charter of pardon, and pay the King as fee for his seal twenty shillings, to make him rich. And so finished this wicked war.'

[1] The *Taxistone* of the MS. is a mistake for *tapison*, a term of venery used of beasts running to earth, like foxes or rabbits.

APPENDIX VI

DOINGS OF THE TRAITOR-ALDERMEN

THE following is the report of the sheriffs and jurors of London in reply to a royal letter bidding them inquire into the opening of London to the rebels. It is dated November 20, 1382.

' Dicunt super sacramentum suum quod tempore male insur-reccionis et rebellionis comunium Kancie et Essexie, videlicet anno regni regis Ricardi secundi post conquestum quarto, Wil-lelmus Walleworth, tunc major civitatis Londoniarum, inde certio-ratus, toto suo animo eis resistere, et ingressum civitatis negare, ac civitatem in pace conservare sategens (*corr.* : satagens), cum avisiamento communis consilii civitatis predicte, ordinavit Johan-nem Horn, Adam Carlylle, et Johannem Ffresch, cives et alder-mannos civitatis predicte, nuncios et legatos ad obviandum eisdem populis sic congregatis contra fidem et ligeanceam suam dicto domino regi debitas, et eisdem nunciis sive legatis dedit specialiter in mandatis quod ipsi eundem populum malivolum tractarent, et ex parte regis et tocius civitatis eis dicerent quod ipsi ad civi-tatem non appropinquarent, in affraiamentum et perturbacionem regis, aliorum dominorum et dominarum, et civitatis predicte, set quod ipsi dicto domino regi in omnibus obedirent et reveren-ciam preberent, ut deberent. Qui vero Johannes, Adam et Jo-hannes nuncium suum non dixerunt prout in mandatis habuerunt, et dicunt quod predictus Johannes Horn ex assensu predicti Ade, non obstante majoris sui mandato supradicto, excedens suum nuncium ac mandatum, cum principalibus insurrectoribus con-spiravit, et predictum populum maleficum pulcris sermonibus versus dictam civitatem vertere fecit, ubi prius in proposito fue-runt ad hospicia sua revertendi, et eisdem maleficis et principalibus insurrectoribus dixit, ex[c]itando et procurando, quod ad civitatem cum turmis suis venirent, asserens quod tota civitas Londoniarum fuit in eodem proposito sicut et ipsi fuerunt, et quod ipsi deberent in eadem civitate ita amicabiliter esse recepti, sicut pater cum

filio et amicus cum amico. Qui quidem malefactores et rebelles,
causa nuncii predicti per predictos Johannem Horn, Adam Carlylle et Johannem Ffresch eis sic false et male facti, hillares
devenerunt, et ob hoc tam obstinati in suis malefactis fuerunt,
quod fines civitatis statim appropinquaverunt, videlicet die mercurii in vigilia festi Corporis Christi anno quarto,[1] et carcerem
domini regis vocatum le Marchalsye ffregerunt. Et eadem nocte
predictus Johannes Horn duxit secum Londonias plures principales insurrectores, et aliorum malefactorum ductores, videlicet
Thomam Hawke, Willelmum Newman, Johannem Sterlyng et
alios qui, ex hoc postea convicti, judicium mortis susceperunt, et
cum eo tota illa nocte in hospicium suum recepti fuerunt felonice
et proditorie. Et idem Johannes Horn, eadem nocte, dixit majori
civitatis predicte quod ipsi insurrectores venirent Londonias, unde
majori ex hoc maxime perturbato idem Johannes Horn sibi (*sic*)
dixit et manucepit quod sub periculo capitis sui nullum dampnum
in civitate nec in ejus finibus facerent. Mane autem facto in
festo Corporis Christi,[2] predictus Johannes Horn venit ad quendam Johannem Marchaunt, unum clericorum civitatis predicte,
dicens eidem clerico verba sequencia vel similia : *Major precepit*
quod tu deberes michi querere unum standardum de armis domini
regis. Qui quidem clericus tale standardum post longum scruti-
neum eidem Johanni Horn deliberavit, ipso clerico omnino nescio
quid idem Johannes Horn inde faceret ; et idem Johannes Horn
predictum standardum in duas partes divisit equales, quarum
unam partem ligavit cuidam lancie, et aliam partem dedit garcioni
suo custodiendam, et sic cum tali vexillo displicato equitavit
usque ad Blakeheth, per se nullum onus nuncii sive legacionis illo
die habens, set solummodo ad complendum promissa eisdem malefactoribus per ipsum prius facta, et ad provocandum eos toto nisu
suo ad civitatem venire felonice et proditorie, sciens expresse
perturbacionem et magnum afflictum domino regi, aliis magna-
tibus et civitatis predicte civibus, in adventu predictorum insurrectorum et domini regis proditorum, adesse. Et dicunt quod
eidem Johanni Horn sic equitando versus le Blakeheth appro-
pinquabat quidam Johannes Blyton, qui missus fuit per dominum
regem et consilium suum eisdem malefactoribus ut ad civitatem
non appropinquarent, et dixit eidem Johanni Horn ista verba vel
similia : *Domine, vellem scire nuncium vestrum, si aliquod habetis ex*

[1] June 12, 1381.   [2] June 13, 1381.

*parte civitatis istis insurrectoribus dicendum, ita quod nuncium meum
quod habeo ex parte domini regis eisdem, et nuncium vestrum, quod
habetis ex parte civitatis, poterunt concordare.* Qui statim, iracundo
vultu eum aspiciens, dixit : *Nolo de nuncio tuo nec tu debes de meo
aliquid intromittere ; ego dicam eis quod mihi placet, et dic tu sicut tibi
placet.* Et postquam predictus nuncius regis cito equitando eisdem rebellibus ex parte regis suum nuncium exposuisset, predictus
Johannes Horn venit et, contrariando nuncium domini regis predictum, in contemptum ejusdem domini regis, felonice, false et
proditorie contra ligeanceam suam, dixit eisdem : *Venite Londonias, quia unanimes facti sumus amici et parati facere vobiscum que
proposuistis, et in omnibus que vobis necessaria sunt favorem et
obsequium prestare,* sciens regis voluntatem et majoris sui mandatum suis dictis contraria fore. Et sic, per verba premissa, excita-
cionem et procuracionem illius Johannis Horn, habentis de suis
coniva, consilio et conspiracione precogitatis Walterum Sybyle,
predicti malefactores et domini regis proditores sic, ut supradicitur,
conjuncti, cum Waltero Tyler, Alano Thedre, Willelmo Hawk,
Johanne Stakpull, principalibus ductoribus et aliis regis proditoribus, venerunt Londonias, currendo et clamando per vicos
civitatis : *Ad Savoye, ad Savoye,* et sic per predictum Johannem
Horn et Walterum Sybyle predicti felones et proditores domini
regis introducti fuerunt in civitatem ; ob quam causam carcera
(*sic*) domini regis de Newgate fracta fuit, arsiones tenementorum,
prostraciones domorum, decapitaciones archiepiscopi et aliorum
facte fuerunt, et alia plura mala prius inaudita perpetrata per
ipsos tunc fuerunt. Et dicunt quod predictus Johannes Horn, cum
eisdem turmis malis et omnino maledictis deambulans per vicos
civitatis, quesivit si aliquis vellet monstrare et sibi proponere
aliquam injuriam sibi factam, promittens eis festinam justiciam
per ipsum et suos inde faciendam, ob quod venit quedam Matilda
Toky coram Johanne Horn, conquerendo versus Ricardum Toky,
grossarium, de eo quod idem Ricardus injuste detinebat rectam
hereditatem ipsius Matilde, ut ipsa tunc dixit, super quo predictus
Johannes Horn, in magna societate rybaldorum et rebellium predictorum, cum eadem Matilda accessit ad quoddam tenementum
predicti Ricardi Toky in Lumbardstrete, Londoniis, et ibidem
idem Johannes Horn, capiens super se regalem potestatem, dedit
judicium aperte quod predicta Matilda predictum tenementum
haberet, et adjudicavit eidem Matilde habenda omnia bona et

catalla in eodem tenemento inventa pro dampnis suis, et sic fecit
super predictum Ricardum Toky disseisinam et predacionem felonice et contra pacem et legem domini regis, in enervacionem regie
corone et, in quantum in ipso fuit, adnullacionem regie dignitatis
ac legis terre ac pacis regis, et regni destruccionem manifestam.
Ac eciam dicunt quod idem Johannes Horn, cum predictis turmis
malis et filiis iniquitatis, quamplures de dicta civitate magnis
mynis vite et membrorum se redimere coegit, inter quos fecit
felonice quemdam Robertum Nortoun, taillour, facere finem et
redempcionem cuidam Johanni Pecche, ffisshmonger, de decem
libris sterlingorum, pro quibus bene et fideliter solvendis idem
Robertus Nortoun plura jocalia posuit in vadium, et si idem
Robertus taliter non fecisset, predictus Johannes Horn juravit
quod eundem Robertum turmis suis traderet decapitandum, et
sic idem Johannes Horn fuit unus principalium insurrectorum
contra regem et principalis eorum malorum consiliator, ita ut per
ipsum et per predictum Walterum Sybyle felonice et proditorie
malefactores prenominati excitati et procurati fuerunt veniendi
Londonias, et in eandem civitatem per ipsum et per predictum
Walterum Sybyle proditorie introducti fuerunt, per quod omnia
mala predicta in dicta civitate et in cunctis locis eidem adjacenti-
bus facta fuerunt et perpetrata, non obstante quod iidem Walterus
Sybyle et Johannes Horn de officio suo aldermanie ad pacem
domini regis ibidem conservandam fuerunt specialius per sacramentum suum astricti.

Item, dicunt predicti jurati super sacramentum suum quod,
ubi predictus Willelmus Walleworth, major, cum deliberacione
predicti communis consilii civitatis predicte, ordinavit ut omnes
aldermanni ejusdem civitatis ad custodiendum civitatem deb[er]ent
esse parati in armis, cum aliis concivibus suis, ad resistendum
malefactoribus supradictis, et ad negandum eis ingressum, et ad
defendendum tam portas quam alios ingressus civitatis predicte,
predictus Walterus Sybyle, tunc aldermannus, sciens et videns
predictum populum ferocem et malevolum in Suthwerk tot mala
facere et fecisse, die jovis supradicto, supra pontem Londoniarum
in armis stetit, parvum vel nullum sibi adquirens adjuvamen, set
plures volentes eundem Walterum Sybyle adjuvasse in resistendo
eisdem idem Walterus Sybyle repulit, verbis reprobis et contu-
meliosis, et eos omnino recusavit, dicens aperte : *Isti Kentenses
sunt amici nostri et regis*.   Et sic dedit eisdem proditoribus supra-

nominatis cum turmis suis liberum introitum et egressum felonice et proditorie, ubi hoc impedivisse debuit et de facili potuit, et quando idem Walterus Sybyle premunitus fuit per aliquos quomodo predicti proditores et rebelles fregerunt carceres regis, fecerunt decapitaciones hominum et prostraverunt quoddam tenementum [1] juxta pontem Londoniarum, idem Walterus Sybyle omnia mala predicta parvipendens, dixit : *Quid ex hoc? Dignum est et dignum fuit everti per viginti annos elapsos.* Et dicunt quod ubi Thomas Cornewayles, dicto die jovis, in magna comitiva armatorum venit et optulit se ad succurrendum eidem Waltero, et ad custodiendum introitum pontis, et ad ibidem restitendum (*sic*) proditoribus predictis, sub omni forisfactura quod forisfacere potuit, idem Walterus Sybyle felonice et proditorie illorum adjuvamen recusavit et eos non permisit aliquam custodiam seu restitenciam contra predictos malefactores ibidem facere, set sine custodia reliquit portas civitatis apertas. Et sic, per maliciam ipsius Walteri Sybyle, conyvam et conspiracionem inter ipsum Walterum Sybyle et Johannem Horn precogitatas, alie porte civitatis aperte fuerunt, et omni clausura caruerunt, unde supradicti malefactores nominati, et alii eisdem consimiles cum turmis suis, per easdem portas liberum introitum et exitum pro libito habuerunt, false, felonice et proditorie, et, quod pessimum fuit, ex hoc dominus rex et tota civitas cum toto regno fuerunt in aperto periculo ultimate destruccionis.

Item, dicunt predicti jurati quod, quando dominus noster rex et major civitatis predicte in maximo periculo constituti fuerunt, in Smethefeld, inter turmas malefactorum, die sabbati proximo post festum Corporis Xti, predictus Walterus recenter recessit ab eisdem, equitando in civitatem per vicos de Aldrichegate et de Westchepe, et clamavit aperte : *Claudite portas vestras et custodite muros vestros, quoniam jam totum perditum est.* Et dicunt quod Walterus Sybyle et Johannes Horn fecerunt portam de Aldrichesgate claudi felonice et proditorie, et, in quantum in ipsis fuit, impediverunt homines ad succurrendum domino regi et majori, scientes illos in tali periculo constitutos, contra ligeanciam et fidem suas domino regi debitas, cui debuissent omni nisu adherere, et eum succurrere, et, omnibus aliis rebus postpositis, defendere, et, si cives civitatis festinancius se non expedivissent, auxilium

---

[1] Clearly the house of ill fame mentioned on pp. 193-4.

domino regi et majori minus tarde advenisset, causa verborum et factorum predicti Walteri Sybyle et Johannis Horn.

Item, dicunt super sacramentum quod quidam Thomas Ffarndon, tempore principii insurreccionis predicte, ivit ex proprio suo capite felonice ad malefactores de comitatu Essexie, et eis conquerendo dixit quod per reverendum militem priorem Hospitalis Sancti Johannis Jherusalem a recta sua hereditate injuste expulsus fuit, ob quam causam malefactores supradicti indignacionem et magnum rancorem habuerunt erga predictum priorem, unde plura dampna et ruinam suis placiis et tenementis in comitatu Essexie fecerunt. Et predictus Thomas Ffarndon, die jovis in festo Corporis Christi supradicto, cum predictis insurrectoribus, ut unus eorum capitaneus, venit Londonias, ducens retro se magnam turbam, et eorum ductor fuit usque tenementum predicti prioris vocatum le Temple, in Ffletestrete, felonice et proditorie, et ibi eis signum fecit ita quod statim eadem tenementa prostraverunt, et cum eis ivit usque ad manerium de Savoye, quousque plene funditum fuit et crematum. Deinde clamans socios suos, eos duxit usque ad prioratum de Clerkenwell, et ibidem predavit et spoliavit prioratum predictum et igne succensit. Accessitque ultra cum eisdem turmis in civitatem Londoniarum et ibidem pernoctabat, et recepit secum noctanter plures principales insurrectores, videlicet Robertum de la Warde et alios, ymaginando illa nocte et cum aliis sociis suis conspirando nomina diversorum civium, que fecit scribi in quadam cedula, quos vellet decapitare et eorum tenementa prostrare. Mane autem facto, die veneris proximo post festum Corporis Christi [1], predictus Thomas cum pluribus complicibus suis ivit usque ad Hybery et ibidem nobile manerium predicti prioris ad nichilum igne perverterunt. Deinde accessit cum maledictis malefactoribus usque ad le Milende, obviando domino nostro [regi], et ibidem ffrenum equi regis nostri felonice, proditorie et irreverenter in manu sua cepit, et sic dominum regem detinendo, dicebat ista verba vel consimilia : *Vindica me de illo falso proditore priore, quia tenementa mea false et ffraudilenter de me arripuit ; fac michi rectam justiciam, et tenementa mea mihi restaurare digneris, quia aliter satis fortis sum facere michimet justiciam, et in eis reintrare et habere.* Cui rex instanter inquit : *Habebis quod justum est.* Deinde idem Thomas, semper continuando suam maliciam, ivit apud Turrim Londoniarum, et felonice

[1] June 14, 1381.

et proditorie ibidem intravit, et noluit cessare quousque tam archiepiscopus quam predictus prior decapitati fuerunt, et deinde circuivit civitatem, querens quos potuit per cohercionem vite et membrorum facere se redimere, et quorum tenementa voluit prostrare. Et tempore quo idem Thomas fuit circa prostracionem tenementi Johannis Knot in Stanynglane, captus fuit et prisone deliberatus, et idem Thomas primus fuit omnium principalium insurrectorum de comitatu Essexie. Et dicunt quod predictus Thomas Ffarndon, a die lune in septimana Pentecostes [1], anno quarto supradicto, usque diem sue capcionis, continuavit maliciam suam in coligendo et congregando predictos insurrectores, et in prosequendo mortem predicti prioris false, felonice et proditorie, contra fidem et ligeanciam suam, in adnullacionem status sui regis et pervercionem regis et regni.

Dicunt eciam predicti jurati quod, postquam Willelmus Walleworth, major supradictus, portam de Algate in vigilia festi Corporis Christi supradicti [2] noctanter claudebat, ne malefactores de comitatu Essexie ibidem ingressum haberent, quidam Willelmus Tonge portam illam male aperuit et communes ibidem intrare permisit contra voluntatem dicti majoris.

Item, dicunt quod Adam atte Welle et Rogerus Harry, bocheres, per quatuordecim dies ante adventum dictorum insurrectorum de comitatu Essexie Londoniis, ipsos insurrectores ad veniendum ad dictam civitatem excitaverunt et procuraverunt, et multa super hoc eis promiserunt, et postea, die jovis in festo Corporis Christi [3], in eandem civitatem ipsos insurrectores proditorie introduxerunt, et ulterius eos in magna multitudine ad manerium domini ducis Lancastrie, dictum Savoye, eodem die perduxerunt, et ad arsuram et depredacionem ejusdem manerii, ut eorum ductores et principales consiliatores, provocaverunt, et exinde plura jocalia, et alia bona, et (*corr.* : ad) valorem et precium viginti librarum felonice asportaverunt. Et, die veneris proxime sequenti [4], predictus Adam quemdam Nicholaum Wyght, in parochia Sancti Nicholai, ad macellas, caput suum pro viginti solidis felonice redimere fecit.'

In another inquest dated Nov. 4, 1382, the sheriffs and jurors write as follows: 'Item, dicunt supra sacramentum suum quod quidam Willelmus Tonge, tunc aldermannus, predicto die mercurii [5], portam de Aldgate per predictum majorem

---

[1] June 3.   [2] June 12.   [3] June 13.
[4] June 14.   [5] June 12.

pro inimicis excludendis clausam, videlicet turbis de comitatu Essexie contra pacem domini regis ex coniva Kentensium levatis, idem Willelmus Tonge ipsam portam de nocte aperuit, et easdem turbas per predictam portam intrare permisit ; qui, statim ut infra civitatem fuerunt, malefactoribus predictis de comitatu Kancie se immiscuerunt ; et omnia mala predicta simul cum illis et eis adherentibus peregerunt. Set si idem Willelmus Tonge dicte porte apercionem fecerit ex sua malicia propria, vel ex coniva predictorum Johannis Horn et Walteri Sybyle, vel ex metu et minis predictorum malefactorum de comitatu Kancie infra civitatem tunc existencium, omnino ignorant ad presens.'

N.B.—I am allowed to reprint these documents from André Réville's copies from the originals in the Record Office, by the kindness of the Société de l'École des Chartes, to whom the copyright of M. Réville's collections belongs.

INDEX